MULTINATIONALS AND THE GROWTH OF THE SINGAPORE ECONOMY

CROOM HELM SERIES THE GROWTH ECONOMIES OF
SOUTH-EAST ASIA

Edited by
Chris Dixon and David Drakakis-Smith

Multinationals and the Growth of The Singapore Economy

HAFIZ MIRZA

ST. MARTIN'S PRESS
New York

Scholarly & Reference Division,
St. Martin's Press, Inc., 175 Fifth Avenue, New York, NY 10010
First published in the United States of America in 1986
Printed in Great Britain

Library of Congress Cataloging in Publication Data

Mirza, Hafiz.
    Multinationals and the growth of the Singapore
economy.

    Bibliography: p.
    Includes index.
    1. International business enterprises–Singapore.
2. Singapore–Economic conditions. I. Title.
HD2903.M57   1986   338.8'885957   85-22302
ISBN 0-312-55264-5

CONTENTS

Contents

Contents

TABLES, MAPS AND FIGURES

Tables, Maps and Figures

Tables, Maps and Figures

TABLES continued

PREFACE

All books are generated by social endeavour and I thankfully acknowledge the many academics, researchers, journalists, government departments and international organisations whose efforts have made this book possible. At a directly personal level my path has been smoothed by many people of whom I would especially like to mention: John Sparkes for his eagle-eyed proof-reading; Peter Buckley for his encouragement; Linda Naylor and her colleagues at Word Express for the preparation of the typescript - without too many grumbles about my handwriting; Sylvia Ashdown for typing earlier versions of some chapters - also without too many grumbles; Gul Chotrani, Patrick Yang, K.W. Koh, Doug Sikorski and K.S. Yeoh for their hospitality and help in Singapore itself; librarians Carol McLaren, Wendy Small, Neil Hunter and two who have gone AWOL for the dirty work; Peter Sowden for his considerable support in preparing this book; Sotos Papadopoulos for the entertainment; and Naina, of course, for everything.

A few general points about style and the use of information and data in this book are worth mentioning here:

In order to conserve space and make passages readable I have occasionally adopted a didactic style and this is particularly the case in chapter five. However, all statements are justified by data, notes and references and the reader is directed to these.

I seldom describe tables at length in the text because this is often superfluous; and it is worth studying them independently, especially since most are as comprehensive, analytical and readable as possible. Most of the tables are based on my own calculations and I have endeavoured to explain the methodology where necessary, although I would be happy to answer specific queries. Incidentally, though many statistics produced by the Singapore authorities are believed to be suspect (see table 5.8, for example) I have found that they can be quite revealing nevertheless.

All values in this book are expressed in US$ and conversions from other currencies are based on average exchange rates calculated by the IMF and published in its International Financial Statistics yearbooks.

Most definitions are to be found in the notes at the end of each chapter and the index therefore refers to these as appropriate. Acronyms are explained in the index.

Chapter two was written before the December 1984 general election and I have resisted all temptations to alter it. The election is, however, referred to in chapter six. Incidentally, the PAP backlash against those who voted for other parties continues to gather pace. In early April, 1985, for example, the government announced that PAP-held districts would get priority in housing maintenance.

Finally, my analysis of the Pacific Community concept, TriCom and the trilateral carve-up of the developing world (pages 214-221, 224-225) may appear paranoid, but I hasten to add that I am not alone! I am gratified to read that Kenichi Ohmae has come to similar conclusions. He was cited as believing, 'the big (Japanese, European and American) manufacturers are actually collaborating with each other; it would appear that the three powerful northern economies have actually divided the international market place among themselves.... Southeast Asia has gone to the Japanese, West Asia and Africa to the Europeans and Central and South America to the United States' (Far Eastern Economic Review, April 11, 1985, page 73.)

Chapter One

INTRODUCTION

Singapore is one of the smallest countries in the world, with a mere two and a half million inhabitants and a surface area barely a third of Greater London's. Yet this smallness is belied by Singapore's increasingly significant role in the world economy. To begin with, as Table 1.1 illustrates, Singapore is one of a handful of countries whose extremely rapid rates of growth have earned them the label "newly industrialising countries" (NICs). Singapore itself has recorded average annual growth rates in excess of eight percent for two decades. In recent years this growth rate has exceeded that of the burgeoning Japanese economy, and has far surpassed the growth rates of all western industrialised economies. As a result, its 1982 GNP per capita of $5,910 compared favourably with that of Ireland ($5,150), Spain ($5,430), Italy ($6, 840) and even the UK ($9,660). (1,2)

The stern discipline and keen scrutiny of the government has helped ensure a consistent, smooth-running economy. In October 1984 Euromoney, basing its judgement on a number of key indicators (see Table 1.2), paid Singapore a considerable compliment by declaring that this resourceless, miniscule island-state had achieved the world's best overall economic performance over the period 1974 to 1984. Not unexpectedly an earlier issue of Euromoney, in the journal's assessment of country risk/credit ratings, ranked Singapore as the 15th least risky country: the best placing for any developing country bar Saudi Arabia; and ahead of industrialised countries such as Denmark, France and Italy.

A major consequence of Singapore's economic performance is the increasinly important role that it is playing in world trade. In 1983 Singapore's

1

share of world merchandise (i.e. visible) trade was
1.2 percent (Table 1.1). This compared very
favourably with the UKs equivalent figure of 5.5
percent,bearing in mind the UKs vastly greater
population. (3). Similarly 1.5 percent of total
world private invisible receipts in 1981 accrued to
entities in Singapore; and, within this, 4.5 percent
of all 1983 international banking activity was
conducted by Singapore based banks. (4)

AN INTERNATIONALISED ECONOMY

Despite all the impressive facts mentioned
above, however, Singapore is not an independent
nascent capitalist economy. Since the mid-sixties
multinational companies (MNCs) have flocked to
Singapore, simultaneously compelled by competition
and attracted by the benefits and inducements on
offer. (5) This remarkable influx of foreign direct
investment (FDI) has resulted in one of the few
truly internationalised countries in the world. (6)
Table 1.3 evinces that foreign corporate and
individual residents presently represent over a
quarter of Singapore's GDP. (7) This overwhelming
level of foreign involvement, unlikely to be
repeated elsewhere, has been achieved in a mere
two decades because of the massive scale of inward
FDI, as illustrated clearly by Table 1.4. In recent
years Singapore has received up to 4.6 percent of
world FDI, and up to 14.6 per-cent of FDI destined
for developing countries. In 1983 only two
developing countries, Saudi Arabia and Brazil,
received more FDI, with the latter barely ahead (3.6
percent of world FDI). The UK, another major
recipient of foreign direct investment, received
about 8.7 percent of the global total, but is a
larger economy. (8) On a per capita basis the
scale of FDI is truly remarkable: this island-state
with only two and a half million inhabitants
annually receives up to a half of all foreign direct
investment in Asia, a continent which includes
highly populated countries such as China, India,
Japan, Indonesia, Pakistan and Bangladesh.
Multinational involvement is particularly
intense in certain key sectors and industries,
including manufacturing, banking and other
services. These will be discussed in detail later,
but Table 1.5 is indicative. Foreign companies
finance the preponderant share of investment in
manufacturing and are responsible for 60 percent of

Table 1.1: Singapore in an International Context.

Country[a]	GNP per capita (US$)	Average annual growth rate of real GDP/GNP (percent)			Share of world trade[b] (percent)			Destination of manufactured exports (percent going to industry market economies)		
	1982	1960-70	1970-82	1984	1960	1970	1983	1962	1978	1981
Singapore	5,910	8.8	8.5	8.9	1.0	0.5	1.3	4	54	49
Hong Kong	5,340	10.0	9.9	8.1	0.6	0.9	1.3	63	83	77
South Korea	1,910	8.6	8.6	7.9	0.3	0.3	1.5	83	74	62
Brazil	2,240	5.4	7.6	3.6	1.1	1.0	1.3	60	53	43
UK	9,660	2.9	1.5	2.2	9.0	6.8	5.5	58	65	62
Japan	10,080	10.4	4.6	5.5	3.4	6.7	8.8	45	47	47
USA	13,160	4.3	2.7	6.7	17.4	15.1	12.1	48	58	54
India	260	3.4	3.6	6.5	1.1	0.7	0.5	56	52	51

Sources: World Bank, World Development Report, 1980 and 1984.
International Monetary Fund, Intnl. Financial Statistics Yearbook, 1984.
OECD, Economic Outlook, July 1984.
South Magazine, February 1985.

Notes: a – Hong Kong, South Korea, Brazil and Singapore are four of the ten-or-so "newly industrialising countries." b – Exports of each country as a proportion of total merchandise exports of all non-socialist countries.

Table 1.2: Singapore's Comparative Economic Performance, 1974-84.

World Rank[a]	Overall Performance [b,c]	The Fastest Growing GDP [d]		The Lowest Rates of Inflation [e]		The Strongest Currencies[f]	
	Country	Country	Average Annual Real Growth Rate (%)	Country	Average Annual Rate of Inflation (%)	Country	Average Annual Change Against SDR (%)
1	Singapore	Singapore	8.40	Switzer-land	3.56	Japan	4.35
2	Taiwan	Taiwan	7.95	Singapore	4.27	Switzer-land	3.36
3	Malaysia	S. Korea	7.81	W. Germany	4.38	Singapore	3.07
4	Hong Kong	Hong Kong	7.60	Burma	4.54	Qatar	2.56
5	S. Arabia	Egypt	7.57	Malaysia	5.36	Bahrain	2.14

Source: Based on Euromoney's third annual survey of a decade of economic performance in Euromoney, October 1984.

Notes: a - Ranking is based on 93 non-socialist countries.
b - Based on Euromoney's weighting of economic growth, inflation, currency strength, export growth and current account performance.
c - Japan was 8th, the USA 26th and the UK 54th.
d - Japan 25th; USA 51st; UK 75th.
e - Japan 7th; USA 19th; UK 45th.
f - Japan 1st; USA 8th; UK 33rd.

Introduction

Table 1.3   Indigenous and Foreign Shares in
             Singapore's Gross Domestic Product
             (GDP)

	1966	1970	1975	1980	1982
Total GDP (US$ mn)	1,086	1,876	5,640	11,302	14,649
Indigenous share (%)	91	82	77	72	74
Foreign share[a] (%)	9	18	23	28	26

Source: Singapore Department of Statistics, Economic
and Social Statistics of Singapore, 1960-1982.

Note: a - share of resident foreigners and resident
foreign companies in GDP.

manufacturing   output   and   70   percent   of
manufacturing exports. (9)

GENERAL CHARACTERISTICS OF FOREIGN INVESTMENT

        Until the 1960's Singapore was a major
entrepot centre within the British Empire and this
meant that most foreign direct investment was U.K.
in origin and orientated towards trade and
distribution. In 1963 Singapore achieved
independence as a member of the Malaysian Federation
and foreign companies, anticipating a Malaysian
common market, increased their local investments.
When Singapore was ousted from the Federation in
1965 many of these companies could have come to
grief, but fortunately discovered that the
government had decided to promote export-oriented
FDI (see Chapter Two). This policy decision
coincided with an embryonic restructuring of the
world production and trading system. Rising labour
costs, high taxes, competition and other factors
were increasingly forcing companies from
industrialised countries to locate production (10)
in developing countries. By creating the
appropriate ambience Singapore has benefited
disproportionately from these trends, as previously
mentioned. Since the late 1960's FDI in Singapore
has expanded at a remarkable rate, as is borne out
by Table 1.6.

5

Introduction

Table 1.4   Singapore's Share of World Foreign
             Direct Investment, 1975-83

	Percent		
	1975	1980	1983
Total Flow of World FDI (US$ billions)	19.1	47.3	43.0
Regional or Country share of World FDI			
- Industrial Countries	58.8	74.7	65.4
- Developing Countries[a]	26.5	25.3	22.1
- Asia	6.4	10.4	10.2
- Singapore	3.1	4.6	3.2
FDI in Singapore as a proportion of FDI in Asia	48.6	44.6	31.8
FDI in Singapore as a proportion of FDI in developing countries[a]	11.7	13.7	14.6

Source: Calculated from data in the International
         Monetary Fund, Balance of Payments Yearbook,
         1982 and 1984.

Note: a - Non oil-exporting developing countries.

Introduction

Table 1.5   Local and Foreign Share in Net
             Manufacturing[a] Investment
             Committments.

	1972	1975	1980	1982
Total (US$ mn)	69.2	129.2	665.5	816.1
Local (%)	20	19	14	31
Foreign (%)	80	81	36	69

Source: Singapore Department of Statistics,
          Economic and Social Statistics, 1960-1982.

Note: a - Investment commitments in
              petrochemicals excluded.

     Foreign   direct   investment   has   played   an
increasingly   major   role in Singapore's development
and amounted to 31 percent of gross domestic capital
formation   (GDCF)   in   1982   (see   Table   1.7). (11)
However   net   borrowing   from   abroad   has   been
relatively   modest   because   most FDI is financed by
earnings   from   very   profitable   existing   foreign
subsidiaries.   For example, Table 1.7 shows that if
all   foreign   earnings   had   been reinvested locally
this   would   have   been   sufficient to finance 75% of
all FDI in that year.
     Until   1970   the main foreign investors were UK
firms   and   Overseas   Chinese   concerns.   However,
because   of   the massive expansion in foreign direct
investment   by   USA , Japanese (refer to Table 1.6),
European   and developing country firms, the range of
source   countries   is now very diverse indeed.   This
is   confirmed   by Table 1.8, although care should be
taken   in   analysing   the information presented. (12)
The   largest   sources   are the USA , the UK, Japan
and   Overseas   Chinese   investors   (probably in that
order).
     Overseas   Chinese subsidiaries play a prominent
role   in   Singapore's   economy   because   it   is   a
predominantly   Chinese   country in a manifestly non-
Chinese   region.   There   are three main sources for
these   investments.   Chinese   countries   and
territories   such   as   Hong Kong and Taiwan; Chinese
companies   in   nearby countries, including Indonesia
and   Malaysia   (13); and the rather shadowy world of

7

Table 1.6   Foreign Direct Investment (FDI) in Singapore, 1960-83.[a]

US$ Millions

Year	Total flow of FDI into Singapore	Inflow of USA FDI	Inflow of Japanese[b] FDI
1963	5		
1964	11		
1965	16	30[c]	
1966	18		31[d]
1967	28	1	
1968	23	15	
1969	37	21	
1970	92	30	9
1971	126	25	8
1972	191	59	42
1973	393	92	81
1974	607	88	51
1975	610	84	55
1976	651	-26	27
1977	335	57	66
1978	739	210	174
1979	941	139	255
1980	1,689	339	140
1981	1,916	635	266
1982	2,093	-17	180
1983	1,390[e]	143	NA
Stock of FDI, 1982/83	11,911	1,803	1,383

Sources: International Monetary Fund, Balance of Payments Yearbook, various issues. U.S. Department of Commerce, Survey of Current Business, November 1984 and unpublished data. Japanese Ministry of International Trade and Industry (MITI), the Overseas Business Operations of Japanese Firms, various issues.

Notes: a - Because the data in this Table is derived from different sources they are not strictly comparable.   b - Figures released by the Japanese Ministry of International Trade and Industry (MITI). Unfortunately the figures are "licensed" amounts (i.e. sums agreed to by the Japanese Government) rather than actual amounts arriving in Singapore. Nevertheless they illustrate the massive increase in Japanese FDI in Singapore during the 1970s. c - Total Inflow, 1946 to 1966. d - Total Inflow, 1951 to 1969.   e - This low figure partly reflects the strength of the USA dollar against the SDR.

Introduction

Table 1.7   Foreign Investment and
             Domestic Capital Formation

	US$ Millions				
	1972	1975	1980	1981	1982
Annual Foreign Direct Invest-ment (FDI)[a] in Singapore	191	610	1,689	1,916	2,093
Stock of FDI[a]	547	2,157	6,512	8,428	10,521
Earnings[b] of Foreign Investors	128	345	1,332	1,519	1,565
"Rate" of Profit[c] (%)	36	22	28	23	19
Gross Domestic Capital Formation in Singapore[d] (GDCF)	1,194	2,208	5,133	6,029	6,747
Net borrowing from Abroad[e]	496	584	1,564	1,382	1,279

Sources: International Monetary Fund, Balance of
           Payments Yearbook, various issues.
           Singapore Department of Statistics,
           Economic and Social Statistics of
           Singapore, 1960-1982.
           Singapore Department of Statistics,
           Yearbook of Statistics, Singapore,
           1982/83.

Notes: a - IMF data. The Stock of FDI is simply
           the sum of the annual flows. b - Mainly
           earnings on foreign direct investment in
           Singapore. c - Earnings of any year
           divided by stock of FDI in previous year.
           d - GDCF = net domestic savings of local
           and foreign entities in Singapore plus
           factor income from abroad plus net
           borrowings from abroad. e - Includes
           various types of short and long term
           capital flows.

Table 1.8 Foreign Establishments^a in Singapore by Country of Origin and Industry, 1982.

Country of Domicile of Parent Company	Total No. of Parent Companies Involved	Total No. of Establishments	Establishments by Industry or Sector^b	
			Agriculture, Forestry and Fisheries	Energy
USA	194	226	–	10
UK	180	369	8	8
Japan	136	129	–	4
Australia & N. Zealand	96	125	1	3
W. Germany	43	46	–	1
The Netherlands	29	40	–	–
Sweden	25	26	–	–
Switzerland	23	23	–	1
France	15	12	–	2
Canada	12	22	1	–
Other Developed Countries^c	33	31	–	–
Hong Kong	66	127	2	1
Malaysia	59	80	2	–
Other Less Developed Countries^d	19	20	–	1
All Countries	930	1,276	14	31

continued

Introduction

Table 1.8 Foreign Establishments[a] in Singapore by Country of Origin and Industry, 1982. (cont.)

Country of Domicile of Parent Company	Establishments by Industry or Sector[b]			
	Extraction and Manufacture of Metals, Chemicals and Minerals	Engineering, Vehicles and Construction	Other Manufacturing	Wholesale Distribution inc. Exports/Imports
USA	43	97	24	5
UK	34	64	37	23
Japan	21	66	14	7
Australia & N. Zealand	19	28	22	11
W. Germany	4	21	4	3
The Netherlands	12	5	7	7
Sweden	4	9	1	1
Switzerland	2	12	1	1
France	2	4	-	3
Canada	-	1	2	-
Other Developed Countries[c]	5	12	2	-
Hong Kong	8	11	11	10
Malaysia	9	16	12	9
Other Less Developed Countries[d]	1	8	2	3
All Countries	164	354	138	83

continued

11

Table 1.8 Foreign Establishments[a] in Singapore by
Country of Origin and Industry, 1982. (cont.)

Country of Domicile of Parent Company	Establishments by Industry or Sector[b]			
	Retail Distribution	Transport and Communication	Business and Finance	Other Services[b]
USA	-	9	33	5
UK	31	39	94	31
Japan	3	8	5	1
Australia & N. Zealand	4	11	21	5
W. Germany	-	4	8	1
The Netherlands	1	7	1	-
Sweden	2	4	4	1
Switzerland	1	-	4	2
France	-	-	1	-
Canada	-	2	16	-
Other Developed Countries[c]	-	3	9	-
Hong Kong	13	18	50	3
Malaysia	3	3	24	2
Other Less Developed Countries[d]	1	2	2	-
All Countries	59	110	272	51

continued

Table 1.8 Foreign Establishments[a] in Singapore by Country of Origin and Industry, 1982. (cont.)

Source: Derived from a frequency count of subsidiaries in Dun and Bradstreet Ltd., Who Owns Whom in Australasia and the Far East, London, 1983.

Notes:
a - "Establishments" include both direct and indirect subsidiaries in Singapore. For example, The Standard and Chartered Bank Ltd. (UK) has a subsidiary in Singapore (INTRACO Ltd.), which has itself spawned about 20 further subsidiaries. (This company is also regarded as a state-owned enterprise). Only majority owned (50-100%) subsidiaries are included.
b - This is normally the industry or sector of the parent company, although the subsidiaries' industry is used where possible.
c - Includes Finland, Austria, Denmark, Norway, Italy, The Soviet Union, Belgium and Yugoslavia.
d - Includes India, Bermuda, Panama, The Philippines etc.

Energy Industries   - Coal, solid fuels, petroleum, nuclear fuel, gas and electricity.

Extraction etc.   - Ore extraction and preparation, iron and steel, ceramics and chemicals.

Engineering etc.   - Simple metal goods, electrical/ electronic engineering, vehicles, shipbuilding, construction and civil engineering.

Other Manu-   - Food, Toys, Textiles, etc.
facturing

Retail   - Also includes Commodity Brokers, Hotel and Catering, etc.
Distribution

Transport   - Sea/air transport, supporting services, storage and warehousing.

Business   - Banking, Insurance, Accountancy, Advertising, Computing and Legal Services.

Other Services   - Research and Development, Education, Cultural and Recreational Services.

International Chinese Capital about which little is known and even less said. More recently there has been an influx of refugee capital from crisis-stricken Hong Kong, but its scale is not known because of its clandestine arrival in Singapore, albeit with the Government's full cognizance.

Foreign investment in Singapore is highly diversified sectorally and industrially (Table 1.8 and 1.9), although the move towards finance and services is fairly recent and reflects shifts in government policy from the early 1970's onwards. A point of particular interest is that source-countries appear to have particular sectoral and industrial preferences. Thus, for example, as Tables 1.8 and 1.9 clearly show, foreign investment from the UK is especially concentrated in services such as banking, insurance, consultancy and trade. This presumably reflects the UK's well known comparative advantage in trade invisibles; this explanation may also apply to similar USA, Australian and Canadian orientations towards service-related FDI. Service-orientated preferences by Malaysian and Hong Kong investors is perhaps explained by noting that these investors are often the local subsidiaries of UK companies.

Foreign investment from most countries is concentrated in the manufacturing sector because Singapore's incentives structure and infrastructural facilities are second to none. In addition there are country-concentrations in some industries because of the existing strengths of companies from certain source countries. Thus, for example, both the USA and Japan are better represented in electrical/electronic machinery than the U.K. (Table 1.9). Similarly, despite the recent establishment of the Sumitomo petrochemicals complex (a Singaporean - Japanese joint venture), petroleum products and petrochemicals remain the domain of companies from the UK, the USA and the Netherlands. The dynamics underlying the establishment of this industry in Singapore will be discussed in chapter five.

CONCLUDING REMARKS

The surge of foreign investment into Singapore has led to a dynamic, expanding and relatively healthy economy where growth is apparently only fettered by full employment. (14) The authorities have reacted to this problem by promoting sectoral

Introduction

Table 1.9   The Industrial Distribution of USA,
            U.K. and Japanese Foreign Direct
            Investment in Singapore.

Percent

Industry	USA.(1982)	U.K.(1981)	Japan[f](1980)
Petroleum	39.7[a]	N.A.[b]	-
Manufacturing	31.3	40.9	73.4
- chemicals	1.2	29.6	8.8
- non-electrical machinery	3.0	0.6[c]	13.2
- electrical machinery	15.4	3.7	14.8
Trade	10.0	21.3	6.0
Banking	7.0	27.2[d,e]	-9
Other Finance, Insurance and Real Estate	9.5	8.0	5.3[h]
Others	2.5	2.5	15.2
Total Amount (US$ mn)	1,803.0	1,169.9[e]	932.2

Sources: U.S. Dept. of Commerce, Survey of Current
         Business, August 1983.
         U.K. Government Statistical Office,
         Business Monitor (MA4), Supplement, Census
         of Overseas Assets 1981, HMSO, 1984.
         Japanese Ministry of Finance.

Notes: a - As well as petroleum distribution this
             includes petroleum refining and related
             activities including manufacture of
             petroleum-related products.
         b - U.K. activities in this area are
             similar to those of USA firms. Most of
             the share appropriate here is included in
             "Chemicals", the rest in "Banking" (because
             the data presentation is intended to avoid
             disclosure of information on individual
             banks or oil companies).
         c - Only mechanical engineering and
             instrument engineering. Presumably other
             data appropriate here is included in other
             manufacturing categories.
         d - Includes Insurance.
         e - Figures for Banking in Singapore is

Table 1.9   The Industrial Distribution of USA,
             UK and Japanese Foreign Direct
             Investment in Singapore. (cont.)

Notes: continued.

             lumped with Banking in Malaysia in the U.K.
             statistics.   Two-thirds of this sum has
             been allocated to Singapore and is included
             in the total amount of UK FDI in
             Singapore.
             f - The Japanese statistics refer to
             approved, not confirmed, amounts of FDI.
             g - Included in "other finance" etc.
             h - Includes Banking and Branch Offices.

diversification (into finance and services) and
higher technology, higher value added industries.
Table 1.10 (see also chapters two to four) attests
to the success of these policies, but the government
continues to urge constant vigilance by the entire
populace.   Given   the   fragile   world   economy,
Singapore's precarious lack of resources, and the
fickleness   of   multinational   enterprise,   this
reasonable paranoia is probably justified.
      Where   Singapore   is   concerned, events progress
rapidly.   As the "Pacific Century" approaches, amid
calls   for   further   regional economic co-operation,
Singapore, whose economy is likely to play a significant role if this international effort succeeds,
is   striving   to   achieve   an   "Information Society"
which will naturally become the "brain centre" and
economic leader of South East Asia. (15) Meanwhile
this small city-state has begun to export weaponry;
local   firms   are   expanding   their   investments
overseas;   and   many   countries   are   attempting   to
emulate its achievements. (16) Sri Lanka has even
turned   to   the   Singapore   authorities   for advice.
(17)
      This   book intends to place Singapore's success
and   predicament   in   context   by: (i) examining the
historical and institutional factors underlying the
influx of foreign companies (chapter two); (ii) des-
cribing the current position and dynamics of MNC's
in   various   sectors   and   industries (chapters three
and   four);   (iii)   explaining   the   island-state's
attractiveness relative to other developing and
industrialised countries (chapters two to four); and
(iv)   analysing   the   national   and   international
determinants   and   consequences   of   the   country's
economic transformation (chapters five and six).

Introduction

This book cannot claim to be definitive, but hopefully it will make some contribution towards understanding the Singapore phenomenon.

NOTES

1. All dollar figures quoted in this book are in United States Dollars.

2. All figures are from the World Bank (1984), World Development Report, Oxford University Press.

3. The U.K.'s population is 55.8 million people.

4. These figures are from, the Committee on Invisible Exports (1983), Annual Report, 1982/1983, p.11, and "International Banking Markets 1983", Bank of England Quarterly Bulletin, March 1984, Table 2. Singapore's share of world net private invisible receipts is even greater at 4.6 percent.

5. For the purposes of this book a multinational company (MNC) is defined very simply as a company with productive facilities (be these in manufacturing, mining, finance or other services) in more than one country.

6. Foreign direct investment (FDI) is one way in which a MNC can operate overseas. It involves the establishment and control of a subsidiary in a foreign country. A multinational company can operate overseas in a number of other ways (e.g. through licensing or franchise), but FDI remains the most important method, not least in Singapore.

7. This fact does not overly affect the validity of GNP per capita figures quoted earlier because most foreign earnings are re-invested in Singapore.

8. These figures were calculated using data from the IMF (1983), Balance of Payments Yearbook, Washington.

9. These figures were calculated using data in, the Department of Statistics (1983), Report on the Census of Industrial Production 1982, Singapore.

10. This term includes finance and services.

11. This is a very rough estimate, especially because the data for FDI and GDCF came from two different sources.

Introduction

Table 1.10 Some "High Value Added" subsidiaries
            in Singapore.

Parent Company	Singapore Company	Products
Air Liquide (France)	Liquide Pte Ltd.	Speciality Gases for electronics industry.
Caltex Petroleum) Corp. (USA)) British Petroleum) Co. Ltd. (U.K.)) Singapore Petro-) leum Corp.(Sing.))	Singapore Refining Co.	Petroleum Products.
WIBAU (W.Germany)	WIBAU-Allatt(s) Pte Ltd.	Road constructio equipment.
Honeywell Inc. (USA)	Honeywell - Synertek Pte Ltd.	Semiconduct ors; Integrated circuits design.
ELXSI Inc. (USA)) Tata Industries) Ltd. (India))	Tata/ELXSI Plc Ltd.	Super-mini computers and related software.
Philips (Netherlands)	Philips Singapore Pte Ltd.	Precision tools and discs, TV sets, radios, cassette recorders, domestic appliances.
Matsushita Electric Industrial Co. (Japan)	Matsushita Electronics(s) Pte Ltd.	Hi-Fi equipment.

Introduction

Table 1.10   Some "High Value Added" subsidiaries
             in Singapore.

Parent Company	Singapore Company	Products
Consolidated Aeronautics Corp. (USA)	Aerospace Industries Pte Ltd.	Aircraft parts and components.
Wild Heerbrug AG (Switzerland)	Wild (Singapore) Pte Ltd.	Surveying Instruments, Stereomicro-scopes.
Beecham Group (U.K.)	Beecham Pharmaceuticals Pte Ltd.	Semi-synthetic penicillins.
Alfa Laval (Sweden)	Alfa Laval (Singapore)	Compressors; Heat Exchangers.
Kanegafuchi Chemical Industry Co. Ltd. (Japan)	Kaneka Singapore (Pte) Ltd.	Amino acids.
Nestle SA (Switzerland)	Eastreco Pte Ltd.	Regional food research centre.
Fuji Oil (Japan)) C. Itoh & Co.) (Japan))	Fuji Oil Singapore	Cocoa Butter replacer plant.

Sources: Singapore Economic Development Board,
          Leading International Companies
          Manufacturing and Providing Technical
          Services in Singapore, 1983.

          Singapore Investment News, September 1983,
          April 1984 and May 1984.

19

NOTES continued.

12. Table 1.8 is derived from a frequency count of subsidiaries listed in Who Owns Whom in Australasia and the Far East. Consequently its coverage is patchy for both countries and industries. Japan and developing countries suffer most in this respect e.g. Toyo Keizai Shinposha (Japanese Multinationals: Facts and Figures 1983, Tokyo) lists well over 400 Japanese subsidiaries in Singapore. This far exceeds the number indicated by Table 1.8. Similarly, subsidiaries are placed, as far as possible, under their actual industry, but where this was not possible to ascertain they have been assigned the industry of their parent company. In addition there are problems of classication and weighting. For example, the Table under-states the importance of petroleum (i.e. energy) subsidiaries which are capital intensive, but overstates the importance of distribution subsidiaries.

13. There are a great number of large Chinese owned companies in South East and East Asian countries such as Thailand, Malaysia, The Philippines, Indonesia and, of course, Singapore. Many of these are family owned businesses of which a good example is the Indonesian based conglomerate empire of the Liem family. (See Anthony Rowley, "Birth of a multinational", Far Eastern Economic Review, April 7, 1983). The Liem's have major (nearly always controlling) stakes in over 30 Indonesian companies and over 20 overseas companies. The overseas companies are based in countries as far apart as the U.S., Liberia, the Dutch Antilles, Hong Kong, the Netherlands and Singapore. These companies are in manufacturing, trading, finance and the services and some are quite large e.g. First Pacific Holdings (Hong Kong, formerly Shanghai land) and Hibernia Bancshares Corp. (U.S., twelth largest Californian bank). Another interesting example of a foreign Chinese company operating in Singapore is Mulpha (Singapore). This is owned by Mulpha International Holdings, a Malaysian company, which is the manufacturing and trading arm of Multi Purpose Holdings Bhd (MPH). MPH is itself 52% owned by Koperasi Serbaguna Malaysia (KSM), the Malaysian Multi-purpose Co-operative Society which is a component of the Malaysian Chinese Association (MCA), a Chinese political party. MPH is a large conglomerate and its structure indicates how complex some of these concerns can be. (See Anthony Rowley, "The Politics of Business", Far Eastern Economic Review, May 10, 1984).

Introduction

NOTES continued.

14. In fact Singapore is now host to a great deal of immigrant labour.

15. See, for example, Michael West Oborne and Nicholas Fourt (1983), Pacific Basin Economic Co-operation, OECD and Peter Large, "Silicon Island Invests in Chinese Brain Power", Guardian, December 8, 1983.

16. See, Rudy Maex (1983), Employment and Multinationals in Asian Export Processing Zones, ILO; S. Kumar, "Today Singapore, tomorrow the world", Straits Times, July 14, 1984 (based on an interview with Professor Raj Aggarwal of the University of Toledo); and U.G. Kulkarni, "Coming out of the closet", Far Eastern Economic Review, June 30, 1983.

17. See "Singapore and Sri Lanka begin to talk shop", South, January 1982.

Chapter Two

THE POLITICS OF ECONOMIC TRANSFORMATION :
AN HISTORICAL OVERVIEW

In a recent article the veteran pro-"free"
market development economist P.T. Bauer declares
that the experience of many East Asian countries
contradicted the view that 'comprehensive central
planning is indispensible for the economic progress
of poor countries' (1) and cited an impressive list
of countries, including Japan, Hong Kong, South
Korea and Singapore, in support of his thesis
However, this conclusion required scant
substantiation for, by quoting statements made by
eminent social scientists in the 1950s and by
referring to the ultimate bogey, "central planning"
Bauer's article effectively groomed and demolished
an "Aunt Sally". (2).

When the role of the state in economic
development is considered in a fairer manner the
evidence is, to say the least, mixed. While the
authorities have played a minimal role in Hong Kong
the role of the state in modern Japan, South Korea
and Taiwan is generally acknowledged to have been
both significant and crucial. (3)

Singapore itself, despite its heavy dependence
on multinational companies, is not the exception
that breaks the rule, a point often stressed by
local economists. (4) Indeed, as this chapter will
show, Singapore is almost a classic example of
growth-orientated interventionary capitalist state
which promotes industrial expansion by (i) ensuring
market liberalisation; (ii) mobilising resources and
establishing an adequate infrastructure; (iii)
orchestrating the various sectors of the economy
(iv) educating and training the work force; and (v)
providing an ideological rationale for acquiescence
by the general populace to the activities of the
government and other privileged groups.

EARLY HISTORY

Although Chinese explorers may have discovered Singapore in 231 A.D., referring to it as "Pu-luo-chung" (the island at the end of the [Malay] peninsula), little is known of its early history. Javanese chroniclers refer to Singapore as "Temasek" ("Sea Town") after an existing coastal settlement, and the Sejarah Melayu (Malay Annals) mention that it was renamed by the Sumatran prince Sri Tri Buana in the 13th century. Upon landing on the island the prince spied a strange beast, probably a Tiger, which his courtiers mistook for a lion. Considering the animal a good omen he promptly renamed the island Singha Pura ("lion city" in sanskrit), a name which it still retains. In the 14th century Singapore became a battleground for Thai-Javanese rivalry and at one stage all settlements were razed to the ground by the Java-based Majapahit Empire. In 1390 the Sumatran prince Parameswara (founder of the Malacca Sultanate) seized control and declared himself ruler, but was forcibly expelled in 1402 by the Ayutthaya (Thai) Empire. Soon after this the island was re-acquired by the Islamic-Malay Malaccan Empire and, upon the empire's demise in 1511, was occupied by the conquering Portuguese in 1526.

By the 19th century Portuguese power had declined and Singapore briefly became a possession of the Sultanate of Johore. However Anglo-Dutch rivalry in the East Indies was at its height and in 1819 Singapore was given to the British East India Company by Sultan Hussein as a reward for their help against his brother, the previous Dutch-installed Sultan of Johore, Abdul Rahman. William Farquar and Thomas Stamford Raffles played a major part in this acquisition and the latter, perceiving a significant military and commercial role for the strategically placed island, lobbied hard for its retention. Within four years Singapore proved to be commercially viable and its trade exceeded that of Penang, hitherto Britain's main port in South East Asia. Impressed, the British arranged and signed two treaties in 1824, one with the Netherlands, the other with the Sultanate of Johore, formalising Singapore's new position in the British Empire. The Sultan of Johore retains property in the Republic of Singapore; and the legal status of the island, although never discussed, remains ambiguous.

In 1826 the East India Company formed the Straits Settlements by uniting Singapore with Penang and Malacca, both territories on the Malay peninsula. In 1867 the Straits Settlements became a Crown Colony on the assumption of direct British rule. Singapore was the major constituent territory and it was from here that British imperialists embarked upon their economic expansion into Malaya, South East Asia and China. Singapore's entrepot trade expanded rapidly and, despite the challenge of Hong Kong after 1842, it retained a key role in the East Asian colonial economy, a position which was enhanced by the opening of the Suez Canal in 1869. Prior to this date vessels from Europe bound for East Asia had to travel via the Cape of Good Hope and, because most ships then took the shortest route between Java and Sumatra (the Sunda Straits), Singapore was often bypassed. The island-port was well positioned on the new route and benefitted accordingly, serving as a conduit of commodity exports from East Asia to Europe and manufactured goods in the opposite direction.

Many companies prospered as a result of Singapore's entrepot activity and firms such as Boustead and Co., Simon and Patterson and Guthrie and Co. can trace their origins back to the early years of Singapore's colonial success. This prosperity derived not only from mercantile activities in a free trade port, but also from more productive pursuits. On the Malay peninsula itself these pursuits included rubber plantations (5) and tin mining, although the latter activity was largely dominated by Chinese immigrants.

Table 2.1   The Population of Singapore, 1819-1983.

(Thousands)

Year	Population	Year	Population
1819	0.2	1947	938.1
1823	10.0	1957	1,445.9
1871	97.1	1970	2,074.5
1901	227.6	1980	2,413.9
1931	557.7	1983	2,502.0

Source: Saw Swee-Hock (1981), Demographic Trends in Singapore, Singapore Department of Statistics.
Singapore Department of Statistics, Monthly Digest of Statistics, May 1984.

Singapore's economic success attracted vast numbers of migrants from nearby countries, the British Empire and, most importantly, from China. Chinese immigrants arrived in Singapore and South East Asia as a result of major socio-economic upheavals in their homeland. The 1842 Treaty of Nanking (in which China ceded Hong Kong to Britain) accelerated economic decline in China's southern provinces of Kwangtung, Kwangsi and Hunan by directing trade from Canton to Shanghai. As well as European encroachment Chinese peasants fled the spate of lengthy insurrections which convulsed China, including the rebellions of the T'ai P'ing (1850-64), the Nien (1853-68), the Miao of Kweichow (1854-72) and the muslim Hui of Yunnan, Shensi-Kansu and Singkiang (1855-73, 1863-73 and 1862-78 respectively).

This Chinese influx resulted in a massive increase in Singapore's population (Table 2.1) and turned a Malay Island into a Chinese dominated state (Table 2.2), although the Chinese population is itself composed of a large number of ethnically-differentiated groups. It is worth mentioning that migration to Singapore continues today and includes "guest" workers, expatriate personnel working for multinational companies, professionals lured by Singapore's prospects and latter day refugees such as the wealthy of Hong Kong. Table 2.2 shows that non-citizens compose over 9 percent of the population.

Table 2.2   The Population of Singapore by Ethnic Group and Residential Status.

Ethnic Group	Chinese	Malays	Indians	Others	Total (1983)
Number (thousands)	1,917	368	161	56	2,502
Percent	76.6	14.7	6.4	2.2	100.0

Residential Status	Singapore Citizens	Permanent Residents	Non-Residents	Total (1980)
Number (thousands)	2,194	88	132	2,414
Percent	90.9	3.6	5.5	100.0

Sources: As Table 2.1

Singapore remains an important entrepot, but the heyday of such activity was certainly the period before the second world war. In addition to these entrepot activities the island served as a major forward base for Britain's military expansion into East Asia. As a bastion it was regarded as the "Gibraltar of the East", a position which the island fulfilled, with declining effectiveness, until the late 1960s. In 1942 the city's ill-equipped forces capitulated to the Japanese and, despite the resumption of British control in 1945, the imperial epoch was over. In Singapore, as elsewhere, imperial nationalism had engendered indigenous nationalism and, armed with the conviction that liberation was possible (a point reinforced by the Japanese interlude), local patriots demanded independence.

FROM INSURRECTION TO INDEPENDENCE

In 1945 the communist led Malayan Peoples' Army (MPA) emerged from the jungles after three years of successful resistance against the Japanese. The Communists were hailed as heroes and participated in victory marches in front of Lord Mountbatten (Malaya) and the King (Britain). Chin Peng (Ong Boon Hua), the Malayan Communist Party's (MCP) secretary-general during the period of insurgency (1948-1960), even received an OBE which was later rescinded. Returning British Forces rapidly disarmed the MPA, but remained anxious about the prestige of the Communist party.

The MCP soon proved to be the most formidable and cohesive political organisation in Malaya (then including Singapore) and the United Kingdom, afraid that a communist regime would endanger British interests in South East Asia, embarked upon a policy of containment or elimination. In the event, the British Army, employing text-book counter-insurgency tactics (6), took twelve years to defeat the Malayan Communist Party which was well entrenched throughout the country and enjoyed a great deal of support. (7)

Left-wing sympathisers were especially numerous in Singapore with its large, urban working class and predominantly Chinese population. (8) The British authorities, confronted by a strong, militant and combative labour force whose call for self-determination was echoed in all social strata, were forced to eschew the military option and resorted

26

instead to repressive labour laws and security provisions in their attempt to maintain an amenable regime.

The People's Action Party

The People's Action Party (PAP), the party of government since 1959, was founded in the mid-fifties amid the turmoil of a colonial society actively demanding its freedom. From the beginning the PAP represented a marriage of convenience between a liberal, English speaking professional elite and a relatively left-wing, Mandarin educated group of leaders with a mass following. Consequently it is not surprising that both constituent parts of the PAP were constantly attempting to outwit each other for control of the party - and national leadership upon independence. In the interim both wings recognised the requirement for mutual support against the colonial authorities. The radical left and the Communists received overwhelming grass-root support from unions, students, Mandarin organisations and ethnic groups. The liberals were well aware of the need to mobilise the non-English speaking, subjected masses in the struggle for freedom. In turn they offered their coalition partners contacts in the establishment, professional expertise and a veneer of respectability. For the left these merits of an umbrella organisation were not to be scoffed at. In June 1948 the British Authorities had banned the Malayan Communist Party and left-wingers, whether communist or not, were subject to frequent arbitrary arrests.

Lee Kuan Yew, the present Prime Minister of Singapore and leader of the PAP since its inception, was a member of the liberal wing and first rose to prominence, as a lawyer, because of his defence of trade union activists in the early 1950s. Born in 1923, the Hakka (9) "Harry" Lee was educated entirely in English at Raffles College and Cambridge where he achieved a double first in Law. Upon his return to Singapore he improved his faltering Mandarin (10) and entered politics at the earliest opportunity. Lee possesses flair, intelligence and cunning, qualities which he adroitly used in his drive to power. He is also known for his determination and some of the methods of his PAP could be mistaken for refined versions of ancient Altaic state-craft. Aided by remarkable associates (notably Goh Keng Swee) he is responsible for

27

The Politics of Economic Transformation

Singapore's "economic miracle". His opponents in
the PAP were mainly radical-left trade unionists of
whom Lim Chin Siong, Fong Swee Suan, Sandra
Woodhull, James Puthucheary, Jamit Singh and S.T.
Bani were among the better known personalities.
Lee's later incarceration and emaciation of these
and other activists, not least the popular and
redoubtable Lim, can be regarded as a tragic chapter
in Singapore's history. They were accused of being
"communists", but:

> There was never any evidence, except Lee
> Kuan Yew's word, to show they were card-
> carrying communists. Their advocacy of
> workers' rights and a socialistic economy
> was communism enough for Lee. While using
> their undeniable mass base for the benefit
> of the PAP, it was Lee's perennial
> preoccupation to prevent the party from
> falling into their hands. He let them
> have the run of trade unions, but insisted
> that the party-machinery was his domain.
> (11)

In 1955, a year after its foundation, four PAP
leaders stood as candidates for the Singapore
Assembly and three of these, including Lim and Lee,
won a seat. Victory in these elections belonged to
the liberal Labour Front which had earlier rebuffed
Lee's pre-PAP collaboration overtures. Although
much-lambasted by contemporaries, and Lee since,
David Marshall's Labour Front did make some progress
towards self government, although he was forced to
resign when Britain began to stall. Meanwhile the
PAP went from strength to strength by espousing
revolutionary causes in all fora, but Lee was
concurrently vying for British favour and attempting
to outwit the left-wing. There is evidence that the
liberal wing of the PAP collaborated with the
authorities against the "pro-communists". Thus, for
example, when David Marshall refused to accept the
Special Branch's advice that three hundred radicals
be put in prison Goh Keng Swee, Lee's crony,
declared the detention of seven people, 'feeble and
lamentable in the extreme'. (12)
  Despite strenuous protestations by Lee against
frequent arrests of "pro-communists" and his release
of prisoners when he came to power, the coincidence
between these arrests and the fortunes of the
liberal faction of the PAP raised many suspicious
contemporary eyebrows. In 1956 when the left-wing

28

had gained four seats on the PAP's twelve-seat
central executive committee (Lim outpolling Lee) and
were attempting to revise the constitution, Lee's
position was rescued by the sudden arrest of three
of the four left-wingers by the post-Marshall Labour
Front Administration of Lim Yew Hock. In 1957 the
left-wing captured six seats and, as Lee stalled,
five of the six, including Lim Chin Siong were
arrested.

In 1959 the United Kingdom decided that the
time was ripe for self-government in Singapore.
Elections were held under universal suffrage for the
first time and the PAP won with 53% of the vote
(Table 2.12). Since Lim and the brightest of the
radical left were languishing in prison, there was
nothing to forestall Lee Kuan Yew's assumption of
power. At 36 he was the youngest Prime Minister in
Asia. The right-left struggle in the PAP was to
continue, however, and when matters eventually came
to a head over the Malaysia issue (see later) the
left-wing broke free and established a new
organisation, the Barisan Sosialis. Barisan's
Secretary was Lim Chin Siong and its formation
reduced the PAP to a skeleton. The PAP lost
thirteen MPs, seventy percent of its membership and
nearly all its branches. Unfortunately for Barisan
Sosialis the PAP and Lee retained control over the
levers of power.

The Winsemius Mission

The looming spectre of potential economic
crisis began to haunt Singapore in the mid-fifties,
just as the PAP's power struggle with the British
commenced. By 1960 it was recognised that the
entrepot sector's rate of expansion was insufficient
to keep pace with the rapid rate of increase of
population, then running at 4% a year. Since the
entrepot sector (trade and related financial,
transportation and other services) accounted for
over 70% of Singapore's GNP (Table 2.3) this was
grim news indeed and a United Nations Industrial
Survey Mission was asked to make recommendations.
(13).

The United Nations Mission, headed by Dutch
economist Dr. Albert Winsemius, arrived in Singapore
in 1961 and presented its report in June 1961 when
internal PAP left-right tensions were at their
height. (14) The report argued that if the
stagnating entrepot and manufacturing sectors were
left to their own devices there was no chance of

Table 2.3 Industrial distribution of Gross
          Domestic Product, 1960-83.

Percent

Industry	1960	1965	1970	1975	1980	1983
Agriculture & Fishing	3.8	3.1	2.3	1.6	1.3	1.0
Quarrying	0.3	0.3	0.3	0.4	0.3	0.6
Manufacturing	12.8	15.3	20.5	21.4	24.1	20.0
Utilities	2.3	2.3	2.6	2.5	2.9	2.9
Construction	3.5	6.3	6.3	6.7	4.7	8.2
Trade	31.2	27.4	28.1	27.0	24.4	23.9
Transport & Communication	13.3	11.1	11.3	14.0	18.3	20.8
Financial & Business Services	11.7	13.8	13.9	17.0	18.0	21.9
Other Services	17.7	17.3	13.6	12.7	11.0	11.0
Imputed Bank Service Charges	-1.5	-1.6	-1.9	-4.4	-6.6	-10.1
Import Duties	4.8	4.8	3.0	1.7	1.7	(a)
Total	100.0	100.0	100.0	100.0	100.0	100.0
Amount (US$ bns 1968 market prices)	0.8	1.0	1.8	3.7	5.7	7.3

Sources: Calculations based on data in:
         Singapore Department of Statistics,
         Economic and Social Statistics, 1960-1982;
         Singapore Department of Statistics, Monthly
         Digest of Statistics, May 1984.
Note: a - Figures for the 1983 column were
         derived from a separate source and the
         amount for import duties is presumably
         allocated between the various industries.

checking rising unemployment. The Mission estimated that 37,000 people were unemployed in 1960 (7-8% of the workforce) and calculated that 214,000 jobs had to be created by 1970. This figure was conservative because while population increase and productivity effects were incorporated in the estimation procedure, underemployment was not - although it was deemed to be considerable. The UN team believed that only manufacturing could generate jobs at the necessary rate and called for an expansionary programme in the industrial and related sectors. This approach was ambitious because in 1960 the manufacturing sector accounted for only 13% of Singapore's GDP and employed a mere 61,000 workers. (15) A number of recommendations were made regarding Markets, Labour, Capital and Entrepreneurs, Organisation and Specific Industries - and these formed the basis of future government policy.

Markets. Malaya, the U.K. and Indonesia were identified as the major markets for Singapore's products, but Indonesia was considered erratic as an importer. It was recommended that industrialisation efforts should primarily be aimed at markets in Malaya, the U.K. and EFTA (the European Free Trade Association). Attempts should also be made to expand exports to nearby countries such as Sabah, Sarawak, Brunei, Thailand and Burma. Singapore initially followed these recommendations by becoming a part of the Malaysian Federation, thereby increasing its "domestic" market considerably. Early efforts at industrialisation were therefore through import-substitution policies, although these efforts were abandoned in favour of export-promotion in 1965 when it became politically expedient for the island to dissolve its union with Malaysia. Interestingly, Singapore's Malaya-oriented policies led to a trade-boycott by the Indonesians and, to this day, political pressures prevent official disclosure of Singapore-Indonesian trade figures.

Labour. In the Mission's opinion Singaporean workers were of a high quality, but their calibre could be improved through education, degree courses, vocational training and overseas visits. However, it was also claimed that 'unrest, low productivity and irrational wage demands' were damaging and needed to be curtailed. This unrest was connected with Singapore's political discord and the declining trend in manufacture was a result of:

> ... political uncertainty, the industrial
> promotion policy in the Federation, the
> instability of the Indonesian market,
> concern of investors over long-term
> political stability, and unfavourable
> industrial relations. (16)

The team recommended industrial relations
improvement with employers becoming more responsive,
unions accepting longer term agreements based on
productivity, and government acting as arbitrator.
The PAP went a shade further. Political stability
and industrial peace was ensured by smashing Barisan
Sosialis, emasculating socialist unions and
establishing a PAP-led National Trade Union Congress
(NTUC).

Capital and Entrepreneurship. The need to attract
considerable amounts of overseas capital, technology
and skills was recognised as a priority and it was
suggested that the Singapore Government facilitate
foreign investment by (i) improving the investment
climate (industrial relations, infrastructure,
double taxation agreements etc.), (ii) increasing
inducements (tax holidays, tariff reductions,
subsidies), and (iii) establishing appropriate
bodies to organise the industrialisation process.

Organisation. Two specific bodies were recommended
by the Winsemius report. One was to be an
Investment Development Bank which was to finance
certain investments, and the other, the Economic
Development Board (EDB), was to oversee the
establishment of industrial companies and assess the
viability of various courses of action. The EDB was
to be divided into a number of interacting
departments, one of which would market Singapore
overseas. Both of these organisations were
later established by the Government.

Specific Industries. Given the skills available in
the workforce, four key industries were considered
worth promoting: shipbuilding and shiprepairing,
metal and engineering products, electrical equipment
and appliances and chemicals. All these industries
today play an important part in Singapore's economy,
although the Government is now attempting to reduce
the contribution of lower-volume added products and
processes. In addition the report also suggested a
short-term crash programme, but this need not
concern us here.

The Politics of Economic Transformation

Quite evidently the UN report played a major role in Singapore's economic policies, not least because Dr. Winsemius has been the Government's chief economic adviser ever since. In addition it provided the PAP with a rationale for subduing the left and entering the Malaysian Federation.

The Federation of Malaysia

By 1957, after ten years of battle, Britain believed that the communist insurgency was under control. Peninsular Malaya was granted independence, but Singapore was retained as a colony and military base, albeit with self-government from 1959. The issue of Singaporean independence was a complex one. Both Britain and Malaya feared that an entirely independent Singapore would become a "communist" controlled bastion - the "Cuba" of South East Asia - and advocated union with Malaya to neutralise the island's left-wing. However UMNO-MCA (the coalition between the United Malay National Organisation and the Malayan Chinese Association), the ruling party of Malaya, was also anxious about the likely effect of a Malaya-Singapore union on the delicate ethnic balance. Tensions were already high between the bumiputra (indigenous Malays) and the economically dominant Chinese minority: the merger with a relatively skilled, predominantly Chinese population from Singapore could well lead to communal violence. (17) In the event Malaya's Prime Minister, Tunku Abdul Rahman, neatly side-stepped the communal problem on 27 May 1961 by proposing a Federation of Malaysia which would consist of Malaya, Singapore, Brunei, Sarawak and Sabah. Brunei did not join, but the indigenous population of Sarawak and Sabah ensured that the Chinese share of Malaysia's population was minimised.

Lee Kuan Yew and the PAP were entirely in favour of the proposed federation and entered into immediate negotiations. In their view entry into Malaysia offered better control over leftist forces, potential PAP expansion into a larger state, access to a large market (as advised by the Winsemius report) and, most importantly, guaranteed independence from Britain. Given these considerable benefits, the PAP took no chances. A referendum was held on 1 September 1962 which offered voters only three choices: (i) merger with Malaysia under terms negotiated by the PAP allowing autonomy in education and labour; (ii) merger under the (less favourable)

33

conditions offered to other Malaysian states; and (iii) merger under the (least favourable) conditions offered to Sabah and Sarawak. Blank votes would count as votes for the PAP proposal and, further, since it was possible to trace individual voters, much of the electorate were obviously intimidated into voting "correctly". Not unexpectedly there was a resounding majority for union with Malaysia, although the Government was infuriated by the blank votes returned by a quarter of all voters. A date was duly set for the establishment of Malaysia, but the PAP feared that a Barisan Sosialis victory in the 1963 elections could yet lead to a reversal of the merger.

In many respects the events of 1963 represent the denouement of the crucial left-right struggle in Singapore. Lee Kuan Yew took a number of measures to ensure the PAP's retention of power. A key weapon in his armoury was the Internal Security Department (ISD) which had virtually unlimited power to detain persons considered risks to security. In February 1963 the ISD organised operation "Cold Store" in which over one hundred members of Barisan Sosialis, the Singapore Association of Trade Unions and other leftist groups were arrested and jailed. (18)

Though this raid incarcerated all the major leaders of the left (Lim, Fong, Puthucheary etc.) and decapitated Barisan, Lee still had a number of other tricks up his sleeve. For example, the Government restricted campaigning to only nine days and ordered simultaneous festivities to celebrate entry into Malaysia. The latter measure had the additional merit of clogging up printing presses, thus impeding the circulation of opposition literature. The PAP had its own literature printed well in advance in Hong Kong.

Despite loading the electoral dice the PAP won only 46.9 percent of the vote on 21 September, but this was sufficient for an overwhelming thirty seven seats. Barisan Sosialis received 33.3 percent of the vote and thirteen seats, a commendable performance under the circumstances. Nevertheless, Lee's tactics had paid off handsomely and Singapore's entry into the Federation of Malaysia, proclaimed on 16 September 1963, was secure.

The election of 1963 marked a turning point for both Barisan Sosialis and the PAP. The left, so certain of popular support, had displayed an amateurish attitude towards the electoral process and thereby allowed Lee to both outmanoeuvre and outflank Barisan. Disgusted by Lee's "legal fixing", Barisan Sosialis MPs resigned their parliamentary seats in 1966 and since then the party has refused to contest any further elections. The PAP meanwhile has built up an almost invincible position in Singaporean political life and continues to win elections with thumping majorities (Table 2.14). The government has been able to maintain the consent or acquiescence of the general public for a number of reasons. First, it has established a very efficient system for responding to popular demand and stifling expectations deemed inappropriate. According to Crouch:

> Since 1965, Citizens' Consultative Committees (CCCs) have been established in every electoral constituency, with the local Member of Parliament as adviser (except in the case of the lone opposition Member of Parliament since 1981), and a network of local management committees of community centres has also been established within each constituency. Through these bodies, the government has been able to keep in touch with popular feeling and respond to those expectations considered appropriate. (19)

Secondly, the integrity, efficiency and success of Lee Kuan Yew's administration cannot be denied; and the possible turmoil and decline arising from the PAP's collapse as a political force plays a major part in the public's acceptance of 'the devil you know'. Thirdly, Singapore's extreme reliance upon foreign investment reduces the country's short-term options dramatically. This allows the PAP to foster simultaneously (a) an antipathy towards domestic and foreign left-wing elements which may "undermine" the system; and (b) a cult of efficiency, achievement and material success. Finally, the depoliticisation inherent in this cult has been reinforced by the government's efforts towards social engineering, including eugenical solutions and social regimentation. (20)

MIRACLE BY DESIGN

On 9 August 1965 the Malaysian Parliament passed a bill terminating Singapore's membership of the Federation. For Lee and the PAP this ignominious separation meant a large-scale reversal of policy, but it was an event of their own making. During Singapore's two year union with Malaysia it maintained an independent stance on both domestic and foreign affairs; Lee Kuan Yew, although a member of the opposition, insisted on the designation, "Prime Minister"; and both Malay and Chinese members of the UMNO-MCA Alliance suspected the PAP of long-term designs on the Federation. On a number of occasions these tensions spilled over into communal violence and Tunku Abdul Rahman eventually decided that the penalty for disobedience was divorce. (21)

After initial traumatic paralysis the newly independent and sovereign Republic of Singapore swiftly re-orientated its economic and political objectives. The chief architects of the post-1965 policies were Lee Kuan Yew himself, Goh Keng Swee, Hon Sui Sen, Ngiam Tong Dow, Albert Winsemius, Devan Nair and S. Rajaratnam. (Further details in note 22.) Now that open access to the larger Malaysian market was lost to Singapore-based companies, import-substitution policies had to be replaced by ones designed to promote exports. In this context it was necessary to attract multinational companies which would produce locally (hence employment, technology transfer) and sell globally or regionally. Given the island's strategic location, well-developed infrastructure and cheap, skilled, plentiful labour-force the chances of attracting investment from such MNCs were considered to be good. Even the country's lack of resources was not a disadvantage because of the nearness of Brunei, Indonesia and Malaysia - all rich in energy, raw materials and agricultural produce. Indeed, Singapore's existing key entrepot role in distributing these commodities meant that it could be an ideal base for preliminary processing and, potentially, forward integration into manufacture.

Although all the omens were good, Lee and the leadership of the PAP realised that MNCs had to be convinced of the suitability of Singapore vis-a-vis other developing countries with a similar profile. A grand strategy (23) was developed to build and maintain foreign confidence in the city-state's economic dynamism and future potential. First, it was decided, industrial and political stability would be "improved"; secondly, infrastructural facilities would be developed yet further; thirdly, inducements would be offered to foreign investors in priority industries; fourthly, key state-owned boards and enterprises would be established to direct the economy; and finally, not only would the investment climate be good - it would be seen to be good. The island would be promoted at all cost, and soon the Republic's emissaries were criss-crossing the continents.

This international marketing of Singapore entered a critical phase when it was discovered that Britain was planning to close its local military base. In 1967, when the withdrawal plan was announced, the base still accounted for 14% of the country's GNP and employed 16% of the work-force. (24) Although the effects on the economy could be minimised, it was feared that the end of an ostensibly strategic British presence in South East Asia could seriously undermine foreign confidence and jeopardise the island's future. Frantic diplomatic activity eventually led to a calmer atmosphere and much of Singapore's militarisation can be traced to this period. (Table 2.5)

As chapter one demonstrated, there was a quantum leap in foreign direct investment soon after this crisis of confidence and employment generation was phenomenal. Singapore's advantages and incentives induced a great deal of multinational investment in manufacturing and this sector's share of GDP rose from 12.8% in 1960 to 20.5% in 1970 and a peak of 24.1% in 1980. (Table 2.3) Since then the sector's share has fallen, but the government plans to boost manufacturing's share to over 30% of GDP by 1990. By the early 1970s Singapore was in a position to diversify its economy further and measures were implemented to expand foreign investment in higher value-added manufacture, finance and services. The Monetary Authority of Singapore (MAS) was established as a major step towards developing the island as an international financial centre and, as Table 2.3 shows, the administration was ultimately successful in this policy. By 1983 Financial and Business Services (chiefly serving multinationals in Singapore and other countries in the East Asian region) accounted for 21.9% of GDP, up from 11.7% in 1960 and 13.9% in 1970. Entrepot activities have also continued to grow in absolute terms and trade still represents a quarter of GDP.

The government's more recent promotion of service industries will be discussed in the next section; and later chapters will outline specific inducements and infrastructural facilities designed to entice foreign investors. The remainder of this section analyses various elements of the PAP's "grand strategy" which was mentioned above.

The Taming of the Unions.

The PAP began to establish its control over the union movement in the early days of its struggle with Barisan Sosialis, much of whose support came from the radical unions. In the run-up to the 1963 election many union officials were arrested during operation "Cold Store", 400 Barisan labour leaders were dismissed from their jobs and the three largest left-wing unions had their bank accounts frozen. The strength of the Singapore Trade Union Congress (STUC) was gradually sapped by a cynical deregistration of member unions under the Trade Union Act of 1946. In 1961 the PAP established the National Trade Union Congress (NTUC) under the leadership of Devan Nair (the present President of the Republic) to challenge the dominance of the STUC. "Legal fixing" assured the NTUCs success and it remains an important instrument for managing the work force. Despite its claims to independence, the NTUC is an integral part of the PAP constituency and all three secretary-generals to date, Devan Nair, Lim Chee Onn and Ong Teng Cheong, have been Cabinet Ministers.

The 1968 Employment Act and Industrial Relations (amendment) Act removed almost all worker rights and enshrined the ascendency of employers and management. According to Pang:

> The Employment Act of 1968 was designed to spread employment and reduce the cost of fringe benefits. It sets out extensive regulations about hours of work, overtime (including maximums), holidays and bonuses. Amendments to the Industrial Relations Act, also made in 1968, made non-negotiable management prerogatives such as promotion, internal transfer, recruitment, retirement, dismissal, and allocation of duties. (25)

Multinational companies were encouraged greatly, but unions discovered that the scope for collective bargaining was greatly reduced by this authoritarian legislation foisted upon them by Lee Kuan Yew, one time defender of union leaders. All disputes were subject to compulsory arbitration at the Industrial Arbitration Court which was required to take into account, 'not only the immediate interests of the parties to the dispute but also the interest of the community as a whole and in particular the condition of the economy of Singapore.' (26) Not unexpectedly, the interest of the economy demanded "wage restraint" and the court accordingly awarded only low pay increases. However even NTUC unions were incensed in 1969-70 when 70 Ministers and members of parliament were awarded salary increases totalling $200,000 per annum - only a month after 19,000 daily-rated workers were denied a wage increase which would have cost the treasury $420,000 (barely twice as much).

The government moved swiftly to defuse the labour unrest and the tripartite (Unions - Government - Employers) National Wages Council (NWC) was formed in 1972. Neither the unions nor the employers have much control over the NWC which sets wage levels annually by decree. Rapid economic progress has meant that the wage awards (usually in line with productivity) have contributed to rising living standards, thus reducing popular discontent and improving the investment climate. Table 2.4 demonstrates the success of government policies aimed at controlling the labour force. Industrial stoppages declined dramatically after the 1963 coup against Barisan Sosialis when 388 thousand man-days were lost: during the period 1978 to 1982 no days were lost at all. Trade disputes have also declined to a small number of minor disagreements; and union membership now only represents 19% of the work force as against 43% in 1962.

Many foreign investors have undoubtedly been attracted by Singapore's clement and stable industrial relations regime, but this pacific climate has been bought at a price and the government may yet reap what it has sown. Thomas Bellows argues:

> There does exist a sizeable group of people who might be activated against the PAP if Singapore should become embroiled in an economic crisis which offers no hope of solution. The overwhelming majority of the now unaffiliated former unionists are pro-Barisan persons who have been deprived of unions and leaders by the government but who have refused to be enticed into joining pro-government or neutral unions. These unaffiliated...[and others]... could during a period of economic decline, be a potential threat to the government. (27)

Table 2.4   Trade Union Membership, Industrial
            Stoppages and Trade Disputes, 1960-1982.

Year	Trade Union Members[a] (Thousands)	Industrial Stoppages (Thousands of man-days lost)	Trade Disputes[b] (Number)
1960	145	152	804
1961	164	411	1,225
1962	189	165	1,064
1963	143	388	967
1964	157	36	792
1965	154	46	801
1966	141	45	702
1967	130	41	790
1968	126	11	649
1969	120	9	449
1970	112	3	486
1971	124	5	765
1972	167	18	1,140
1973	191	2	997
1974	204	5	1,091
1975	209	5	709
1976	222	3	694
1977	229	1	640
1978	237	-	548
1979	250	-	577
1980	244	-	484
1981	224	-	392
1982	214	-	311

Source: Singapore Department of Statistics,
          Economic and Social Statistics, 1960-1982.

Notes: a - Employee class only.
          b - Excluding disputes or refusals to
          negotiate and union membership from 1979.

Although the memories of Barisan must be
dimming twenty years on, the PAP is aware that only
continued economic success will ensure its survival
in the long run.

International Relations and World-Wide Sourcing.

Three key issues dictate the bulk of
Singapore's international diplomatic activity.
First, Singapore is a small, wealthy, relatively
industrialised Chinese city-state surrounded by

large, under-developed non-Chinese neighbours. It
is heavily dependent on these neighbours for
markets, trade and raw materials, but it's
technological and economic dominance in the region
is a natural source of tension. Most of these
neighbours (especially Malaysia and Indonesia) have
large Chinese minorities with potent interests in
the business sector and this further fuels tensions.
Consequently much of Singapore's foreign policy is
designed to allay the fears of neighbouring
countries, but this is difficult because much of
Singapore's well-being directly depends on its
economic hegemony in South East Asia. Secondly, the
country is sustained by a massive influx of foreign
direct investment from the West and it expends
considerable diplomatic and promotional activity in
ensuring continued high levels of overseas
investment. Finally, the authorities promote the
view that any potential (domestic) left-wing (28)
challenge to the PAP's domination of the state must
be anticipated and eliminated because (i) foreign
confidence in the island's economy is fragile and
(ii) neighbouring right-wing countries, alarmed as
they are by their own Chinese minorities, view
Singapore as a possible fifth column. (The People's
Republic of China is, of course, the nearest
superpower.) Singapore's strident anti-communist
international stance is therefore, amongst other
things, both a subtle method of manipulating
domestic attitudes and a sop to foreign pressures.
During the fifties and early sixties Lee Kuan
Yew played the role of a radical nationalist and
accordingly was heavily involved with the non-
aligned movement. He met with Nasser, Nehru,
Kenyatta and other Afro-Asian figures in the non-
aligned hall of fame. Lee still maintains that his
administration is neutral, but while support for
western capitalist states is strong, communism is
officially regarded as the major enemy. Further,
the convergence of interests between the economy and
multinational companies means that Singapore's
support for developing countries in international
fora is somewhat ambiguous. For example, although a
member of the group of 77 which represents the
developing countries during all major negotiations
regarding the New International Economic Order
(NIEO), Singapore's position during the 1983 United
Nations Conference on Trade and Development
(UNCTAD VI) was generally in favour of the status
quo. (29) Since the status quo preserves western
domination of the international trading system - a

domination from which Singapore and other newly industrialising countries benefit - this stance is readily comprehensible and is consistant with the PAP's "grand strategy".

After withdrawal from Malaysia the English-educated PAP leadership initially attempted to attract investment from the United Kingdom and Old Commonwealth countries such as Australia and Canada. This strategy signally failed because Commonwealth MNCs, especially those happily ensconced in Malaysia were unwilling to make precipitative and unnecessary investments in a newly sovereign firebrand of a nation. (30) Singapore responded to this set-back by encouraging USAand Japanese investment instead. This volte-face jolted even the most seasoned of foreign policy analystsbecause of Lee's abhorrence for all things American or Japanese. Americans were considered brutal and crass; the Vietnamese war was imperialistic; and in 1965 Lee declared that he would offer Singapore as a military base to the Soviet Union if US troups were ever stationed in Malaysia. (31) The Japanese were hated because of their ill-treatment of the local Chinese population during the war.

USA and Japanese FDI may have been accepted with reluctance, but Lee and his team correctly discerned the direction of the dynamic international economy. From the early sixties multinational companies began to operate a policy of world-wide sourcing. Products began to be manufactured (32), in whole or in part, at the global site where the cost of inputs (be these raw materials, capital or labour) was lowest. In the late sixties, as labour costs exploded dramatically in most industrialised countries, firms responded variously in their struggle to maintain low costs of production. West German and Swiss companies imported cheap labour from less developed mediterranean countries; most companies encouraged research into more capital intensive methods of production; and Japanese and USA MNCs led the wave of investors who moved their factories to cheap labour developing countries - especially to those in Latin America and East Asia. This structural change in the world economy (33) was fortuitous for Singapore and corresponded almost exactly to the requirements of the "grand strategy". In order to maximize its receipt of foreign investments the Singapore Economic Development Board stepped up its overseas promotional activities; and Lee Kuan Yew visited the US (October 1967) and Japan (November 1968). He came back a changed man, wedded to the American dream and anti-Vietnamese to boot. Some of this was merely the confirmation of economic realities, of course, because Singapore was already a major trading partner with South Vietnam. In any case the USA, Japan and Britain are still the largest investors in the island today, although a policy of source-country diversification is consciously followed.

The Association of South East Asian Nations (ASEAN) is a political-economic organisation which could, in principle, resolve all of Singapore's international problems. First, as a regional economic unit and trading bloc it contains a large market, is exceptionally well endowed in resources, and is a major factor in attracting foreign investors to Singapore (which serves as a production platform or regional headquarters). Secondly as a right wing military grouping, ASEAN is invaluable in quelling internal dissent and reducing the threat of communist subversion. Finally, as a co-operative venture, ASEAN helps reduce regional tension, including the communal problems associated with the South East Asian Chinese.

These regional tensions were in fact the principal raison d'etre for the organisation's establishment in August 1967. Until this date the region was wracked with disputes such as the Philippine's claim to Sabah (a Malaysian state) and Indonesia's "Konfrontasi" with Malaya and Singapore over the establishment of Malaysia. Previous regional organisations had all failed, often because of the intransigence of Indonesia which was the largest, most populous state in South East Asia - and left-wing.

In this context General Suharto's 1965 coup, which shifted Indonesia to the right, was recognised as a major opportunity and ASEAN was established two years later. The founding members were Indonesia, Malaysia, the Philippines, Singapore and Thailand. Brunei joined in 1984. (Map 2.1).

Almost two decades later the early promise of ASEAN has not yet been realised, although the Bali Summit of 1976 is generally regarded as a crucial turning point in ASEAN relations because of its cool and collected recognition of the political and economic interdependence of member states. (34) There has been some progress in economic affairs (see later chapters), but intra-regional rivalries and differences, admittedly much subdued, still chequer the international horizon and hinder effective co-operation among the ASEAN states.

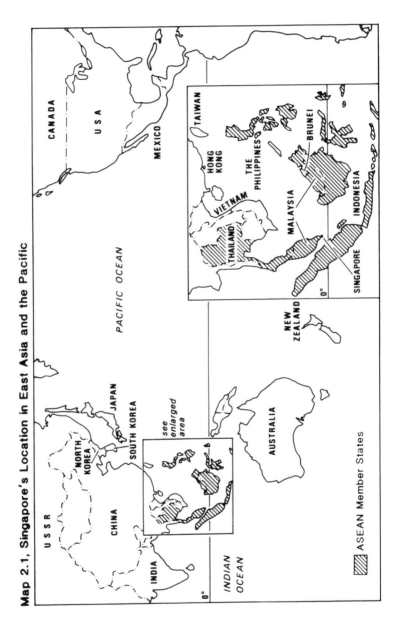

Map 2.1, Singapore's Location in East Asia and the Pacific

The Politics of Economic Transformation

Recent rifts have occurred over trade issues,
Vietnam's invasion of Cambodia, the Indo-Chinese
refugees, East-West rivalry (Thailand and the
Philippines are formally aligned with the USA.) and
the concept of a Pacific Community (Singapore is in
favour). The root causes of these rifts are the
large ethnic, religious, political and economic
disparities between the ASEAN nations. These are
highlighted by Table 2.5
     The two countries economically most divergent
from the norm are oil-rich Brunei and the NIC
Singapore. However, while Brunei is simply the
lucky recipient of oil-generated wealth and enjoys
pacific relations with its neighbours, Singapore's
position has been achieved by hard graft - albeit
with a little help from MNCs and the resources of
ASEAN - and its economic and political relationships
bridle with potential conflict. One source of
conflict is Singapore's cavalier attitude towards
its commitments. A good recent instance is
Vietnam's revelation in 1984 of high levels of trade
(about $200 million) with Singapore. Indonesia and
Thailand took umbrage and repeated their accusation
that the high level of trade with Vietnam
(officially conceded to be $82 million) was
'Incompatible with Singapore's highly vocal hard
line against Hanoi's presence in Cambodia, and that
it undermines ASEAN solidarity.' (35) Apart from
this economic "pragmatism" there is a more
fundamental and historically determined source of
friction between the island and neighbouring
countries. Buchanan puts it thus:

> Singapore's essential role as focus and
> clearing house for foreign economic
> interest in the Malay world remains the
> same: capital and enterprise gather in the
> island-state, and spread outwards; a
> colonial pattern of trade persists with
> Singapore as the middleman; the region's
> markets and raw materials are exploited,
> through Singapore. The Republic's
> relationship with its Malaysian and
> Indonesian hinterland remains a colonial
> one, but the structure of colonial
> influence is changing: from a British and
> Dutch Domain the Malay World is being
> transformed into an American and Japanese
> one - with the increasing interest in
> Indonesian and Borneo mineral resources, a
> neo-colonial relationship between the

Table 2.5 The ASEAN Countries, 1982

	Population (millions)	Area (thousands of square kilometres)	GNP per capita (US$)	Main Religion	Raw Materials and Energy	Manufacturing Production as proportion of GDP (%)	Life Expectancy (Years)
BRUNEI	0.3	6	17,700[d]	Islam	Abundant Major oil-exporter	N.A. (small)	N.A.
INDONESIA	152.7	1,919	580	Islam	Abundant Major oil-exporter	13	53
MALAYSIA	14.7	330	1,860	Islam	Abundant Oil-exporter	18	67
SINGAPORE	2.5	1	5,910	Mixed[b]	None	26	72
PHILIPPINES	50.7	300	820	Christianity[c]	Moderate amounts	24	64
THAILAND	48.5	514	790	Buddhism	Moderate amounts	19	63

Table 2.5 The ASEAN Countries, 1982 - continued

Source: The World Bank, World Development Report 1984.
          ABECOR Country Report, Brunei, November 1983.

Notes: a - 1981 figure;
          b - the percentage breakdown is: Chinese composite
          (Buddhism/Taoism/Confusiaism) - 56%, Islam - 16%, Christianity - 10%,
          Hinduism - 4%;
          c - the muslims of Mindanao are in active rebellion.

Chinese "head-link" city and the Malay
countryside is hardening. (36)

Ten years later Buchanan's analysis remains
essentially correct and is reinforced by Singapore's
recent expansion as the region's financial and
services centre. The PAP's latest strategy to
attract "brain" services to the island (see next
section) will further perpetuate the country's
metropole - periphery relations with other South
East Asian economies. Thus, unless Singapore can
help weave ASEAN into a cooperative and sufficiently
wealthy system, future conflict appears inevitable.

The Creation of a Garrison State

Singapore is one of the most militarised
countries in the world. In 1983 its armed forces
stood at 55,000 regular troops and 37,000
paramilitary personnel. (37) This compares very
favourably with the levels of militarisation in
other countries as can be seen from the following
figures:

	Number of Regular Troops	Population (millions)	Number of Troops per Thousand of Population	Military expenditure as percent of GNP
Singapore	55,000	2.5	22	6
Malaysia	99,700	14.5	7	5
United Kingdom	320,600	55.8	6	2
South Korea	622,000	39.3	16	6

Compared to much larger countries Lee's city-state
is positively bristling with troops and armaments.
Tiny Singapore could fight Malaysia to a standstill
(especially if paramilitary forces are included); it
spends a greater proportion of GNP on "defence" than
a nuclear power such as the U.K.; and it possesses
more troops per thousand of the population than
South Korea - a country with a massive army.
Since there is no immediate external threat to
Singapore's security the country's level of

militarisation has often been a source of puzzlement to observers. In fact the creation of a garrison state intensely reflects PAP ideology and strategy and its existence serves four functions. First, domestic dissent, particularly from unions and socialist groups, is stifled thereby reasurring foreign investors and right-wing neighbours such as Malaysia and Indonesia. Secondly, young Singaporeans are kept "out of mischief" during their impressionable years and disciplined into appropriate modes of behaviour. Thirdly, and partly as a consequence of military training, an orderly, disciplined and efficient society is promoted. Finally, the garrison state allows ethnically isolated Singapore to promote itself as the 'Israel of South East Asia' - and perhaps serve as the linchpin of western influence in the region. This final function may appear fanciful, but the island's location remains strategically important. With the collapse of South Vietnam, Cambodia and Laos, ASEAN represents the major regional bulwark against the perceived communist threat - and Singapore lies at the geographic heart of the region.

Table 2.6 shows clearly that Singapore's heavy commitment to defence began after Lee Kuan Yew's visit to the United States in October 1967. Indeed at a meeting in Zurich during the same month Lee declared that his government had opted for an Israeli model of development after studying a number of small, cohesive countries surrounded by large neighbours. (38) In 1968 Israeli officers disguised as "Mexican advisers" arrived in Singapore; the military establishment was reorganised; and military expenditure soared, expanding from 5.0% of the main budget in 1965, to 17.6% in 1968 and to an all time high of 31.2% in 1983/84. Meanwhile the widely-defined Welfare category declined precipitously from 58.1% in 1965 to as low as 18.1% in 1980/81. Of course Welfare expenditure has increased in absolute terms since 1965, but the priorities of the PAP are quite clear.

The Role of the State

The Singapore state apparatus is one of the most powerful in the third world and can indeed be regarded as the epitomy of the "hard state" described in development literature. The government uses the apparatus to exert considerable control over the economy (39) and this is reflected in the

Table 2.6   Defence and Welfare Expenditure as a
             Proportion of Government Main
             Expenditure, 1960 - 1983/84

Percent

	1960	1965	1968	1971/72
Defence[a]	14.1	5.0	17.6	29.6
Welfare[b]	45.4	58.1	38.2	22.3

	1974/75	1977/78	1980/81	1983/84[c]
Defence	24.6	28.3	22.7	31.2
Welfare	23.1	21.1	18.1	28.4

Source: Calculations based on data in: Singapore
           Department of Statistics, Economic and
           Social Statistics, 1960-1982; Singapore
           Department of Statistics, Monthly Digest of
           Statistics, May 1984.

Notes: a - includes Justice and Police.
           b - Education, Health, Social and
               Community Service.
           c - estimates.

scale of state expenditure, the activities of state-
owned enterprises and even in the rate of national
savings.
     Table 2.7 shows that government expenditure is
divided between a main budget and a development
budget.   The former is largely concerned with
current and capital expenditure on general
government activities such as Education, Defence and
Social Services; and the latter is targetted at
capital projects specifically designed to promote
investment and improve economic performance by
domestic and foreign companies.   Infrastructural
development, industrial estates, free trade ports,
industrial training, incentive schemes and a range
of other activities all come under the purview of
the development budget; and the phenomenal growth of
such expenditure since 1960 explains the increasing
share of the GDP accounted for by certain sectors

Table 2.7   Government Main and Development Budgets,
1960-83/84

Year	Main Budget (US$ millions)	Main Budget as proportion of GNP (%)	Development Budget (US$ millions)	Development Budget as proportion of GNP (%)	Loans to Statutory bodies[a] as a proportion of the Development Budget
1960	79.5	11.1	11.7	1.6	N.A.
1965	127.8	12.9	60.1	6.0	61.8
1968	227.9	15.9	73.5	5.1	41.6
1970 /71	398.5	19.3[b]	125.6	6.0[b]	59.6
1975 /76	1,207.8	21.3	626.7	11.1	73.5
1980 /81	2,702.0	22.6	1,729.8	14.4	62.1
1983 /84[c]	4,197.4	26.8[d]	3,652.3	20.1[d]	62.4

Sources: Calculations based on data in Singapore
Department of Statistics, Economic and
Social Statistics, 1960-1982;
"Singapore", Europa Yearbook 1984;
Singapore Economic Development Board,
Singapore Investment News, 1984.

Notes: a - These include statutory boards and
enterprises.
b - Proportions from 1970/71 calculated
using a simple average of the GNPs of each
year.
c - Estimates.
d - Proportions calculated using the 1983
estimated GNP.

and industries, including utilities, transport,
communications and construction (see Table 2.3).
Since 1960 both the main and development budgets
have grown more rapidly than the economy itself.
The scale of the main budget as a proportion of GNP
has increased from 11.1% in 1960 to 26.8% in
1983/84; the respective increase for the development
budget is an impressive leap from a mere 1.6% to a
massive 20.1%. In 1983/84 (if the estimates prove
correct) the total government budget amounted to
46.9% of GNP. Further, if allowance is made for
additional expenditures of statutory boards and
state-owned enterprises (40) and the actual output
of these bodies, then state expenditure must
constitute well over 50% of GNP. It seems that in
order to maintain the Singapore economic miracle the
government is being forced to play an ever larger
role in the economy. However the PAP will not be
overly disturbed by greater state activity because
it is not committed to a private market economy by
any matter of principle. In addition, it is only
fair to add that the post 1977 increase in the
development budget is in fact mainly due to the
government's attempt to attract large scale foreign
direct investment in high technology and service
industries (see next section); and the resulting
increase in GNP - if the policy is successful - will
of course proportionately reduce the state's role in
the economy.

Though all governments differ in how they
derive their revenues from various sources (Table
2.8), Singapore is peculiar in a number of respects.
First, a comparatively low proportion of its revenue
is derived from taxes on income, goods, services or
international transactions: a consequence of
attracting tax-avoiding multinational companies by
"liberalising" the trading environment. Secondly,
the yield from property taxes is very high because
the government takes advantage of the country's land
shortage - a shortage which has actually resulted in
the reclamation of land from the sea, especially in
and around the business and financial district of
Singapore City. Thirdly, there is a great deal of
property income which mainly derives from (i)
commercial and user-charge profits of state-owned
enterprises; and (ii) the dividends, profits and
other returns from the government's large holdings
of overseas portfolio and direct investments.
Government concerns play a relatively major role in
the Singapore economy and will be referred to again

Table 2.8   Government Revenue by Economic Type,
            Selected Countries, circa 1981.

Percent of Total Revenue

Economic Type	Country					
	Singapore	U.K.	U.S.	India	Korea	Mexico
Taxes on Income & Profit	31.9	39.1	52.6	19.2	22.8	37.1
Social Security Contributions	nil[a]	16.7	29.9	nil	1.0	14.4
Employers Payroll & Manpower Taxes	1.6	3.4	nil	nil	nil	0.9
Taxes on Property	9.0	1.5	1.2	0.6	0.9	0.4
Taxes on Goods & Services	12.6	26.9	5.5	40.5	44.3	31.8
Taxes on International Trade & Transactions	5.0	neg.	1.4	21.9	13.8	29.1
Other Taxes	3.3	0.1	nil	nil	0.6	0.3
Non tax Revenue	26.1	11.9	9.4	16.6	13.6	6.2
Property Income	14.5	7.7	6.8	7.1	7.3	4.2
Total Revenue[b]	100.0	100.0	100.0	100.0	100.0	100.0

Source and Notes overleaf.

Table 2.8   Government Revenue by Economic Type,
            selected countries, circa 1981. cont.

Source: International Monetary Fund, Government
            Finance Statistics Yearbook, 1983.

Notes: a - However workers contribute to the
            Central Provident Fund (CPF) which is a
            major holder of the government bonds.
            b - Components may not sum to 100 because
            of adjustment items and unallocated
            transactions.
            neg - negligible.

---

later in this section. Finally, the state seems to
obtain no social security receipts whatsoever, but
in actual fact such contributions are paid directly
into the semi-autonomous Central Provident Fund
(CPF) and indirectly play a highly significant role
in financing government borrowing requirements.

The Central Provident Fund was established in
1955 as a compulsory savings scheme for all workers.
Initially it was intended to finance old age
pensions and also benefits to those permanently
incapacitated; but more recently as balances have
built up (Table 2.9), members have been allowed to
use a part of their savings towards buying housing,
shares in Singapore Bus Service Ltd and other
approved schemes. As Table 2.9 further shows, net
annual contributions to the fund now constitute an
incredible 11% of GNP and it is therefore not
surprising that the CPF plays such a large role in
government borrowing. Nearly all of the Fund
balances are used to purchase state-issued bonds and
securities and a preponderant 50-60% of government
debt is financed by this device. The CPF thus
constitutes an ingenious mechanism for generating
national savings and harnessing them for the state's
development efforts. However neither employee nor
employer is enamoured by these enforced savings
which are very high by international standards. In
1984, for example, the joint employee/employer
national insurance contribution in the UK was
about 20% of the employees earnings, while the
monthly equivalent joint CPF contribution in
Singapore was a massive 50% of earnings - a
phenomenal increase from a mere 10% in 1965.

The state channels its economic activities
through a number of government units and state-owned

Table 2.9   The Role of the Central Provident Fund.

Item	1965	1970	1975	1980	1982
Net Contributions by members[a] (US$ billions)	0.02	0.05	0.35	0.95	1.64
Members' Balances (US$ billions)	0.12	0.25	1.36	4.44	7.32
Contribution Rates (%)					
- employee	5	8	15	18	23
- employer	5	8	15	20	22
Net Contributions as proportion of GNP (%)	1.7	2.5	6.1	8.8	11.5
Government Securities held by Fund as proportion of Members' Balances (%)	N.A.	97.5	88.7	95.1	62.9[b]
Government Securities held by Fund as proportion of Government Debt	N.A.	37.6	50.4	61.9	47.6[b]

Sources: Calculations based on data in Singapore
Department of Statistics, Economic and
Social Statistics, 1960-1982;
The Monetary Authority of Singapore, Annual
Report 1982/83;
Tan Chwee Huat (1981) Financial
Institutions in Singapore, Singapore
University Press.

Notes: a - Members' contributions plus interest
and investment earnings and minus
withdrawals. b - However US$ 2.5 billion
was deposited with the Monetary Authority
of Singapore as advanced subscription to
future Government bond issues. This would
increase the 62.9% to 97.4%.

enterprises, the most important of which are listed
in Tables 2.10 and 2.11. Central government units
with their own budget and state-owned enterprises
are semi-autonomous, the chief difference being that
the latter behave, as far as possible, as commerical
concerns. The most important of these semi-
autonomous organisations are responsible for key
aspects of Singapore's economic strategy and in
1983/84, in addition to their expenditure from other
sources, they accounted for 62.4% of the development
budget (Table 2.7). The most important of these
organisations include: the Economic Development
Board (EDB) which since 1961 has masterminded and
overseen the country's industrialisation strategy;
the Jurong Town Corporation (JTC) which runs the
island's 21 industrial estates or export processing
zones (including the Singapore Science Park) and is
developing fifteen more; the Port of Singapore
Authority (PSA) which is responsible for the free
trade zones; the Development Bank of Singapore (DBS)
which provides financial assistance to manufacturing
and other industries; Neptune Orient Lines Ltd.
which is the national shipping line; the Monetary
Authority of Singapore (MAS) which has played a
major role in developing the city-state as an international financial centre; and INTRACO (International Trading Company) which coordinates and
expedites the search for overseas markets for
locally produced manufactures. The activities of
specific statutory boards and state-owned enterprises will be analysed more fully, and as
appropriate, in later chapters.

There are a large number of government enterprises not listed in Tables 2.10 and 2.11, many of
them subsidiaries of listed statutory boards and
state-owned concerns. Thus, for example, both
Neptune Orient Lines and the Development Bank of
Singapore (DBS) have about twenty subsidiaries each.
In addition as Singapore has developed and become
more complex state-owned enterprises have had to
expand their operations, often in unexpected
directions, and now constitute an intricate,
interwoven web that encloses, stabilises and directs
the economy (see also chapter three, pages 109ff).
New and innovative enterprises are being established
constantly. Thus, for example, INTRACO (itself a
joint subsidiary of the state, DBS and Standard and
Chartered Bank (UK)) recently formed a liquid bulk
installation business with PSA, and a computer
consultancy with the Indian MNC Tata Consultancy

Table 2.10   Units of Central Government

1.   Presidency, Prime Minister's Office,
     Parliament, Judiciary, Attorney General's
     Chambers, Audit Department, Cabinet Office,
     Presidential Council, Public Service Commission
     and 14 Ministries.

Central Government Units with own Budget.

2.   Applied Research Corp.
3.   Economic Development Board.
4.   Family Planning and Population Board.
5.   Institute of Education.
6.   Institute of Southeast Asian Studies.
7.   National Maritime Board.
8.   National Productivity Board.
9.   National Statistical Commission.
10. National Theatre Trust.
11. National University of Singapore.
12. Ngee Ann Polytechnic.
13. People's Association.
14. Preservation of Monuments Board.
15. Science Council of Singapore.
16. Singapore Institute of Standards and Industrial
     Research.
17. Singapore Polytechnic.
18. Singapore Science Centre.
19. Singapore Sports Council.
20. Singapore Tourist Promotion Board.
21. Timber Industry Board.
22. Vocational and Industrial Training Board.

Source: International Monetary Fund, Government
          Finance Statistics Year Book, 1983.

Table 2.11 Major State Owned Enterprises

1.   Non-Financial Enterprises.

Chartered Industries of Singapore (Pte.) Ltd.
Civil Aviation.
Commercial and Industrial Security Corp.
Hotel Premier.
Housing and Development Board.
Jurong Bird Park (Pte.) Ltd. (tourism).
Jurong Shipyard.
Jurong Town Corp.
Keppel Shipyard (Pte.) Ltd.

Table 2.11   Major State Owned Enterprises. cont.

1.   Non-Financial Enterprises. cont.

National Engineering Services (Pte.) Ltd.
Neptune Orient Lines Ltd.
Port of Singapore Authority.
Primary Industries Enterprises (Pte.) Ltd.
Primary Production Department (agriculture).
Public Utilities Board.
Resource Development Corp. (Pte.) Ltd.
Sembawang Shipyard (Pte.) Ltd.
Sentosa Development Corp.
Singapore Airlines Ltd.
Singapore Broadcasting Corp.
Singapore Corp. of Rehabilitative Enterprises.
Singapore Electronic and Engineering Ltd.
Singapore National Printers (Pte.) Ltd.
Singapore Pools (Pte.) Ltd. (gambling).
Singapore Zoological Gardens.
Singmanex (Pte.) Ltd.
Telecommunication Authority of Singapore (including
   postal services).
Urban Redevelopment Authority of Singapore.

2.   Financial Enterprises.

Monetary Authority of Singapore.
Board of Commissioners of Currency.
Central Provident Fund.
Credit Post Office Savings Bank (Pte.) Ltd.
Development Bank of Singapore.
Export Credit Insurance Corp. of Singapore Ltd.
Government of Singapore Investment Corp.
Post Office Savings Bank.

Source: International Monetary Fund, Government
          Finance Statistics Year Book, 1983.

Services - two concerns poles apart, but deemed
necessary for Singapore's continued success.

TOWARDS A SECOND INDUSTRIAL REVOLUTION

     If Japan is 'a fragile lotus blossom on a
storm-tossed sea', Singapore's lot is infinitely
worse!   Though both countries are dependent on
overseas mineral resources and international trade,

the latter lacks even a moderately sized domestic market or a significant level of home-sprung technology. (41) Consequently the island's economy was buffetted constantly by the critical global events of the 1970s; and the authorities were forced to address themselves to two thorny problems: the loss of international competitiveness and the local repercussions of the world economic crisis.

By the early 1970s Singapore had fully reaped the fruits of the first industrial revolution (42), including high levels of capital investment, nigh full employment and a substantial increase in GNP per capita. For a period the importation of cheap labour from nearby developing countries such as Malaysia, Indonesia and even Sri Lanka prevented wage rises and maintained rapid rates of expansion in manufacturing, finance and the services, but such a policy was only good for the short term. It was recognised that in the long run genuine progress could only be achieved through the restructuring of the economy into labour saving, higher value added industries and sectors. The imperative to restructure was reinforced by four other trends or events: (i) competition from emulative developing countries attempting to attract MNCs on the basis of cheap labour and incentives; (ii) the oil crisis which raised energy costs and threatened Singapore's large petroleum processing industry; (iii) growing unemployment and the consequent slackening in wage demands in industrialised countries which coincided with rising industrial wages in NICs and narrowed the labour cost differential between Singapore and the west; and (iv) the advent of revolutionary cost-reducing micro-electronics technology which insidiously eliminates the need for cheap labour. (43) The Economic Development Board recognised the competitiveness crisis at an early stage and in 1979 the authorities unveiled an ambitious plan to meet this challenge: Singapore would become an "information society" and the "brain centre" of South East Asia by upgrading its technology and services. Critics may consider this hubris, but Lee is determined.

The world economic crisis has been a tricky period for trade-reliant Singapore. The genesis and evolution of the crisis has been complex, but the relevant trends are outlined by Table 2.12. The rate of economic expansion in industrialised countries entered a slow phase in the late sixties, although some countries fared better than others

The rate of growth of GNP fell from an average of 4.9% in the 1960s to a nadir of -0.1% in 1982. Unemployment spiralled upwards, private and industrial consumption declined and, as trade plummetted, the developing countries were also ultimately affected. The metropole-periphery relationship between industrialised and developing countries has meant that the effects of the crisis on the latter have been very grim. Exports, commodity prices, export earnings have all fallen heavily (see Table 2.12); and the decline in earnings, allied with record interest rates, has triggered an international debt crisis. (The developing countries' ratio of debt to GNP rose from 13.3% in 1970 to 26.7% in 1983. [44]) Though Singapore rode the various recessions of the last decade well (chapter one), the government has been forced to respond actively to the slow down in trade and the increasing level of international protectionism, especially now that UNCTAD VI and other fora have failed to extract an expansionary policy from the industrialised countries.

Singapore's response has been four-fold. First, there has been considerable activity to increase south-south trade, especially among ASEAN countries. (45) Although there has been some progress in this effort (54% of the island's exports went to developing countries in 1982 - an increase of 6% over 1976), the world crisis is a major impediment. The fall in foreign exchange earnings affects the amount developing countries can import; and in many cases (Indonesia in 1983, for example) a fall in exchange rates has positively discouraged Singaporean exports: the Singapore dollar is one of the world's strongest currencies. Secondly, the concept of a Pacific Basin Economic Community has been promoted quite strongly by the PAP leadership because of the obvious benefits of belonging to a "growth club". However this is a long term aim and will be discussed further in chapter five. Thirdly, the Economic Development Board has followed a broadly Keynesian policy in maintaining a high level of domestic demand. Thus, for example, the sky-line is littered with half-constructed hotels; and the Mass Rapid Transit (MRT) rail system is being built by companies from Japan, Britain, France, Belgium and the USA (46) This policy has worked quite well because it can be used as a means of expanding the country's capital stock and infrastructural facilities. The fourth and final response coincides

Table 2.12 The World Economic Crisis

Percent

					Change from preceding year					
	1960-73	1967-76	1977	1978	1979	1980	1981	1982	1983	1984[a]
Real GNP Growth of all Industrialised Countries	4.9	3.7	3.9	4.1	3.5	1.3	1.6	-0.1	2.3	3.6
World Trade[b]	13.1	7.5	5.0	5.5	7.0	1.5	1.0	-2.5	2.0	5.5
Exports[b] from Developing Countries	N.A.	6.5	2.4	4.2	5.3	-2.5	-4.1	-7.4	0.6	7.5
Imports[b] by Industrialised Countries	N.A.	7.6	4.4	5.1	8.6	-1.5	-1.9	-0.5	4.1	6.5

Sources: International Monetary Fund, World Economic Outlook, June 1984
World Bank, World Development Report, 1984
GATT, International Trade, 1982/83

Notes: a - estimates. b - change in volume.

with the authorities' strategy for an "information society": technological upgrading and sectoral diversification and specialisation allows the economy to compete more effectively. Thus, for example, more sophisticated components and products can bypass tariffs and other protectionist measures imposed by industrialised countries; and the establishment of advanced technical, financial, consultancy and other services should provide a further boost to Singapore's regional trade, particularly if the prospective up-turn in world trade proceeds as envisaged.

Singapore as an International Business Centre

Singapore's ambitious strategy to restructure radically its economy was compelled by a fundamental transformation in the world economy and a concomitant rise in international competition. The evolution of this strategy can be traced to the early seventies when the authorities introduced incentives to attract financial services, but the broad outlines of the present approach only became apparent after the economy had suffered the multiple hammerblows of trade disruption, oil shocks and a slump in national productivity growth. In March 1978 Goh Chok Tong (Senior Minister of State for Finance) declared:

> Singapore's manufacturing sector has now reached an intermediate level of development..... We will now have to accelerate our programme to diversify into higher technology industries..... we must try to encourage greater local entrepreneurship in the manufacturing sector..... we should exploit our comparative advantage in trade related services and our strategic location to the maximum. More attention will now be devoted to make Singapore an export oriented services centre. (47)

As a first step towards restructuring, the National Wages Council (NWC) awarded pay rises of 20% per annum in 1979 and 1980. The 1981 award was reduced to 6% after pressure from employers, but pay rises have remained fairly high since. This move from a low-wage to a high-wage policy is intended to encourage a move into higher value added, less labour-intensive industries and is a tactical move designed to upgrade the level of technology employed in Singapore by multinational companies. (48) This preliminary step was followed by policies and plans of increasing sophistication until the Ministry of Trade and Industry unveiled its definitive "economic development plan for the eighties" in 1981.

The plan first argued that, 'our wages must be related to the labour market. In a full employment economy, low wages will lead to an overtight labour market' and, 'a low wage does not bring out the best in a worker. It discourages training'. (49) Armed with this justification for a high-wage policy it then outlined the major poblems facing Singapore in the eighties. These were: (i) slow growth in the labour supply; (ii) rising expectations for better wages which could only be afforded if higher skilled jobs were created; (iii) continuing dependence on foreign skills, technology and markets; (iv) a declining rate of savings; (v) slow growth and protectionism in industrialised countries; (vi) high oil prices; and (vii) international competition. Given these problems and Singapore's heavy dependence on the international community, it was deemed necessary to maintain a liberal trade regime, further diversify the economy, and continue to attract foreign direct investment allied with overseas professional, technical and industrial skills. Five targets were outlined:

> (a) Real GDP growth of eight to ten percent per annum to reach present Japanese per capita GNP by 1990.
> (b) Productivity increases of six to eight percent per annum.
> (c) Full and better paid, higher skill employment.
> (d) Inflation lower than the world rate.
> (e) Healthy Balance of Payments. (50)

To meet these targets the plan promised to raise the levels of skills appropriately and provided tax and other incentives to promote mechanisation, automation, computerisation and research and development. Most effort was to be aimed at a number of key pillars of growth, including:

Manufacturing. The plan envisaged an increase in this sector's share of GDP from 23 percent to 31 percent by 1990. Higher value added/high technology industries were to be encouraged. The initial impulse was likely to derive from MNCs, but provisions were made to expand the role of local entrepreneurs in better industries. Manufacturers not willing to upgrade their labour-intensive plant would be forced overseas by higher wages. Incentives would encourage certain priority industries including petrochemicals, pharmaceuticals, industrial machinery, consumer electrical equipment, high-grade electronic components, technical services and transport equipment such as vessels and aircraft.

Trade. Export of higher value added and technology goods was expected especially by MNCs, but also by local entrepreneurs supported appropriately by the Ministry of Trade. Trade documentation procedures would be simplified and local manufacturers and traders would be encouraged to group together and form large trading companies.

Computer Services. The computer industry and other "brain services" (e.g. consultancy and medical services) were deemed desirable because they are knowledge-intensive, non-polluting and required little manpower or energy. Computers in particular could raise the productivity and technology of sectors; "brain services" in general could become a major export item because of general regional underdevelopment and Singapore's good infrastructure, telecommunications and strategic location. The plan detailed ways in which computerisation would be stimulated in the private and public sectors, for example by allowing accelerated depreciation on computers and peripheral equipment.

Financial Services. These would be expanded further by developing Singapore as a "financial supermarket". Offshore banking and loan syndication in Asian Currency Units (ACUs) were to be encouraged. The plan also outlined the intention to establish or promote promising markets such as those in futures or gold.

If successful the economic development plan will turn Singapore into a nascent, independent international business centre. However the success of this "second industrial revolution" depends on a variety of supporting policies, not least the manpower development programme.

Education and Training.

Singapore is pouring an incredible level of resources into manpower development, but this is essential if it is to achieve its simultaneous aims of (i) generating real GDP growth rates of 8-10 percent per annum and (ii) supplanting foreign workers with home grown talent. Expansion is occurring in four main areas and these are described below. (51)

Higher Education. The production of graduates, especially engineers and professionals, is being stepped up considerably. The National University of Singapore (NUS) was established in 1980 through the merger of the University of Singapore and Nanyang University. (52) The number of students at NUS are to increase from 11,750 in 1982 to 13,938 in 1985. Nanyang's old site has been allocated to the Nanyang Technological Institute (NTI), established in 1981, whose student numbers are to increase dramatically from 600 in 1982 to 2,442 in 1985/86 and 2,799 in 1990/91. By 1985 the engineering students at NUS and NTI combined will number 4,493, up from 2,700 in 1982. Student numbers at Singapore Polytechnic will increase from 5,553 in 1982 to 7,623. Ngee Ann Polytechnic is also up for expansion, but figures are not available; this institute houses Singapore's new Centre for Computer Studies. The irony of the island's higher education policy (as with many other plans) is that excellent new facilities are not enough: expatriate staff are required to train faculty and students intended to supplant all foreign workers.

Vocational Training. The Vocational and Industrial Training Board (VITB) has also stepped up its activities. Ten major projects extending old institutes and building new ones are now almost all completed (53) and will extend the VITB's existing capacity of 15 full time institutions/centres and 24 night and weekend centres. Enrolments are expected to increase from 10,316 in 1982 to 24,100 in 1986. VITB courses are designed with the co-operation of employers and are aimed at school-leavers who need some sort of vocational training. There are advisory committees monitoring all major industries to ensure that courses are relevant.

Skills Development Fund (SDF). The SDF was established to reimburse employers who in some way sponsored their employees for training or skills upgrading. The Fund's resources are in fact derived from a 4% payroll tax which in itself encourages a move towards less labour-intensive methods of production. The SDF is supervised by the VITB and used in a number of ways. For example, the SDF has financed the upgrading of employer's training facilities: at the end of 1982 there were 12 VITB approved employer-based training centres. In other instances the Fund has been used to grant employers up to 70 percent of the cost of training workers on apprenticeship schemes leading to VITB qualifications.

EDB Industrial Training Courses. The Economic Development Board has established, (i) three training centres in collaboration with leading MNCs (Tata, Brown-Boveri and Philips) and one with the Japanese government; (ii) three technical institutes with the help of foreign governments (Germany, France and Japan); and (iii) two training units jointly with two MNCs, Computervision Corporation from the USA and ASEA AB of Sweden. These centres train some thousands of Singaporeans and represent an interesting approach to technology transfer - one that deserves future scrutiny. Table 2.13 outlines the courses on offer at these foreign - Singapore collaborative ventures in education and training.

The Japanisation Programme.

The PAP's admiration for Japan knows few bounds and Lee Kuan Yew has even declared that, "Japanese society is an illustration in Darwinist evolution, the survival of the most resilient organisation". (54) Given Lee's predisposition towards eugenics (see chapter six), it is not surprising that Singapore has turned towards Japan as a model for its present phase of social engineering. Thus, for example, students at the Japan-Singapore technical centre begin their day with Japanese-style calisthenics; the Singapore Institute of Standards and Industrial Research (SISIR) has been authorised to inspect exports bearing the Japan Industrial Standards (JIS) mark, the Japanese symbol of quality (55); the government is constantly prodding local companies to establish joint general trading houses similar to the

Table 2.13   The Economic Development Board's
              Industrial Training Courses and
              Technical Institutes.

Training Centres	Courses
Tata-Government Training Centre	Tool and Die-Making (Press Tools) Precision Machining
Brown-Boveri Government Training Centre	Tool and Die-Making (Press Tools and Injection Moulds) Production Machining Toolroom Machining Precision Mechanics
Philips-Government Training Centre	Precision Machining
Japan-Singapore Training Centre	Tool and Die-Making (Injection Moulds) Electrical Trade Consumer and Industrial Electronics Instrumentation and Control Industrial Machinery Maintenance

Technical Institutes	Courses
German Singapore Institute of Production Technology	Diploma courses in Production Technology with emphasis on: Design (Tool and Die, Jigs and Fixtures) Cutting Technology and CNC techniques Production Processes and Industrial Engineering
French Singapore Institute of Electro-technology	Diploma course in Electro-technology with emphasis on: Industrial Electronics Instrumentation Automation and Control

Table 2.13   The Economic Development Board's
             Industrial Training Courses and
             Technical Institutes. cont.

Technical Institutes cont.	Courses cont.
	Computer and Micro-Processor Applications
Japan Singapore Institute of Software Technology	Diploma course in Systems Analysis Programming Systems Analysis Engineering

Training Units	Courses
Computervision-EDB CAD-CAM Training Unit	CAD-CAM applications in: Mechanical Design and Drafting Numerical Control Printed Circuit Board Design Integrated Circuit Design Structural Analysis
ASEA-EDB Robotics Training Unit	Robotics Appreciation courses Robotics Applications/Project Engineering courses Robotics Programming and Operation courses Robotics Maintenance and Servicing courses

Source: Ministry of Culture, Singapore Facts and
          Pictures 1983

Japanese   Sogo   Shosha;   and   company   unions   are
encouraged.
     Given   the   PAP's   ideological   bent   it is   not
surprising   that the Japanisation programme has gone
furthest   in   industrial   relations   and   worker
motivation. As early as 1972 the Employment act was
amended   on   the   recommendation   of   the   NWC   to
recognise the concept of a thirteenth month payment,
thus   stabilising   the practise   of paying a bonus as

an important benefit of employment. (56) More recently, however, the National Productivity Board (NPB) has been systematically introducing Japanese concepts such as "productivity will", quality control circles and non-adversarial labour management relationships (in addition to other ways of increasing productivity). The NPB inculcates Japanese methods through activities such as study missions (to Japan Productivity Centre, Sophia University, Nomura Research Institute, Matsushita's PHP Institute etc.), managerial and supervisory training, specific productivity schemes, in-house training and the establishment of a resource centre. (57) In 1982 7,665 people participated in the NPB's courses on performance appraisal, quality control circles and joint labour-management consultation (up from 1,170 in 1981); and by March 1983 525 quality control circles were in operation with a membership of 3,821. (58) Of particular interest is the systematic way in which the NPB is inculcating "productivity will". The NPB recognises that Japanese companies adopted "productivity will" after the 1958 Rome Conference of the European Productivity Association and that quality circles as a concept originated in USA companies. The 'long-term, systematic and continuous education of the Japanese people' (59) is being repeated with Singaporeans. In-company training of all new employees (using methods based on Japanese firms such as Isetan Department Store) is being recommended to all local firms.

The Plan for the Eighties: an Initial Assessment

The early years of Singapore's second industrial revolution have been a qualified success and the government is optimistic. On a macro-economic level, foreign direct investment in Singapore has increased rapidly in recent years despite the recession and the high-wage policy; the GDP growth rate has remained high (despite a plunge to 6% in 1982) at 7.9% in 1983 and 10% in early 1984 (60); and the labour productivity growth rate recovered dramatically - it fell from 7.9% in 1966-71 to as low as 3.3% in 1973-78, but was 5.0% in 1983 and 7.4% in the first quarter of 1984. (61) The main contributors to the 1983 growth in GDP were Financial and Business Services (34%), Construction (20%) and Transport and Communications (17%), largely in line with the government's strategy. (62)

Manufacturing only contributed 5% because it was most seriously affected by world recession (output actually fell by 6% in 1982), but the outlook was good because of a productivity increase of 11%. (63) However the contribution of high value added industries to the total value added in 1982 was only 2.5% up on 1979 (74.7% as opposed to 72.2% of total), but judgement should be reserved until the sector has recovered a little from its recent drubbing at the hands of the world economic crisis.

On a microeconomic basis there have been many signs that Singapore's strategy is paying off. The following are a few recent instances:

- Computer vendors increased in number from 36 in 1979 to 114 in 1982. Nearly 45% were owned by foreign companies, the majority dealt in hardware and software, and three quarters of them were computer services companies 'providing software, consultancy contract programming, bureau services, time sharing facilities management and... turnkey projects'. (64)
- IBM established a regional health industry centre in Singapore to design and develop applications software for health management for the local, regional and international markets in March 1984. (65)
- In 1982 Nestle established its eastern food research centre (Eastreco) in Singapore. Eastreco is the Asian equivalent of Westreco in North America and Latinreco in South America. (66)
- In April 1984 Ciba-Geigy transferred its Asian medical centre to Singapore from Hong Kong. The centre will collect, generate and provide data on developments in the pharmaceuticals and medical fields in Asia. (67)
- Bell Helicopter established a product support facility in Singapore in 1984. (68)
- Six Sheng-Li (69) companies pooled resources in a partial merger to form the Singapore Technology Corporation in 1984. The company has a $100 million capital base and 4,500 employees of whom 800 are engineers, technicians and executives.
- Arthur D. Little International opened a professional office in Singapore in January 1984. (70)
- The American Bureau of Shipping, a leading international classification society, established a new regional headquarters in Singapore in September 1984.

Table 2.14 General Elections Since 1955.

Date	Number of Seats	Number of Parties Contesting	Party Returned	Number of Seats Won	Percentage of Votes Won
Legislative Assembly					
1955 April 2	25[a]	5 and 11 independents	Labour Front	10	26.74
1959 May 30	51	10 and 39 independents	PAP	43	53.40
1963 Sept 21	51	8 and 16 independents	PAP	37	46.46
Parliament					
1968 April 13	7+(51)[b]	2 and 5 independents	PAP	58	84.43
1972 September 2	57+(8)	6 and 2 independents	PAP	65	69.02
1976 December 23	53+(16)	7 and 2 independents	PAP	69	72.40
1980 December 23	38+(37)	8	PAP	75	75.55

Source: Ministry of Culture, Singapore 1983.

Notes: a) The 1955 Legislative Assembly consisted of 1 Speaker, 3 ex-officio members, 25 elected members, and 4 nominated members.
b) Uncontested seats in brackets.

71

The above impressionistic examples are intended to convey Singapore's dynamic progress as an international business centre. A more thorough analysis will be conducted in chapters three to five.

CONCLUDING REMARKS

The history of modern Singapore is completely intertwined with the development of the People's Action Party (PAP) of Premier Lee Kuan Yew. Founded in 1954 as a revolutionary independence-seeking organisation, the PAP's complexion was entirely transformed during the course of the fifties as Lee's liberal faction ruthlessly suppressed the party's left-wing. Aided surreptitiously in this task by the British colonial authorities, the liberals proceeded to the reins of power in 1959. The rout of Barisan Sosialis and the unions in the early sixties established the PAP as the dominant political force in Singapore and, since emerging as the government of an independent sovereign state after the short lived union with Malaysia, the party has energetically pursued export-oriented economic expansion based on a massive influx of foreign capital. Despite the claims of its critics, however, Singapore is neither a fascist nor a corporatist state. "Fascist" is an overly used word and even the highly authoritarian nature of the PAP does not warrant such a designation; though the leadership's attitude towards eugenics and socio-biological engineering is a grim reminder that the dividing line between authoritarianism and fascism is precariously thin - and easily breached. As for corporatism, Singapore's polity does not constitute, 'a system of interest representation in which the constituent units are organised into a limited number of singular, compulsory, non-competitive, hierarchically ordered and functionally differentiated categories, licensed (if not created) by the state and granted a deliberate representational monopoly within their respective categories in exchange for observing certain conditions in their selection of leaders and articulation of demands and proposals'. (72) It is significant that the nigh-feudal exchange of rights and obligations inherent in corporatism is notably absent in the case of Singapore. Thus, at one extreme, the state is beholden to the largesse of multinational companies; and, at the other extreme, the regime has near complete control over the National Trade Union Congress (NTUC). Milne correctly observes:

> In a small country like Singapore, which has a determined and efficient government, groups are well aware of the political milieu in which they operate, and they adapt accordingly. The inference is that while corporatism may be useful in some countries in helping the state preserve its autonomy vis-a-vis powerful groups, this is unnecessary in Singapore; the groups are already under control, without any need to erect a corporatist framework. (73).

Singapore's authorities would find it more difficult to refute the charge of comprador, but even here the PAP represents a comprador with a difference. It is generally recognised that the government has effectively buffered itself against pressure from both the masses and the business community and is consequently able to follow relatively independent policies. (74) Nevertheless it is also true that the regime has aligned its interests with those of powerful multinational corporations and Singapore therefore represents a stable and efficient vehicle for the western exploitation of South East Asia. The PAP's leadership is in fact best characterised as a group of unrepentant cynics and total pragmatists willing to veer in any direction, provided their medium and long term goals are achieved. Of course their aims are also liable to change, and this unprincipled nature of the PAP leadership was highlighted by the expulsion of the party from the Socialist International in 1976 (75) - in the name of socialism Lee and his cronies had established an authoritarian state, disregarded human rights and crushed the genuine left.

The PAP does have one redeeming feature, however. Its origins as an anti-colonial movement steeped in idealistic, indeed revolutionary, fervour has left the legacy of a well disciplined, zealous, honest and efficient organisation whose cadres are now highly motivated technocrats. (76) Ruthlessness combined with honesty and efficiency is one of the hallmarks of the PAP which, though unloved, at least commands the grudging respect of the populace and external observers. The Singapore economic miracle is, after all, the result of these PAP strengths, combined with the party's capacity to control and manipulate a small, highly populated, ethnically homogeneous island towards a prescribed destiny. (77) Bauer was patently mistaken in his claim (78) that Singapore's status as a newly industrialising country is based on the government's attachment to a free market economy; indeed the island-state often resembles his ultimate bogey - the command economy. Statutory bodies and state-owned enterprises play a prominent and significant role in the Singapore economy and their involvement is increasing. Further, Singapore's success owes much to sound planning and nothing at all to a blind invocation of the laissez faire doctrine: by crushing the left and creating a "stable" regime, by harnessing effectively the island's scant resources, and by rigorously attracting MNCs, the Singapore state provided the necessary impetus for the island's industrialisation and development.

The country's manifest economic success does not necessarily translate into popularity for the regime. Although it is difficult to gauge the degree of support the PAP enjoys, table 2.14 indicates that a core of opposition remains. For example, although the PAP won all 75 of the island's constituencies in 1980, 24% of the voters preferred other parties - an extremely high proportion since half of the seats were not even contested by opposing candidates. The defeat of the PAP candidate in the 1981 Anson by-election also highlighted public concern over the government's high handed policies. The Anson seat had been vacated by Devan Nair on his appointment as third President of the Republic and it was this partisan move by the government (Nair was the first Secretary General of the PAP-led National Trade Union Congress) which galvanised the opposition parties into a potent force. They pooled their resources and Mr Jeyaratnam (Workers' Party) was duly elected as the first opposition MP for nearly twenty years. This event jolted the PAP out of its complacency and provoked renewed effort in the party's long-term ideological battle for the people's minds. The main components of the government's strategy in this respect are: (i) to maintain a highly successful economy - this minimizes discontent and means that sections of the population which remember the traumatic events of the early sixties (a group gradually declining in number) have few issues around which to foment opposition; (ii) to stress the benefits of the economic miracle as a concrete example of the value of the PAP's political hegemony; (iii) to promote a disciplined, regimented, efficient society (for example through military training and the Japanisation programme, as previously discussed), very much in the PAP's own image; and (iv) to sustain an atmosphere of crisis. This last tactic is particularly effective as the following extract shows:

> Lee's warnings to his fellow countrymen are as frequent as they are dire. The tranquility and prosperity of their 'little island', as he calls it, are still far from assured. Singapore is vulnerable, Lee tells his people again and again, and only growth, reform and change can reduce that vulnerability. Says a Westerner who sees Lee often: 'He is always running scared'. Sociologist John Clammer of the National University suspects that Lee's image as a brooding worrier is at least partly cultivated as a political technique. By maintaining 'a permanent sense of crisis', Clammer explains, Lee can justify the need for order, conformity and discipline. 'The crisis mentality forms an essential part of the ideological system'. Banker Hughlynn Fierce, former head of Chase Manhattan's Singapore operations, sees it as a shrewd business tactic. 'It's smart to run scared. Like the chief executive officer of any successful company, Lee has to worry that his people are going to become complacent'. (79)

NOTES

1. P.T. Bauer (1983), "Is planning the answer?", Singapore Business Yearbook 1984, Times Periodicals Pte, Ltd.
2. Bauer quotes works by Gunnar Myrdal and H. Kitamura published in 1956 and 1954 respectively.

Notes

3. The role of the state in East Asian development is discussed in, for example, W.W. Lockwood (Ed.) (1965), The State and Economic Enterprise in Japan, Princeton University Press; Takafusa Nakamura (1983), Economic growth in prewar Japan, Yale University Press; Chalmers Johnson (1982), MITI and the Japanese Miracle, Stanford University Press; L.P. Jones and Il Sakong (1980), Government, business and Entrepreneurship in Economic Development: The Korean Case, Harvard University Press; and Roy Hofheinz, Jr. and Kent E. Calder (1982), The East Asia Edge, Basic Books, Inc.

4. Arecent article by a Singaporean academic along these lines was Pang Eng Fong and Tsao Yuan (1983), "Macro matters in our success", Singapore Business Yearbook 1984, Times Periodicals Pte. Ltd.

5. The wild Brazilian rubber plant was cultivated in Singapore's botanical gardens and then transplanted to Malaya.

6. Indeed text books were written based upon the British Army's Tactics!

7. Despite a higher rate of Chinese involvement, the MCP was non-communalist and was supported by people from all ethnic groups.

8. The Japanese had cultivated the Indians and Malays, while persecuting the Chinese. As a result a high proportion of Chinese were involved in the resistance and the Malay Communist Party.

9. The Hakka's are a despised Chinese minority which originally inhabited a part of north China. To what extent, if at all, this explains Lee's personality is unknown. Interestingly, Hung Hsiu-ch'uan, leader of the T'ai P'ing rebels was also a Hakka.

10. Though he did not attempt to perfect his Mandarin until a PAP candidate was crushingly defeated by a Hokkien (another Chinese dialect) speaking rebel in a 1960 by-election. He also set about improving his own Hokkien.

11. T.J.S. George (1973), Lee Kuan Yew's Singapore, Andre Deutsch, page 41.

12. Ibid., page 41.

13. The United Nations Industrial Survey Mission, A Proposed Industrialisation Programme for the State of Singapore, 13 June 1961.

14. Barisan Sosialis was formed on July 26, 1961.

Notes

15. The figure for employees is actually for 1957 and includes both large and small firms.

16. U.N. Industrial Survey Mission, A Proposed industrialisation Programme ... op.cit., page iii.

17. The Chinese constitute about a third of the population of peninsular Malaya, but their economic dominance of Malaysia - real enough in tin mining and commerce - is often exaggerated. See for example the discussion in Iain Buchanan (1972), Singapore in South East Asia, G. Bell and Sons Ltd, pages 43-47 which shows that the bulk of Malayan Chinese were also deprived.

18. To ensure complete secrecy the operation was naturally launched from Johore (in Malaya) and indicates the connivance of Malayan leaders. Most of those arrested were not released until the 1970's or early 1980's and Lim Chin Siong himself was held in prison for seven years.

19. Harold Crouch (1984), Domestic Political Structures and Regional Economic Co-operation, Institute of Southeast Asian Studies, page 16.

20. For further discussion of Lee's social engineering see Chapter 6. See also the section on Singapore's militarisation later in this chapter.

21. For a good account of the Malaysia - Singapore split see T.J.S. George (1973), Lee Kuan Yew's Singapore, Andre Deutsch, Chapter 5.

22. Goh Keng Swee (First Deputy Prime Minister and presently Minister of Education) and Dr. Albert Winsemius (the Dutch economist who led the 1961 UN Mission) are generally regarded as the brains behind the coherent export/foreign investment orientated policies that Singapore has followed. In this respect Lee Kuan Yew was largely a co-ordinator, but Singapore's foreign policy can be largely ascribed to him and S. Rajaratnam (Second Prime Minister). Devan Nair, Secretary-General of the PAP-led National Trades Union Congress (NTUC) from 1962 to 1979 and now President of the Republic, played a key role in defeating the radical unions. Although individuals have been singled out in this brief account it must be stressed that the leadership of the PAP (and a few outsiders) worked as a team - and this unity is one of their major strengths. Hon Sui Sen (the Minister of Finance) who played such a major role in establishing Singapore as a financial centre died in 1983.

Notes

23. Of course the concept of a "grand strategy" is an oversimplication of events. In actual fact the "strategy" resulted from a complex interaction between the values of Lee's team, the force of domestic and international events, rational economic planning and Singapore's historically determined socio-economic characteristics - all of these actually spanning a period from the fifties through to the late sixties. Nevertheless all the characteristics of a "grand strategy" were present by the mid-sixties and the idea of a coherent plan is justified as a "necessary fiction" for analytical purposes.

24. Iain Buchanan(1972), Singapore in Southeast Asia, L. Bell and Sons Ltd, pages 86-87.

25. Pang Eng Fong (1982), Education, Manpower and Development in Singapore, Singapore University Press, page 44.

26. Industrial Relations Act, Section 34 (1) (a). Mentioned in Tan Boon Chiang (1982), "Labour relations and development in Singapore" in International Labour office, Labour Relations and Development: Country Studies, Geneva, Page 74.

27. Thomas Bellows (1974), The People's Action Party of Singapore: Emergence of a Dominant Party System, Yale University Press, page 122.

28. Cynics would argue any challenge to the PAP -left or right, moderate or militant.

29. For further information on the New International Economic, Order (a concept which encapsulates the developing countries demands for a greater access to the worlds' economic, financial and technological resourses) see, Hafiz Mirza (1984), "The New International Economic Order" in P.J. Buckley and M.Z. Brooke (eds.), Handbook of International Trade, Kluwer Publishing; Brandt Commission (1983), Common Crisis, Pan Books.

30. Of course many British and Commonwealth firms were already well established in Singapore.

31. T.J.S. George, Lee Kuan Yew's Singapore, op.cit., page 160.

32. Though the concept of world-wide sourcing can be generalised to include finance and the services.

33. Singapore's role in this "new international division of labour" is discussed in chapter five.

Notes

34.   See   various chapters in Alison Broinowski
(1982), Understanding ASEAN, Macmillan Press Ltd.
35.   V.G.   Kulkarni   (1984), "Under the Counter
Trade",   Far   Eastern   Economic   Review, April 5,
page 54.
36.   Iain Buchanan Singapore in Southeast Asia,
op.cit., page, 248.
37.   All   figures for troop levels and military
expenditure are derived from individual Country
data   in   the   Europa   Year   Book   1984, Europa
Publications Limited.
38.   Switzerland   and   Finland   were   also
considered.
39.   And   also over society and politics as has
already been mentioned.
40.   Loans   by   central government only cover a
part   of   the   expenditure of these bodies and
enterprises.
41.   Even   other NIC's, Hong Kong excepted, are
better off in this respect.
42.   In   other   words   the   post 1960/1965
expansion into the manufacturing sector.
43.   In   a   recent   issue, Global Electronics
Information   Newsletter   (No. 25, October 1982)
compared manufacturing costs per device in Hong Kong
and   the U.S. and showed that while the cost per
device immensely favoured Hong Kong when manual
processes were involved (25 cents compared to 75
cents i.e. a cost saving of 67%). this advantage
evaporated as increasingly automated processers were
employed.   When fully automated equipment was used
the cost reduction was a mere 11% (16 cents rather
than 18 cents), thereby making the advantage of
producing in cheap labour countries such as Hong
Kong or Singapore a marginal affair.
44.   World Bank (1984), World Development
Report, Oxford University Press, page 31.
45.   The   south in this context refers to the
developing   countries,   the   "north"   being the
industrialised capitalist and communist states of
the northern hemisphere.
46.   According   to Lincoln Kaye, "Catching the
Gravy Train", Far Eastern Economic Review, April 26,
1984, page 148-149, the largest awards to date have
gone to Japan (68% of the total) and Britain (10%).
Kawasaki   Heavy   Industries has received the largest
share.

Notes

47. Goh Chok Tong, Senior Minister of State for Finance, "Singapore: next ten years", speech delivered at the annual dinner of the Economic Society of Singapore, March 30, 1978.

48. See Goh Chok Tong, Minister for Trade and Industry "Singapores' economic strategy in the 80's." speech delivered at the Young Presidents' Organisation 4th Trans-Pacific Area Conference, November 10, 1979.

49. These quotes and most of the rest of the information on the plan are taken from "Highlights of Singapore's economic development plan for the eighties", Economic Bulletin, Oct - Dec, 1981. See also, Goh Chok Tong, "We must restructure our economy", speech delivered at the Third Asia-Fiet Ordinary Conference, July 17, 1980; and the Economist Intelligence Unit, Singapore: Economic Prospect, to 1986, special report no. 130, London, 1982.

50. "Highlights of Singapore's economic development plan for the eighties" op.cit., pages 5-6.

51. This summary of Singapore's manpower development programme is based on the following sources: Ministry of Culture, Singapore - facts and Pictures, 1983; Pang Eng Fong (1982), Education, Manpower and Development in Singapore, Singapore University Press; Ministry of Culture, Singapore 1983; Vocational and Industrial Training Board, Annual Report, 1982/83; "New Legislation in Singapore, 1981", Science and Technology Quarterly, January 1982; and Linda Lim and Pang Eng Fong, "Labour Strategies and the High-Tech Challenge: the case of Singapore", Euro-Asia Business Review, April 1984.

52. The PAP took this opportunity to kill off Nanyang University which, as a Mandarin speaking institution, was a major centre of opposition to Lee and his professionals during the 1950's and 1960's. Considerable opposition however ensured that the name Nanyang was retained for the technological institute.

53. At an expense of near $55 million.

54. ASEAN Briefing, no. 26, September 1980, page 2.

55. Singapore Investment News, May 1984, page 1.

Notes

56.   Tan Boon Chiang, "Labour Relations and Development in Singapore" in International Labour Office (1982), Labour Relations and Development: Country Studies on Japan, the Philippines, Singapore and Sri Lanka, Geneva, page 83.

57.   National Productivity Board (1983), Tomorrow shall be Better Than Today, Singapore.

58.   Singapore Department of Statistics, Yearbook of Statistics, Singapore 1982/83, page 70.

59.   NPB, Tomorrow Shall be Better ..., op.cit., page 24.

60.   Singapore Investment News, March and May 1984.

61.   Ibid and Economist Intelligence Unit, Singapore ..., op.cit., page 13.

62.   "Economy Resilient" in (Times Periodicals Pte Ltd) Singapore Business Yearbook, 1984, page 73.

63.   Singapore Investment News, March 1984, page 1.

64.   Industry Development Department, National Computer Board (1983), Singapore Computer Industry Survey, Singapore National Printers, page 49.

65.   Singapore Investment News, March 1984, page 4.

66.   Singapore Investment News, April 1984 page 3.

67.   Singapore Investment News, May 1984, page 3.

68.   Ibid., page 2.

69.   Singapore Investment News, July 1983, page 2. Sheng-li is the investment arm of the Ministry of Defence and the six companies involved (which maintain their separate identities) are: Chartered Industries of Singapore (CIS), Singapore Automotive Engineering (SAE), Ordnance Development and Engineering (ODE), Singapore Automotive Leasing (SAL), Singapore Computer Systems, (SCS) and Unicorn International. This is another example of the state's involvement in the economy; the first three firms are the Republic's technologically agressive defence equipment manufacturers.

70.   Singapore Investment News, October 1983, page 4.

71.   Singapore Investment News, September 1984, page 4.

Notes

72. Philippe G. Schmitter, "Still the Century of Corporatism?", Review of Politics, 1974, pages 93-94 (cited in Stephen Milne, "Corporatism in the ASEAN Countries", Contemporary South East Asia, 1983).

73. Stephen Milne, "Corporatism in the ASEAN Countries", op. cit., page 178.

74. For a discussion of how the Singapore government has insulated itself from pressure from above and below see Harold Crouch (1984), Domestic Political Structures and Regional Economic Co-operation, Institute of Southeast Asian Studies.

75. Ironically (because of the role that the Dutchman Dr. Albert Winsemius has played in Singapore's economic policies) the memorandum recommending the PAP's expulsion was circulated by the Dutch Labour Party.

76. Although it is worth asking whether the second-wave of technocratically moulded leaders such as Suppiah Dhanabalan (Foreign Afairs), Tony Tan (Trade and Industry), Goh Chok Tong (Defence) and Lim Chee Onn are made of the same stern yet pliant stuff of Lee's elder generation.

77. The aid of outside powers such as Britain, Malaya, the US, Japan and Israel should also be mentioned.

78. Refer to the beginning of this chapter.

79. Time Magazine, "Into the Ranks of the Rich", January 25, 1982, page 12.

Chapter Three

MULTINATIONAL ENTERPRISE
IN THE MANUFACTURING SECTOR

Since the early sixties Singapore's strategy
for economic development has hinged upon an
expanding export-oriented manufacturing sector
dominated by multinational companies (MNCs). An
increasingly sophisticated manufacturing sector
remains at the heart of government policy, even
though finance and the services have received
considerable promotion since the early 1970s. In
fact the authorities hope that manufacturing will
constitute a third of the island's economic activity
by the 1990s - substantially up from the present
quarter of GDP. Given the sector's continuing
importance, this chapter shall examine: (i) the
specific institutions and instruments employed by
the state to promote investment in industry; (ii)
the characteristics of manufacturing foreign direct
investment in Singapore and (iii) the nichal role of
indigenous enterprise.

FREE ZONES AND THE INVESTMENT CLIMATE

Chapter Two has already documented Singapore's
economic difficulties during the fifties and
sixties; and the consequential orientation towards
export-oriented development. This effort was based
upon the establishment of "free zones" which are
defined as 'geographic areas offering tariff, tax
and/or regulatory relief to businesses located
within their boundaries' (1) and may be classified
as follows:

Free Trade Zones (FTZs): delineated areas where
unrestricted Trade is permitted with the rest of the
world. Merchandise may be moved in and out of FTZs
free of customs duty, stored in warehouses for

varying periods, opened for inspection and repackaged as needed. (2)

Export Processing Zones (EPZs): industrial estates located outside the customs barrier offering foreign investors duty-free movement of goods in and out of the zone. Other fiscal and regulatory incentives are also offered. (3)

Free Ports: zones where FTZs and EPZs have been supplemented with tourist hotels, housing projects, shopping centres, marinas and other services. (4)

Enterprise Zones: elements of regional policy designed to expand employment and investment in distressed areas. (5)

Free Banking Zones: off-shore banking centres designed to attract non-resident foreign currency denominated business by relaxing or eliminating foreign exchange controls, interest rate payment ceilings on deposits and reserve requirements. (6)

In terms of the above classification Singapore is essentially a free port with well established FTZs, EPZs and other integrated services. Being a small economy, enterprise zones (as here defined are unnecessary; and offshore banking and services will be discussed in the next chapter.

The island's export processing zones are run by the Jurong Town Corporation (JTC) which was established in 1968. By 1983 21 EPZs were in operation, covering over 7000 hectares and housing 2,895 foreign and indigenous companies (table 3.1) Map 3.1 shows that while EPZs are concentrated in Jurong they are to be found throughout the island especially near ports. Nearly 212,000 employees work on JTC industrial estates which probably makes Singapore's EPZs the most successful world-wide. In recent years the Corporation has begun to develop specialised industrial estates in order to promote high-technology industries. These include the Singapore Science and Technology Park (to encourage research and development), Loyang and Seletar industrial estates (near Changi airport as the country's first centres for manufacturing aircraft components and parts, and for airframe assemblies and the International Petroleum Centre. The Corporation's Jurong Marine Base is intended to support and service South East Asia's oil and gas

ultinational Enterprise
n the Manufacturing Sector.

able 3.1 Export Processing Zones in operation,
983

ame	Total Area (Hectares)	Number of Firms	Number of Companies in Production	Estimated Labour Force (Thousands)
ng Mo Kio	13.1	37	36	3.6
yer Rajah	24.9	100	96	7.8
edok	6.4	39	37	3.2
urong	5889.4	1,606	1,451	114.5
allang Basin	101.5	611	597	36.7
allang Park	8.0	39	39	1.2
ampong Ampat	2.0	3	3	0.3
ranji	119.7	53	37	5.0
oyang	188.6	12	9	0.4
edhill	4.3	47	44	2.3
t. Michael's	0.8	18	18	1.4
ims Avenue	0.7	26	26	1.1
cience Park	50.2	1	-	-
ungei Kadut	376.9	149	122	4.6
anglin Halt	16.8	50	50	5.1
g Rhu	1.5	2	2	0.3
elok Blangah	5.7	39	37	3.6
iong Bahru	4.9	75	73	7.6
oa Payoh	6.3	98	98	9.5
oodlands East	170.2	60	31	1.7
ew Tree	25.5	96	89	1.8
otal	7,017.4	3,161	2,895	211,790

ource: Jurong Town Corporation, Annual Report,
        1982/1983

ote: Fifteen other EPZs with a total area of
        2008.6 hectares are under preparation.

xploration and production industry.

The Port of Singapore Authority (PSA) oversees
ingapore's ports, free trade zones and various
elated services such as warehousing. There are six
TZs situated at the five major ports (Keppel,
anjong Pagar, Jurong, Pasir Panjang and
embawang) and Changi airport. Singapore's free

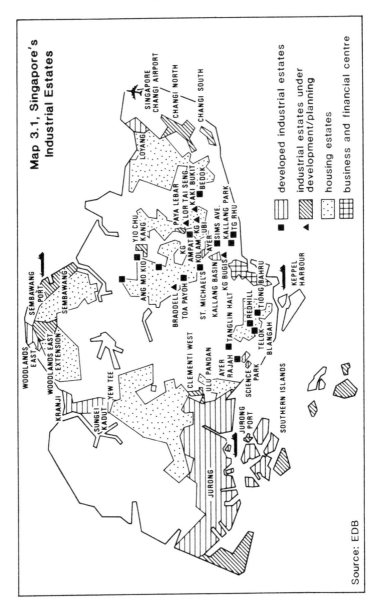

Map 3.1, Singapore's Industrial Estates

Source: EDB

rade zones have undoubtedly boosted the country's
ntrepot trade and sea-borne cargo throughput in
hese zones nearly tripled from 16.6m tonnes in 1973
o 39.5m tonnes in 1982. In addition Changi FTZ
established in 1981) contributes about 0.2m tonnes
f air-borne cargo. (7)

The Economic Development Board (EDB)
o-ordinates the whole effort: it determines
riorities in manufacturing and related sectors,
ffers a variety of supportive and international
ervices, and markets Singapore abroad. While many
asks (e.g. provision of infrastructural facilities
nd specific services) are left to bodies such as
he PSA and JTC, it is the EDB which decides on the
cale and format of taxes and other incentives.
able 3.2 indicates the main tax incentives
resently available to manufacturing companies.

Chapter one mentioned that Singapore is
enerally regarded as a low-risk, credit worthy
ountry and that Euromoney's 1984 table of country
isk ratings (8) placed the island in 16th position,
n the rank of developed countries (9). Chapter two
howed how this favourable investment climate was
he result of deliberate government policy to ensure
olitical stability, economic expansion and
ndustrial efficiency. A 1979 study produced by the
sian Wall Street Journal showed that the PAP was
ssentially correct in its assessment of elements
rucial to a good investment climate (10).
ompanies deemed the following factors most
mportant in their decision process: political and
conomic stability; stable labour force; stable
urrency value; ready availability of foreign
xchange; access to local finance; existence of a
ood joint venture partner; taxation incentives; and
uty-free imports. (11) On this basis the study
ound that Singapore had the best investment climate
f all ASEAN countries (12) and it is readily
iscernible why the island-state attracts more FDI
han other NICs. Hong Kong, for example, is sill
edevilled with the "1997 question" (despite the
984 treaty); South Korea has a recent history of
olitical instability allied with strained relations
ith North Korea and an economic policy biased
owards indigenous firms; and Taiwan still
onstantly looks over its shoulder at the threat
osed by the People's Republic of China.

However, despite an excellent investment
limate the country does not possess such
pportunities for investment as a large local

87

Table 3.2 Tax Incentives offered to Manufacturing Companies.

Tax Incentives	Qualifying Activities	Statutory Conditions	Tax Concessions
Pioneer Status	Projects entailing large capital expenditures and sophisticated, especially knowledge-based, technologies.	No statutory conditions but the EDB generally imposes fixed investment conditions to be achieved by 4th or 5th year of production.	1. Exemption of 40% tax on profits arising from pioneer activity. 2. Tax relief period is 5-10 years.
Expansion Incentive	As above	Minimum investment of S$10 million in productive equipment and machinery.	1. Exemption of 40% tax on profits in excess of pre-expansion level. 2. Tax relief period of up to 5 years.
Export Incentives	As above and deepsea fishing products.	EDB generally imposes fixed asset investment conditions to be achieved.	1. 90% exemption of tax on export in excess of a specified base. 2. Tax relief period is 3 years for pioneer companies and 5 years for non-pioneer companies.

cont.

Table 3.2 cont. Tax Incentives offered to Manufacturing Companies.

Tax Incentives	Qualifying Activities	Statutory Conditions	Tax Concessions
Investment Allowance Incentive	1. Manufacturing. 2. Specialised engineering & technical services. 3. Research and development activities. 4. Construction. (This incentive is increasingly being used to promote the upgrading and mechanisation of existing operations.)	Qualifying period of up to 5 years within which investments must be made.	Tax deduction equal to a specified proportion (up to 50%) of new fixed investment.
Warehousing and Servicing Incentive	Warehousing, technical or engineering services.(This incentive aims at encouraging warehousing of engineering or other technical products as a stepping-stone to manufacturing.)	1. Minimum fixed investment in warehouse buildings and equipment of S$2 million. 2. Goods must be traded by company.	1. 50% exemption of tax on profits in excess of a fixed base. 2. Tax relief period of 5 years.

cont.

Table 3.2 cont. Tax Incentives offered to Manufacturing Companies.

Tax Incentives	Qualifying Activities	Statutory Conditions	Tax Concessions
International Consultancy Services Incentive	Consultancy services in respect of overseas projects. These include technical assistance, design, engineering, fabrication of equipment and data processing.	Minimum revenue of S$1 million per annum.	1. 50% exemption of tax on profits in excess of a fixed base. 2. Tax relief period is 5 years.
Approved Foreign Loan Scheme	Manufacturing and related activities.	1. Minimum loan of S$200,000 from a foreign lender for purchase of productive equipment.	Exemption of witholding tax on interest.
Approved Royalties	Manufacturing and related activities.	Tax relief should not result in an increase in tax liability in the foreign country.	50% or 100% exemption of witholding tax on royalties.

Source: Singapore Economic Development Board, Annual Report, 1982/83.

market, raw materials or even low cost labour. (13)
Consequently Singapore promotes itself as an
"ideal" location for internationally and regionally
oriented industries and services. (See chapter two.)
In manufacturing the role of free zones is essential
and Spinager has mentioned that although Singapore
provides less investment incentives than other
developing countries, these are spread over a longer
period. Moreover they are 'but another part of a
package designed to attract investment to a
strategically located economy already (virtually)
free of import/export regulations, with a high level
of infrastructure as well as an efficient labour
market and stable political conditions'. (14) The
"efficient labour market" is, of course, also the
result of careful government planning including
training/retraining provisions (see chapter two).

Table 3.3 indicates the significance of tax
incentives and their importance in attracting
foreign manufacturing investment. Pioneer status
(i.e. tax exemption : see table 3.2 for definition)
has been accorded to a large proportion of foreign
firms, especially larger ones (15) and in 1981
pioneer firms employed 72% of the personnel,
produced 94% of the output and owned 83% of the
assets of all foreign firms operating in the
Republic (16). Although it is always dangerous to
assign specific causes to events, tax incentives
have undoubtedly influenced the level of investment
in Singapore. In addition to political stability,
pacific labour relations and investment incentives,
MNCs are attracted by good economic performance.
Table 3.4 reiterates how well Singapore has
performed in recent years when compared to
industrialised countries, or even most NICs. Not
surprisingly, foreign manufacturing investors are
keen to participate in the economy's combination of
high growth, low inflation and rapid productivity
increase (7.2% in manufacturing in 1983).

The only cloud to mar Singapore's manufacturing
horizon is the continuing protectionist tendency in
the United States and the resulting wrangle over tax
incentives. The US department of commerce maintains
that incentives offered by the EDB amount to unfair
competition and has threatened to impose
countervailing duties. Thus, according to the
Economist, 'Singapore faces a dilemma'. It may have
to sign the subsidies code of the General Agreement
on Tariffs and Trade (GATT) to stop America imposing
countervailing duties on its exports. Yet, if it

Table 3.3   A Comparison of Foreign and Pioneer^a Establishments, 1981

	Foreign	Pioneer	Pioneer as a Proportion of Foreign (%)
Number of Establishments	883	432	49
Persons Employed (Thousands)	163	117	72
Output (US$ bn)	11.5	10.8	94
[Gross Fixed] Assets (US$ bn)	4.1	3.4	83

Sources: Singapore Department of Statistics, Yearbook of Statistics, 1982/83.

Singapore Department of Statistics, Report on the Census of Industrial Production, 1981.

Note: Pioneer Status is accorded to certain establishments (mainly foreign) as an incentive to set-up in Singapore. Tax relief for up to 10 years is available to these firms which are chosen on the basis of technological sophistication and size of capital expenditures.

Multinational Enterprise
in the Manufacturing Sector.

Table 3.4   Performance of the Singapore Economy Compared to Selected Countries.

Percentage Change

Country	1982			1983		
	Real GNP/GDP	Inflation	Productivity	Real GNP/GDP	Inflation	Productivity
Singapore	6.3	3.9	1.2	7.2	1.1	4.6
NICs						
Hongkong	2.4	10.6	2.4a	5.7	11.2	–
South Korea	5.3	7.3	2.6a	8.9	4.7	8.7a (Jan–Jun)
Taiwan	3.9	4.0	1.3a	6.5	4.6	2.2a (Jan–Jun)
Selected OECD Countries						
US	-1.9	6.1	-1.0	3½	4	2¼
Japan	3.0	2.7	1.9	3	1½	1¼
West Germany	-1.1	5.3	0.7	1¼	3	3¼
France	1.9	11.8	1.9	½	9¼	1¼
UK	2.0	8.6	3.8	2½	6	3¼

Source: Prime Minister's National Day message.
Note: a. Productivity figures are not published by these countries but derived from GDP divided by employment. The latest employment figures for the other countries however are not available for productivity growth calculation.
b. Private consumption deflators are used for OECD countries.

signs, it will have to phase out incentives that
have attracted investors to Singapore. (17)

FOREIGN INVESTMENT AND THE GROWTH OF THE MANUFACTURING SECTOR

Tables 3.5 and 3.6 show that manufacturing FDI
in Singapore increased manifold over the period 1965
to 1982; and that the source country and industrial
composition of foreign assets (18) altered
considerably. In 1965 the UK was the largest
investor because of historical and colonial ties.
Most foreign investment was in food, beverages,
rubber processing and petroleum - the last industry
having raised its share of FDI because of a single
major investment in petroleum refining by Shell.
Because Shell is a joint UK-Dutch company this
explains why the Netherlands had a 25.5% share of
foreign manufacturing investment in the same year.
The Japanese share was also large, but this chiefly
consisted of many small, low-technology investments
geared towards the Malaysian market. The late
sixties saw an upsurge in foreign investment inflow,
particularly from US MNCs increasingly investing in
off-shore production sites. The US share of
manufacturing FDI in Singapore jumped to 34.5% in
1970, chiefly because of investment in petroleum and
electrical/electronic machinery - a level which it
has since maintained. The share of all other
countries, especially Japan, declined as a
consequence, although both the UK and the
Netherlands maintained a share of about a fifth each
because of Shell's continuing investment in
petroleum. In fact petroleum and petroleum
products' share of FDI in Singapore was a massive
55.7% in 1970 and still remains at the 40% mark.
The late sixties saw a wage explosion in many
industrialised countries and foreign investment to
cheap labour sites leapt as a result. A
particularly large outflow from Japan means that its
share of manufacturing FDI in Singapore now stands
at 16%, in rough parity with the UK and the
Netherlands, but well behind the USA. FDI from
other industrialised countries, including Germany,
Sweden, France, Italy and Switzerland, has also
increased in recent years. In earlier years FDI
from developing countries mainly came from Malaysia,
but more recently many other countries (e.g. South
Korea, Taiwan, Hong Kong, Indonesia and India)

Table 3.5 Distribution of Manufacturing Foreign
Direct Investment[a] by Country of Origin, 1965-82

	Percent			
Country	1965	1970	1975	1982
USA	14.6	34.5	33.1	34.0
Japan	17.2	6.8	13.4	16.4
UK	28.7	20.0	14.2	16.3
Netherlands	25.5	18.4	14.0	14.7
Germany	N.A.	0.3	3.1	2.3
European Community[b]	N.A.	42.5	32.8	35.7
Sweden	N.A.	0.3	0.7	1.3
Switzerland	N.A.	1.2	0.9	1.8
Others	14.0	16.2	18.9	10.4
Total Amount (US$ bn)	0.1	0.3	1.4	4.5

Source: Calculated from the Singapore Economic
Development Board's, Annual Report, various
years.

Note: a - in terms of Gross Fixed Assets
(excluding land).
b - including the above EC countries.
N.A. - Not available.

have entered the picture.
By 1982 most manufacturing FDI was in
petroleum, electrical and non-electrical machinery
(Table 3.6), but the composition varied between
source countries. Table 3.7 shows how FDI from
individual source countries is concentrated in
certain industries, though it should be interpreted
with care because the size of individual
establishments is not indicated. Thus, for example,
only 11 establishments engaged in petroleum (Table
3.7) possess 40% of foreign manufacturing assets
(Table 3.6) and produce 40% of Singapore's
manufacturing output (Table 3.8). Bearing this in
mind, it can nevertheless be seen that firms from
Singapore and other developing countries tend

Table 3.6 Distribution of Manufacturing Foreign
Direct Investment[a] by Industry Group, 1970-82

	Percent		
Industry Group	1970	1975	1982
Chemicals and Pharmaceuticals	6.1	5.1	6.1
Petroleum and Petroleum Products	55.7	42.2	40.4
Plastics	0.8	1.2	1.6
Non-electrical Machinery	N.A.	7.4	9.6
Electrical/ Electronic Machinery	8.2	10.5	19.4
Transport equipment	5.1	6.2	5.1
Instruments	1.7	4.2	2.5
Others	22.4	23.0	15.3
Total Amount (US $ bn)	0.3	1.4	4.5

Source and Notes: See table 3.5

towards low value added industries such as food and
apparel; while firms from industrialised countries
tend towards higher value added industries. US and
Japanese firms are especially prevalent in
electronic products and non-electrical machinery;
the Germans also prefer the latter, while UK firms
are concentrated in chemicals and food; and "other"
European countries veer towards electronic products
and transport equipment.
     The evolution of foreign investment in specific
industries will be analysed more fully in chapter 5;

Multinational Enterprise
in the Manufacturing Sector.

Table 3.7 Manufacturing establishments by country of origin and industry, 1982

Number of Establishments

Country of Origin	Food Products	Textiles/ Apparel	Wood/Paper Printing	Chemicals	Refining/ Petroleum Products	Plastic Rubber Products	Mineral Products	Metal Products	Non-electrical Machinery	Electrical Machinery	Electronic Products	Transport Equipment	Instruments	Others	Total
Singapore	263	515	569	62	4	191	66	332	205	53	58	250	14	109	2,691
USA	5	1	6	9	3	2	6	1	31	8	25	6	7	-	118
UK	9	2	8	14	1	3	-	9	7	7	5	5	2	1	73
Japan	6	5	5	8	-	11	4	28	21	20	49	7	12	7	183
Germany	-	2	1	1	-	1	-	5	8	4	5	2	-	-	29
Switzerland	1	1	3	-	-	-	-	4	4	2	2	1	3	-	21
Other Europe	1	2	3	6	2	-	2	6	6	7	11	9	-	1	56
Australia	1	1	7	5	-	4	1	13	1	4	3	2	2	2	46
Hong Kong	6	18	7	16	-	3	2	4	5	1	10	2	3	8	85

cont.

Table 3.7 cont. Manufacturing establishments by country of origin and industry, 1982

Number of Establishments

Country of Origin	Food Products	Textiles/ Apparel	Wood/Paper/ Printing	Chemicals	Refining/ Petroleum Products	Plastic/ Rubber Products	Mineral Products	Metal Products	Non-electrical Machinery	Electrical Machinery	Electronic Products	Transport Equipment	Instruments	Others	Total
Malaysia	5	15	17	2	1	7	2	13	8	1	2	5	-	1	79
Taiwan	-	3	1	-	-	1	1	1	1	2	2	-	-	3	15
Others	8	32	28	9	-	25	4	21	17	5	14	6	5	16	190
Total	305	597	655	132	11	259	88	445	314	114	186	295	48	148	3,586

Source: Based on Table 3.1 in the Singapore Department of Statistics, Report on the Census of Industrial Production 1982

Multinational Enterprise
in the Manufacturing Sector.

here it is sufficient to say that FDI in Singapore
arrived as a result of: (i) competitive forces
necessitating low cost bases, (ii) the lure of
regional opportunities, especially since the
establishment of ASEAN (19), and (iii) the
availability of local opportunities. The transfer
of parts of the electronics industry to developing
countries is a good example of the first motivation;
as is AVIMO's 1972 decision to transfer the
production of sophisticated optical instruments from
the UK to Singapore because of Japanese competition.
The island's petroleum industry is largely
regionally oriented and supplies much of its output
to Hong Kong, Japan and ASEAN (see chapter 5).
Local opportunities also abound and foreign firms
(especially those from South Korea, Japan and the
UK) are benefitting greatly from major construction
projects. As mentioned earlier, Japanese companies
have obtained the lion's share of all contracts
related to the MRT (Mass Rapid Transport) system to
date; and Ssangyong Construction of South Korea
recently clinched a $300m contract to build the
superstructures of the massive Raffles City Complex
(20).
    The influx of manufacturing FDI since the early
sixties has resulted in a seventy-fold increase in
manufacturing output in nominal terms (fifteen-fold
in real terms) since 1961. Table 3.8 shows that
most of the output in 1982 came from just six key
industries: petroleum and petroleum products (40% of
output), electrical and electronic products (17%),
metal products (11%), non-electrical machinery (7%),
transport equipment (6%) and food products (6%). Of
these, the MNC-dominated higher value added
industries (petroleum, electrical and non-electrical
machinery) are the fastest growing. In general the
outlook for manufacturing is good, especially in the
electronics sector:

        This sector, currently consisting of around
        200 firms, is rapidly abandoning basic
        products in favour of computers and
        computer peripherals as well as
        communications and process control
        equipment. This development reflects
        successful efforts to upgrade technology
        since the end of the seventies, although
        further progress could be hampered by a
        lack of skilled labour. (21).

Table 3.8   The Expansion of Manufacturing Output,
1961-1982

Industry	Index Numbers: 1972 = 100			1982 output: (US$ bn)
	1961	1967	1982	
Food and Beverages[a]	34	81	300	1.0
Textiles and Apparel[b]	4	17	306	0.6
Wood Products	13	35	276	0.4
Paper and Printing	26	42	461	0.4
Chemicals/ Pharmaceutical	10	31	620	0.5
Petroleum Products	Neg	22	855	6.7
Rubber and Plastic Products	13	31	531	0.3
Mineral Products[c]	23	44	724	0.4
Metal Products	17	46	601	1.9
Non-electrical Machinery	8	14	1,139	1.2
Electrical and Electronic Products	2	6	807	2.8[d]
Transport Equipment and Oil Rigs	6	14	445	1.0
Instruments	0	0	428	0.1
Others	9	45	375	0.2
Index for Total Manufacturing	9	29	623	16.7

Source: Calculated from Singapore Department of
         Statistics, Economic and Social Statistics
         of Singapore, 1960-1982.
Notes: a - Includes tobacco. b - includes leather
         goods and footwear. c - includes ceramics,
         cement and construction material. d - $2.3
         billion of this figure constitutes
         electronic goods and components.

Multinational Enterprise
in the Manufacturing Sector.

The Productivity and Profitability of Foreign
Firms.

Table 3.9 confirms that the chief objective of
MNCs from most source countries is to utilize
Singapore as a relatively cheap, strategic and
secure base for regional and global exports. In
1982 only Taiwanese and Australian firms exported
less than 50% of their total output (on par with
indigenous enterprise). In contrast, companies from
most other countries exported the bulk of their
output and this is especially the case for German,
Swiss and other European firms. Naturally some
output is sold locally to final consumers; and the
rapid expansion of the manufacturing sector has also
meant an increase in the sale of intermediate goods,
especially chemicals and petrochemical products.

In general firms from industrialised countries
are more productive than indigenous firms or those
from other developing countries (Table 3.9).
Further, although it is difficult to compare (22),
the productivity of MNCs in Singapore is similar to
that in their respective source countries. This
certainly seems to be the case for US and Australian
companies. The lower productivity for German and
Japanese firms is because low technology processes
have been exported to Singapore, e.g. for the
assembly of electronic components; while the higher
productivity for UK firms in Singapore results from
the large share of local output accounted for by
Shell's petroleum complex. (23)

Table 3.9 also compares foreign firms'
profitability in Singapore (i.e. pre-tax profit as a
share of value added) with their profitability in
respective source countries. In the source country
profitability is shown both in terms of gross
operating surplus (column A) and net (post-tax)
operating surplus (column B) because foreign firms'
status as pioneer establishments (see table 3.3 and
text) implies little difference in pre- and post-tax
profits and profitability in Singaporean operations.
Either way it can be seen that foreign manufacturing
firms are considerably more profitable in Singapore
than in their countries of origin. This fact goes a
long way towards explaining Singapore's relative
attractiveness as a host country.

Table 3.9   Manufacturing Productivity and Profitability of foreign firms in Singapore and Source Country, 1982.

Country of Origin	Total Output[a] (US $ bn)	Productivity[b] (US $ Thousands)		Profitability[c] (%)			Direct Exports to Total Sales (%)
		Singapore[d]	Source[e] Country	Singapore[d]	Source Country[e] A	Source Country[e,f] B	
Singapore	6.3	12.1	-	57	-	-	44
USA	2.9	22.6	23.4	72	13	23	65
UK	0.5	31.4	10.5	74	8	19	56
Japan	1.4	11.5	20.3	57	-	44	62
Germany	0.1	10.9	19.5	52	17	27	83
Switzerland	0.3	20.8	-	70	-	-	87
Other Europe[g]	4.2	50.4	-	84	-	-	78
Australia	0.1	17.6	19.3	58	14[h]	27	41
Hong Kong	0.5	11.1	-	54	-	-	80
Malaysia	0.3	16.1	-	65	-	-	52
Taiwan	0.1	12.5	-	43	-	-	43
Others	0.4	7.9	-	42	-	-	56
All Firms	17.1	15.9	-	65	-	-	40

Source: Derived from tables 6 and 11 in Singapore Department of Statistics, Report on the Census of Industrial Production, 1982; and OECD, Historical Statistics 1980-1981.

cont.

Table 3.9 cont. Manufacturing Productivity and Profitability of foreign firms in
Singapore and Source Country, 1982.

Notes: a – In Singapore.
        b – Value added per employee.
        c – Company profits (operating surplus) as a proportion of value added. The
              Singapore figures are gross operating surplus as a share of gross value
              added.
        d – Productivity or profitability of foreign or indigenous firms in
              Singapore.
        e – Productivity or profitability in the manufacturing sector of each set of
              foreign firms' home economies.
        f – A – net operating surplus as a share of net value added (i.e. post-income
              tax);
              B – gross operating surplus as a share of gross value added (i.e.
              pre-income tax).
        g – Including EC and non EC firms.
        h – 1976 figure. (–) – Not available or inapplicable.

All source country figures are for 1981.

THE RELATIVE CONTRIBUTION OF INDIGENOUS AND FOREIGN
FIRMS TO SINGAPORE'S MANUFACTURING SECTOR.

Table 3.10 highlights the preponderant role that
MNCs play in Singapore's manufacturing sector.
Though only 25 percent of manufacturing
establishments are foreign owned, these employ 55
percent of the industrial work force, produce 65
percent of the value added and export 72 percent of
all direct manufacturing exports. Two thirds of
capital expenditure in manufacturing is accounted
for by multinational companies and, accordingly,
they receive 70 percent of all profits. However, as
table 3.11 shows, foreign and indigenous companies
are dominant in different manufacturing industries
indicating that local establishments have filled
specific niches in which MNCs are unwilling or
unable to compete. The more important industries
are discussed below. (24)

Foreign Capital Dominated Industries.

Petroleum and Petroleum products. This industry is
84 percent foreign owned and in 1982 contributed one
sixth ($756 million) of the total value added of the
manufacturing sector. (Much of the remaining 16
percent ownership is accounted for by state-owned
enterprises: see table 3.12). Because of its high
capital intensity, productivity and worker
remuneration (see Table 3.11), this industry is
almost entirely closed to indigenous entrepreneurs.
In any case the future is uncertain because of the
present oil glut (two thirds of the industry's
output is exported) and the decline in third party
processing. With respect to the latter, Indonesia
is reducing the amount of its oil being refined in
Singapore's petroleum complexes by increasing its
own refining capacity.

Electrical machinery and Electronic Products. The
total capital invested in these two rapidly
expanding industries is preponderantly (77 percent
and 83 percent) foreign; and this will remain the
case given the continuing influx of MNCs in these
fields. The Electronic Products industry is
particularly important because it employs 60
thousand workers or about one fifth of all employees
in manufacturing. In theory both these industries
should produce vertical linkages with indigenous
firms (in servicing, component production and

Multination Enterprise
in the Manufacturing Sector

Table 3.10   Contribution of Foreign and Indigenous
Companies in Manufacturing, 1982

Item	Amount	Indigenous Contribution (%)	Foreign Contribution (%)
Establishments[a] (Number)	3,586	75	25
Worker employed (thousands)	275	45	55
Output (US $ bn)	17.0	37	63
Value Added (US $ bn)	4.4	35	65
Direct Exports[b] (US $ bn)	10.2	28	72
Employees renumeration (US $ bn)	1.5	43	57
Undistributed Pre-Tax profits (US $ bn)	2.9	30	70
Capital Expenditure (US $ bn)	1.0	37	63

Source: Calculated from Singapore Department of
        Statistics, Report on the Census of
        Industrial Production, 1982, table 6.

Notes: a - those with 10 workers or more.
         b - i.e. excluding entrepot trade.

Multinational Enterprise
in the Manufacturing Sector.

Table 3.11 Selected Characteristics of Foreign and Local Capital Dominated Industries, 1982.

Industry	Average Size of firm (Number of workers per establishment) [	Value Added per Worker Thousands of US Dollars	Remuneration per Worker	Assets per Worker	Capital Expenditure per Worker]	Direct Exports to Output Ratio (%)
Total Manufacturing	77	16	6	16	4	60
Local Capital Dominated	59	13	6	11	3	40
Food	36	15	5	18	4	52
Beverage	162	25	7	25	5	23
Wearing Apparel	70	5	3	2	½	70
Printing and Publishing	42	13	6	8	3	17
Plastics	41	9	4	12	4	23
Cement and Concrete	59	26	7	8	5	-
Iron and Steel	107	37	9	22	9	12
Metal Products	52	14	6	14	4	28
Transport Equipment	104	15	7	14	4	54
Others	44	7	4	9	7	25

cont.

Table 3.11 cont. Selected Characteristics of Foreign and Local Capital Dominated Industries, 1982.

Industry	Average Size of firm (Number of workers per establishment)	Value Added per Worker	Remuneration per Worker	Assets per Worker	Capital Expenditure per Worker	Direct Exports to Output Ratio (%)
		Thousands of US Dollars				
Foreign Capital Dominated	104	19	6	19	4	66
Textiles	67	8	5	13	1½	46
Wood Products	60	9	5	13	2	52
Furniture	54	7	4	7	1	41
Paper Products	48	13	6	21	6	18
Chemicals/ Pharmaceuticals	54	35	8	28	12	56
Petroleum Products	344	200	17	353	39	64
Non-electrical Machinery	76	20	7	13	4	73
Electrical Machinery	126	13	6	10	4	63
Electronic Products	327	11	5	7	2	86
Instrumentation	120	10	4	9	4	97
Others	N.A.	17	6	14	3	35

Source: Singapore Department of Statistics, Report on the Census of Industrial Production, 1982.

assembly), but in practice this does not
particularly appear to be the case (table 5.15.).
The question of linkages will be discussed more
fully in chapters five and six. Table 5.15 also
shows the relative size of indigenous and foreign
establishments: the former are mainly in the range
of 10-50 employees; the latter are generally much
larger, often consisting of 1000 workers or more.

Chemical and Pharmaceutical Products. Most of the
output of this industry is accounted for by a small
number of large pharmaceuticals producers, all
foreign in origin. While indigenous firms abound in
some simpler chemical products, the pharmaceuticals
industry is a research-intensive field with
considerable barriers to entry: it is likely to
remain dominated by MNCs for the forseeable future.

Local Capital Dominated Industries.

Transport Equipment. This industry is the second
largest both in terms of value added ($470 million)
and employment (30 thousand workers). Most of the
value added in 1982 was accounted for by indigenous
firms involved in shipbuilding and repairs. These
activities respond to a market world-wide in scope
and reflect the internationally competitive position
of local firms; although it must be mentioned that
much of the necessary technology originally came
from abroad (chiefly Japan). However the indigenous
dominance of this sector is in decline as a result
of a fall in demand for shipbuilding and repairs;
and the simultaneous expansion of MNC dominated
aircraft equipment manufacturing and aircraft
servicing. The government has played a major role
in encouraging this expansion, but it is unlikely
that aircraft equipment manufacturing/servicing
technology will be readily transferred to local
firms.

Food Industry. Fifty one percent of this industry's
output was sold locally in 1982; and much of the
rest in the South East Asia region. It is therefore
not unexpected that indigenous firms possess a
comparative advantage over MNCs in the Food Industry
because of their knowledge of the local market and
its requirements.

Wearing Apparel. This industry is important because
it employed about 29 thousand workers in 1982.
However, it is an industry that the Singapore

authorities would like to restructure because it has
the lowest value added per worker ($5 thousand), the
lowest assets per worker ($2 thousand) and the
lowest remuneration per work ($3 thousand). (Table
3.11). Singapore's high wage policy is forcing some
upgrading into high value added fashion garments,
but there is likely to be severe competition from
other developing countries as well as from firms
from industrial nations.

CONCLUDING REMARKS: THE SIGNIFICANCE OF STATE-OWNED
ENTERPRISES.

The foregoing analysis has shown that Singapore's
manufacturing sector, and hence the economy (25), is
very heavily dependent on the local operations of
multinational companies. MNCs dominate in terms of
assets, value added, employment, remuneration and
exporting (tables 3.10 and 3.11) and have forced
indigenous companies into low technology, low value
added industrial and product niches (table 3.11).
Although local firms are very slowly working their
way up the technology ladder they are constrained by
lack of technology, experience, entrepreneurship and
size. The importance of this last factor should not
be under-stated for, though there are some large
private indigenous firms (e.g. the Robin Group), the
average size of establishments in local capital
dominated industries is only 59 workers per
establishment (Table 3.11). The average size in
foreign capital dominated industries is 104 workers
per establishment (a figure which includes large
numbers of indigenous firms); and in key industries
(e.g. Petroleum Products, and Electronic Products)
the average size is very much greater. Further,
even if the local subsidiary of a multinational
company is relatively small, it is nevertheless part
of a much larger international network.
    The comparative uncompetitiveness of indigenous
enterprise is of very great concern to Lee, and the
PAP because , in the final analysis , a MNCs loyalty
is to its shareholders or source country.
Consequently the Singapore state has evolved a
number of ways to encourage indigenous firms. These
measures include the Small Industries Finance Scheme
(SIFS), technical assistance to small local
establishments and help in establishing joint
ventures with foreign companies. In addition
specific state-owned enterprises, such as INTRACO,

help Singaporean firms in servicing foreign markets
(26).   However, despite these efforts, local
entrepreneurs are unhappy about the level of state
assistance . A good example is the recent award of
contracts for the mass rapid transit system:
indigenous contractors and financiers complained
bitterly that foreign concerns (chiefly the
Japanese) received the lion's share of the spoils
(27).

In addition to support for the private sector,
the PAP promotes the indigenous stake in the economy
by pursuing a remarkable strategy of state
entrepreneurship. (28) State-owned enterprises help
Singapore circumvent such common developing-country
problems as a dearth of entrepreneurial,
technological and even capital resources by
concentrating the economy's efforts. All
state-owned enterprises (and statutory boards) are
run as profit-making concerns and the enthusiasm and
zeal of the PAP's cadres stands the country in good
stead. (29)   It is estimated that state-owned
corporations and statutory boards generated a return
of \$5-7 billion in 1983 (30) - equivalent to a
massive <u>third</u> of total GDP or a <u>half</u> of indigenous
GDP.

Table 3.12 (page 114) illustrates the scale of
state involvement in manufacturing and other sectors
of the economy. (31)   It can be seen that the
government's control over the economy is exercised
through minority ownership of strategic private
(domestic and foreign) companies, as well as through
majority-owned concerns. In many respects the
driving forces behind the economy's industrial
restructing are the larger (32) state-owned
enterprises. In tandem with statutory bodies, (33)
companies such as Singapore Airlines, Straits
Trading Co., INTRACO, Neptune Orient Lines, The
Development Bank of Singapore and Keppel Shipyards
are promoting Singapore's diversification into
higher technology, higher value added products and
services. Kathryn Davies essentially agrees:

> Singapore's flexibility in response to
> changing external conditions, as
> exemplified by Keppel, (34) is widely
> believed to be the secret of its success up
> to now. The two major government holding
> companies, Temasek (civilian) and Sheng-Li
> (ministry of defence), have adopted an
> entrepreneurial approach to the running of

their businesses which has helped to create the image of 'Singapore Inc.'. Two home grown industries grouped under Sheng-Li show particular promise: the manufacture of small-arms for an international market; and manufacture, repair and service of aircraft as a significant input to the government encouraged aerospace industry, in which Sheng-Li companies are taking an extremely aggressive part. (35)

One final point should be made. Given the nature of the PAP a military-industrial complex is undoubtedly on the cards. Sheng-Li companies such as Chartered Industries of Singapore (CIS), the largest domestic employer in manufacturing, and Singapore Shipbuilding and Engineering (SSE) already produce and export weapons and ships; and Singapore Aircraft Industries (SAI) expects to build its own aircraft within a decade. Further CIS and five other Sheng-Li companies combined in 1984 to establish the Singapore Technology Corporation (STC) which through subsidiary companies such as the Singapore Computer Systems (SCS) is likely to be valuable in developing sophisticated military products. (36)

NOTES

1. Sabre Foundation (1983), Free Zones in Developing Countries: Expanded Opportunities for the Private Sector, A.I.D. Program Evaluation Discussion Paper No. 18, page 3. The classication of zones in this chapter is also based on this discussion paper.
2. Ibid., page 3
3. Ibid., page 3
4. Ibid., page 4
5. Ibid., page 4
6. Ibid., page 4
7. Port of Singapore Authority, FTZ Progress Review Committee, Free Trade Zones in Singapore, Annual Report 1982/83, pages 2 - 5.
8. Euromoney, October 1984, page 304.
9. In fact Singapore has had to resist attempts by the UN to redefine the island as an industrialised economy - a label warranted by its high per caput income.

NOTES continued.

10. Barry Wain (Ed.) (1979), The ASEAN Report, Volume 1, The Asian Wall Street Journal , Dow Jones Publishing Co., pages 135-145.

11. Ibid., page 135

12. Ibid., page 139

13. Although, as discussed earlier, Singapore's position in ASEAN means that a large market is accessible and raw materials are plentiful.

14. Dean Spinager (1984), "Objectives and Impact of Economic Activity Zones - Some Evidence from Asia", Weltwirtschaftliches Archiv, Bd.CXX, Band 1, pages 68-71.

15. Pioneer status is only one of the many incentives offered by Singapore.

16. Not all pioneer firms are foreign, but most are.

17. The Economist, "Gatt and Singapore", December 3, 1983, page 77.

18. The Singapore statistical department's definition of FDI in terms of gross fixed assets (as used in this chapter) differs considerably from the IMF definition as employed in chapter one. Unfortunately there is no easy way of relating the two.

19. See for example Barry Wain (Ed), The ASEAN Report, op. cit., page 69. The report shows that 44% of MNCs establishing bases in Singapore quoted competitive pressures and 23% mentioned the need to secure or maintain a regional base.

20. This complex includes a 71 storey hotel tower, a 42 storey office tower, a 28 storey twin-core hotel tower and a 7 storey podium. For further details see, "South Korean firm clinches S$671 in Raffles City deal" in Times Periodical Pte Ltd. (1983), Singapore Business Yearbook, 1984, Singapore, page 101.

21. ABECOR Country Report, Singapore, 1984.

22. Because the composition of firms, industries and technology varies enormously between the source country and the manufacturing activity of its companies in Singapore.

23. "Other" European companies also have a high productivity in Singapore because of reasons similar to those underlying high UK productivity.

24. Most of the figures relating to individual industries are taken from the Singapore Department of Statistics, Report on the Census of Industrial Production 1982, Singapore, pages vii-x.

25.   Because other sectors - especially
construction, finance and services - are very
dependent on the manufacturing sector.
26.   See, for example, Singapore Economic
Development Board, Annual Report 1982/83; Chng Hak
Kee, "The Development of Small Enterprises", AISEC
Business Executive, Volume 2, 1983; and Patrick Yang
Pah   Tsing,   "Reference   Materials   for   the
International   Conference   on   Small   Enterprise
Policy," 1983/84, Singapore, Unpublished.
27.   See Cathering Ong, "Finding Fuel for the
Railway," Euromoney, September 1983.
28.   This is, of course, in addition to the
state's role in promoting foreign and domestic
activity in the economy through incentives and
supply/demand management.
29.   For the origin of this zeal see the
conclusion to chapter two. Not only "lackeys" serve
in state enterprises: most government ministers also
hold down directorships in these companies.
30.   See Jay Lee, "How MAS directs Singapore
Inc.", Euromoney, September 1984, page 103.
31.   Not all subsidiaries are included in table
2.12; nor are many recently inaugarated enterprises
including the Sumitomo/government led petrochemical
complex at Pulau Ayer Merbau and the mass rapid
transit company (MRTC).
32.   Comparatively large: even the largest
Singaporean company (Singapore Airlines) is only
59th in South's developing country 500. See South,
July 1984, pages 49-66.
33.   Including the Economic Developing Board,
the Monetary Authority of Singapore and Jurong Town
Corporation.
34.   At Davies' time of writing Keppel had just
diversified into commercial banking and insurance at
home and abroad.   This included a fully-licensed
Bank in the Cayman Islands.
35.   Kathryn Davies, "Singapore adjusts to world
recession", The Banker, July 1983, page 103.
36.   For further details see: Chris Sherwell,
"Singapore builds up defence industry in economic
strategy", Financial Times, November 30, 1983; V.G.
Kulkarni, "Coming Out of the Closet", Far Eastern
Economic Review, July 30, 1983; and "Six companies
form S$200 million high-tech corporation", Singapore
Business Yearbook, 1984, Time Periodicals Pte Ltd.

Multinational Enterprise
in the Manufacturing Sector

Table 3.12 State Owned Enterprises

Name	Year Incorporated	Govenment Shareholding[a] (%)
A. Holding Companies		
Temasek Holdings Pte Ltd	1974	100
Sheng-Li Co Plc Ltd	1974	100
MND Holdings Pte Ltd	1976	100
B. Manufacturing		
1. Food Manufacturing		
Cerebos (S) (Pte) Ltd	1968	45
Intraco Plantations (S) (Pte) Ltd	1981	50
Primary Industries Enterprises (Pte) Ltd	1970	100
Sugar Industry of Singapore	1963	40
2. Textiles		
Singapore Textiles Industries Ltd.	1963	67
3. Wood and Wood Products		
Berwin Timber (Pte) Ltd	1970	66.7
Forest Development (Pte) Ltd	1970	60
Hexa Timber (S)(Pte)Ltd	1976	100
Metrawood (Pte) Ltd	1972	n.a.
4. Printing and Publishing		
Singapore National Printers (Pte) Ltd	1973	100
5. Chemicals & Petrochemicals		
Chemical Industries (FE) Pte Ltd	1962	22.9
Damei Plastic Singapore Ltd	1978	49
Denka (S) (Pte) Ltd	1980	20
Ethylene Glycols (S) Pte Ltd	1982	50
Petrochemicals Corporation of Singapore	1977	48
Phillips Petroleum Singapore Chemicals (Pte) Ltd	1980	28.5
Polylefin Co (S) (Pte) Ltd	1980	26

Table 3.12 Continued.

Name	Year Incorporated	Govenment Shareholding[a] (%)
B. Manufacturing Continued.		
United Industrial Corporation Ltd	1963	16.5
6. Iron and Steel and Metal Products		
National Iron & Steel Mills Ltd	1961	19.7
Metraco (Pte) Ltd	1965	100
Tata Elxsi (Pte) Ltd	n.a.	15
7. Electrical & Electronics		
Aema Electrical Industries Ltd	1965	12.2
Hitachi Electronic Devices (S) Pte Ltd	1978	30
8. Engineering		
Applied Ordnance Co of Singapore (Pte) Ltd	-	60
Chartered Industries of Singapore (Pte) Ltd	-	100
Ordnance Development & Engineering Co of Singapore (Pte) Ltd	-	100
Singapore Automative Engineering (Pte) Ltd	-	100
9. Shipbuilding & Repair		
Argus Shipping (Pte) Ltd	1978	75
Keppel Shipyard (Pte) Ltd	1968	71.3
Jurong Holding (Pte) Ltd	1973	44.5
Jurong Shipbuilders (Pte) Ltd	1968	100
Jurong Shipyard Ltd	1963	79
Mitsubishi Singapore Heavy Industries (Pte) Ltd	1973	49
Sembawang Holdings (Pte) Ltd	1973	100
Sembawang Shipyard Ltd	1968	100
Singapore Shipbuilding & Engineering Ltd	1968	86.8

Table 3.12 Continued.

Name	Year Incorporated	Govenment Shareholding[a] (%)
C. Banking and Finance		
DBS Bank Ltd	1968	48.7
DBS Nominees	1969	100
DBS Finance Ltd	1970	100
DBS Trading Ltd	1978	100
Export Credit Insurance Corp of Singapore Ltd	1975	57
General Securities Investments Ltd	1974	49.6
Government of Singapore Corporation (Realty) (Pte) Ltd	1981	100
Insurance Corporation of Singapore Ltd	1969	-
International Bank of Singapore Ltd	1974	25
Intraco Securities	1978	100
Intraco-Wang Engineers (Pte) Ltd	1981	n.a.
National Discount Co Ltd	1972	48.8
Orient Leasing Singapore Ltd	1972	30
Reinsurance Management Corporation of Asia (Pte) Ltd	1976	30
RMCA Holdings (Pte) Ltd	1981	51
SAL Leasing (Pte) Ltd	1981	100
Singmanex (Pte) Ltd	1966	100
Singapore Factory Development Ltd	1948	100
Singapore Gold Clearing House (Pte) Ltd	1978	20
Singapore Reinsurance Corporation Ltd	1973	8.5
D. Services		
1. Shipping		
Neptune Orient Lines Ltd	1968	67.7
2. Trading		
Colex (S) Pte Ltd	1971	24
Fullerton (Pte) Ltd	n.a.	100

Table 3.12 Continued.

Name	Year Incorporated	Govenment Shareholding[a] (%)
D. Services Continued.		
Goodwin Timbers (Pte) Ltd	1969	50
Intraco Ltd	1968	55.2
National Grain Elevator Ltd	1963	37
Orion Construction (Pte) Ltd	1969	50
Polsin (Pte) Ltd	1975	25
Rotraco Exports (Pte) Ltd	1973	40
SAF Enterprises (Pte) Ltd	n.a.	100
Singapore Airport Duty Free Emporium Pte Ltd	1974	100
Singapore Food Industries (Pte) Ltd	1973	100
Singapore National Oil Co Pte Ltd	n.a.	100
Singapore Offshore Petroleum Services Pte Ltd	n.a.	66.6
Singapore Pools (Pte) Ltd	1968	100
Singapore Resources (Pte) Ltd	1980	51
Unicorn International (Pte) Ltd	n.a.	100
Yaohan Singapore (Pte) Ltd	1973	16.7
3. Air Transport		
Singapore Airlines Ltd	1972	90.5
Singapore Aircraft Industries (Pte) Ltd	1981	100
Singapore General Aviation Service Co Ltd	1974	20
4. Transport		
Container, Warehousing & Transportation (Pte) Ltd	1970	60
Singapore Bulking Co Pte Ltd	1982	49
Van Ommeren Terminal (S) (Pte) Ltd	1980	23

Table 3.12 Continued.

Name	Year Incorporated	Govenment Shareholding[a] (%)
D. Services Continued.		
5. Tourism and Leisure		
Hotel Premier	1970	100
Jurong Bird Park Pte Ltd	1970	100
Parkland Golf Driving Range Pte Ltd	1975	100
Singapore Zoological Gardens	1971	100
Trident Travels Pte Ltd	1980	85
6. Services		
DBS Chartered On-Line (Pte) Ltd	1972	50
DBS Trustee Ltd	1975	100
Heller Factoring (S) Ltd	1974	25
Intraco Metal Box Packaging Pte Ltd	1983	60
Intraco Warehousing	1981	52
Simalco Enterprise Pte Ltd	1980	51
E. Construction and Real Estate		
Cluny Hill (Pte) Ltd	1977	100
Construction Technology Pte Ltd	1980	100
DBS Land (Pte)	1978	100
DBS Realty (Pte) Ltd	1969	100
General Warehousing (Pte) Ltd	1981	100
Glen Orchid Properties Pte Ltd	1981	66.7
International Development & Consultancy (Pte) Ltd	n.a.	n.a.
Corporation (Pte) Ltd	1972	66.7
Intraco Realty (Pte) Ltd	1981	100
Intrabuild Construction Singapore (Pte) Ltd	1982	n.a.
Ladyhill (Pte) Ltd	1977	100
Loyang Valley (Pte) Ltd	1982	65
National Engineering Services (Pte) Ltd	1973	100

Multinational Enterprise
in the Manufacturing Sector

Table 3.12 Continued.

Name	Year Incorporated	Govenment Shareholding[a] (%)
E. Construction and Real Estate Continued.		
Oriental Concrete (Pte) Ltd	1980	14.6
RDC Construction (Pte) Ltd	1982	100
Resource Development Corporation (Pte) Ltd	1976	100
Property Management (Pte) Ltd	1978	100
Plaza Singapura (Pte) Ltd	1982	100
Raffles City (Pte) Ltd	1979	10.3
Raffles Centre (Pte) Ltd	1971	100
Raffles Holdings (Pte) Ltd	1979	100
Singa Development Corporation (Pte) Ltd	1979	100
Singapore Treasury Building (Pte) Ltd	1974	100
Swiss Club Park (Pte) Ltd	1977	100
Thomson Plaza (Pte) Ltd	1977	100
Wan Tien Realty (Pte) Ltd	1973	100
Warehousing Investment (Pte) Ltd	1981	100

Source: Registry of Companies, Singapore.
Note : a - Includes share holdings of state
owned enterprises and statutory boards.

Chapter Four

THE ROLE OF MULTINATIONAL COMPANIES IN BANKING, FINANCE AND THE SERVICES

In the early seventies, apparently motivated by the putative axiom that success is an ephemeral phenomenon, Singapore began to promote itself as an international centre for offshore banking, finance and other services. Many observers questioned the wisdom of this move, especially since the expansion of manufacturing was only then beginning to gather pace, but these doubting Thomases were proved wrong by the events of the seventies and eighties. Singapore is, traditionally, an entrepot economy, but the service sector's (1) share of GDP shrank considerably during the sixties because of the rapid growth of manufacturing. However table 2.3 (page 30) indicates that this relative decline was checked by the boom in financial and business services (and Transport and Communication) in the 1970s and early 1980s. Table 4.1 shows that in 1982 the services sector constituted 62% of the island's GDP. This proportion of GDP is about the same as that for Hong Kong (another externally-oriented city-state), but is far greater than that for most developing countries, be these Singapore's ASEAN partners, NICs, or even service oriented countries such as Greece.(2) Only industrialised countries such as the UK and the US have sectoral profiles similar to those of Singapore and Hong Kong, but the underlying determinants are different. (3)

The significance of the MNC-led expansion in the island's service exports cannot be understated. In 1982 Singapore earned a net $5.7 billion in its invisible trade (table 4.2), making it the world's fifth largest surplus country. (See Table 4.2, note a, on the difference between "services" and "invisibles".) The statistics are even more daunting on a per capita basis. Singapore's 1982 net earnings per head of population were $2,280 well

The Role of Multinational Companies in Banking,
Finance and the Services

Table 4.1   The Share of Services in the Gross
             Domestic Product of Selected Countries,
             1982

Country	GDP (US $b n)	Share (%)
Singapore	14.6	62
Hong Kong	25.9	65
Malaysia	25.9	47
Indonesia	90.2	35
Thailand	36.8	50
India	150.8	41
South Korea	68.4	45
Greece	33.9	52
USA	3,009.6	64
UK	432.2	65
Japan	1,061.9	54

Sources: World Bank, World Development Report
           1984. Lloyds Bank Group Economics Report,
           Hong Kong 1983.

ahead of Switzerland ($1,062), the USA ($202), the
UK ($194) and France ($135). This surplus in
invisible trade is very valuable in reducing the
economy's perennial deficit in the balance of
merchandise trade. In 1970 the services sector
financed about a third of the deficit in merchandise
trade: by 1983 the rapid rate of growth in
invisible exports during the intervening period
meant that almost the entire deficit was so
financed. (Table 4.3).

Not surprisingly, the government is intent on
maintaining a fast rate of expansion in
international tradeable services. Tony Tan,
Minister for Finance (and Trade and Industry),
recently declared the state's continuing commitment
to a gamut of services, including finance,
consultancies, aircraft servicing, tourism,
recreational services and support services for
regional oil and engineering activities (4). (See
also chapter two). In addition to the many
incentives offered to enterprises from all sectors
(e.g. the 100 per cent depreciation on computer
equipment, double taxation agreements with source
countries of foreign investors, and the option of

The Role of Multinational Companies in Banking,
Finance and the Services

Table 4.2 Net Invisible Trade[a] Balances, 1982

US$ b n

Largest Surplus Countries		Largest Deficit Countries	
United States	47.0	Saudi Arabia	-20.0
United Kingdom	10.8	Japan	-16.9
France	7.3	Brazil	-16.6
Switzerland	6.8	West Germany	-16.3
Singapore	5.7	Canada	-13.8

Source: British Invisible Export Council, Annual
Report 1983/84.

Note: a - By and large this is equivalent to
services trade, but "invisibles" also
include "factor services" such as the
repatriation of earnings from direct or
portfolio foreign investments. Since
Singapore has a net deficit in such items
the actual balance of services is even
better than that shown by this table.

Table 4.3 Singapore's Balance of Payments

US$ b n

	Year			
	1970	1975	1980	1983
Balance of merchandise trade[a]	-855	-2,400	-4,229	-5,879
Balance of services[b]	291	1,855	2,716	5,026
Balance of Capital account[c,d]	165	541	1,635	2,613
Errors, omissions, counterpart items	585	199	626	-975
TOTAL CHANGE IN RESERVES	186	195	748	785

Source: International Monetary Fund, International
Financial Statistics, Yearbook, 1984.

Notes: a - Exports minus imports of manufactured
goods and raw materials. b - includes all
types of invisibles: banking, insurance,
tourism , port facility hire etc. c - Both
long term and short term capital movements
including foreign direct investment. d -
Unrequited transfers are also included.

accelerated three year depreciation of equipment),
various inducements, are also available for specific
service industries. These will be discussed, as
appropriate, in later sections.

For the purpose of this chapter services are
divided into four categories: (i) business (or
producer) services which include banking, insurance,
consultancies and real estate; (ii) distributive
services including trade, transportation and
communications, (iii) personal services such as
recreation and tourism; and (iv) social services
which include health, welfare and education. (5)
The role of multinational companies will be
discussed in each of these service categories,
although most emphasis will be placed on business
services in which the impact of foreign investment
is greatest.

BANKING AND FINANCE

In many respects, Singapore's development as an
international financial centre and the East Asian
base of the Asia dollar market has been highly
fortuitous. First, nothing engenders success quite
like success and the earliest foreign banks were
probably more interested in servicing MNCs
manufacturing in Singapore than regional or
international financial markets. Secondly, the
economy's entrepot past, its location at the axis of
ASEAN and its time-zone advantage bridging Europe,
Asia and the Pacific makes it an obvious candidate
for international banks seeking a regional base for
operations. Finally, the Monetary Authority of
Singapore (MAS) began to promote Singapore in the
early 1970s, just as GNP and investment growth rates
in industrialised countries began to slow down: a
fall in demand (6) from their major markets, allied
with an excess of petrodollars deposited by OPEC
countries after the 1973 "oil crisis", forced
western banks to expand radically their
international operations. The only economies
growing rapidly enough to absorb this expansion of
international bank lending were the developing
countries, especially the newly industrialising
countries (NICs) of East Asia and Latin America.
Singapore and Hong Kong were the East Asian
beneficiaries of a global financial realignment:
both were strategic bases for banks lending to
swiftly industrialising countries such as South

Korea, Taiwan, Malaysia, Indonesia and (later) China. However the perceptiveness of Singapore's strategic planners should not be overlooked. A good example of the government's foresight is provided by Tan:

> In the late 1960s, economies in the Southeast Asian and the East Asian regions were booming. The Bank of America was exploring the possibility of setting up a foreign currency unit in Asia, similar to its Eurocurrency unit in London. The objective was to mobilize the pool of US dollars available in Asia and lend them to its Asian borrowers. The bank was considering possible centers such as Hong Kong, Tokyo and Singapore. The Hong Kong Government was not prepared to grant exemption to its 15% withholding tax on offshore currency transactions. The Japanese Government insisted on its strict exchange regulations. The Singapore Government, on the other hand, was receptive to the idea and had the vision that this could enable it to play a regional financial role. It provided incentives to the initiator of the suggested scheme. In 1968, tax laws were amended to exempt from tax the interest derived from non-resident deposits. Other banks, both local and foreign banks, were convinced and joined in to form their own Asian Currency Units. The Asian Dollar Market was born. Subsequent development placed Singapore on the world financial map. (7)

The Monetary Authority of Singapore.

The Monetary Authority of Singapore (MAS) was established in 1971 and acts as a regulatory body as well as a central bank. In its regulatory functions it supervises financial markets and institutions (i.e. commercial banks, discount houses, finance companies, merchant banks, insurance/re-insurance companies, factoring companies (8), leasing companies and international money brokers). (9) It has a reputation of conservativeness combined with shrewdness and its creation of a stable regime is highly appreciated by the financial community.

There have, however, been some rumblings of
discontent in recent years regarding the MAS's
ostensible intentions to expand into
financial services itself and its attitude to
various issues such as the internationalisation of
the Singapore dollar. These matters will be
discussed later in the chapter.

The MAS and the state have promoted Singapore's
expansion into international finance in a number of
ways. First, a "favourable" investment climate has
been created by the implementation of various
measures and, in particular, through the removal of
all exchange controls. This liberalisation was
completed in 1978 and since then all capital
movements to or from Singapore are unrestricted.
Another measure with major impact was the decision
to abolish witholding taxes on all dividends.
Secondly, major international banks and other
financial institutions have been attracted by
offering differential treatment to offshore
activity. (10) Thus, for example, the tax rate on
interest income received from overseas loans was
reduced from 40 percent to 10 percent in 1972. This
incentive was gradually extended to encourage other
financial services as the need arose and is
presently available to nearly all Singapore-based
financial institutions. As a result the
Asiacurrency market (11) has been greatly boosted
and most banks operate an Asian Currency Unit (ACU)
to obtain deposits and make loans in foreign
currencies. (12) In 1983 the government attempted to
promote the Asiacurrency market yet further by
promoting syndicated loans: the budget of that year
offered a five year tax exemption on such loans.
(For a further discussion of loan-syndication see
the section on Singapore - Hong Kong rivalry.)
Finally, the MAS has simultaneously boosted
international financial services and protected the
domestic market from excessive foreign competition
by employing various legal devices. The most
important device is probably the license required
for operations in Singapore. In commercial banking,
for example, the MAS licenses three types of banks:
(i) full banks which are allowed to operate local
branches and carry out the entire range of banking
activity (all Singaporean banks are full banks as
are a selected number of foreign banks); (ii)
restricted banks (all foreign) which are not allowed
to compete for local deposits and rely on inter-bank
funds for local loans; and (iii) offshore banks

are almost entirely geared towards foreign
operations both for their borrowing and lending.
Thus as a result of these licensing categories many
foreign banks cannot compete in Singapore itself and
operate only in the Asiacurrency market.

The Overall Expansion of Financial Services

As a result of factors mentioned earlier
financial services have grown very rapidly since the
early 1970s. Table 4.4 shows how a wide variety of
financial institutions have expanded remarkably in
number in little over a decade. For example, the
number of commercial banks tripled between 1970 and
1983, while other institutions (especially merchant
banks, insurance companies and Asian Currency Units)
grew even more rapidly. Most of the new
establishments are foreign in origin: 108 out of 121
commercial banks in 1983 were foreign owned; 52 out
of 80 insurance companies were foreign (see page
146); and nearly all international money brokers are
local branches of overseas concerns. Most merchant
banks are joint ventures between local companies and
MNCs; and the majority of Asian Currency Units
(ACUs) are operated by foreign investors. Table
4.24 (page 185) shows that most overseas financial
institutions operating in Singapore are well known
multinational firms, although many lesser known
companies have also been lured by the prospects of
the East Asian region.
The increase in the number and variety of
institutions has been matched by a growth in their
activities (table 4.5 and later sections). Thus,
for example, the assets of commercial banks
increased from $1.6 billion to $26.9 billion between
1970 and 1983; while merchant bank assets increased
from $0.5 billion to $11.2 billion. Much of this
expansion was impelled by a search for international
markets and, as a consequence, the foreign loans and
assets of Singapore-based banks surged from only
$0.5 billion to $88.2 billion between 1970 and 1983
(13) - about 4 percent of global international
banking activity (table 4.11). 70 out of 108
commercial banks (table 4.4) are in fact only
licensed to conduct offshore (international)
activity and may only operate domestically in the
inter-bank market.
Statistics on the source-country distribution
of financial activity and ownership are not readily
available, especially on a comparative basis. Table

The Role of Multinational Companies in Banking,
Finance and the Services

Table 4.4   Number and Type of Financial
             Institutions in Singapore, 1970 - 1983.

Institution	1970	1975	1980	1983
Commercial Banks	37	70	100	12
Local [a]	11	13	13	13
Foreign	26	57	87	108
- Full Banks	26	24	24	24
- Restricted Banks	-	12	13	14
- Offshore Banks	-	21	50	70
Representative offices [b]	8	38	50	59
Merchant Banks	2	21	39	50
Asian Currency Units [c]	14	66	120	157
Discount Houses	-	4	4	4
Finance Companies	36	36	34	35
Insurance Companies [d]	N.A.	69	74	80
International Money Brokers	-	5	7	9

Source: Monetary Authority of Singapore, Annual
          Report, various years.

Notes: a - all local banks are full banks.
          b - in 1983 there were 55 representative
          offices of commercial banks and 4 of
          merchant banks.
          c - of these 108 belonged to commercial
          banks, 47 to merchant banks and 2 to other
          institutions in 1983.
          d - in 1983 6 of these were Life Insurance
          companies, 64 General Insurance and 10 Life
          and General Insurance.

The Role of Multinational Companies in Banking,
Finance and the Services

Table 4.5   Financial Institutions: Assets,
             Productivity and Profitability.

Industry	Number of Establishments[a]	Assets (US$ bn) 1970	Assets (US$ bn) 1983	Remuneration to value added (%)	Value added per worker (US$ thousands)
Commercial Banks[b]	355	1.6	26.9	24	46
Government[c]	4	N.A.	N.A.	36	17
Discount Houses	4	Neg	1.1	10	94
Merchant Banks[b]	35	0.5[d]	11.2	23	74
Insurance Companies	542	0.1	0.7[e]	35	17
Finance Companies	85	0.2	3.1	16	44
Investment Companies	651	N.A.	N.A.	68	19
Representative Offices	44	N.A.	N.A.	68	26
Brokers	49	N.A.	N.A.	34	73
Others	561	N.A.	N.A.	37	24
Total	1788	-	-	24	40

Sources: Singapore Department of Statistics
         (1982),Report on the Survey of Services
         1980; Singapore Department of Statistics,
         Economic and Social Statistics of
         Singapore, 1960 - 1982; Singapore
         Department of Statistics, Monthly Digest of
         Statistics, May 1984.
Notes: a - 1980 figures. b - Include Asian
         Currency Units. c - The MAS, Post Office
         Savings Bank (POSB), CPF and the Currency
         Board. d - 1974 figure. e - 1981 figure.

4.6 uses paid-up-capital as a proxy for ownership
and indicates that firms from particular countries
are inclined towards certain financial industries.
There is very little foreign participation in
finance companies, investment companies and general
broking. Local companies also dominate the discount
houses, but here both US and UK companies are well
represented. Foreign companies are preponderant in
commercial and merchant banking and in insurance.
US and Canadian banks are particularly well
represented in commercial banking, evincing the
present Pacific-rim interest in Singapore; but the
high proportion of UK and Hong Kong ownership in
insurance derives instead from the continuing
importance of institutions established during the
common colonial-entrepot past of the UK, Hong Kong
and Singapore. The ownership of merchant banks is
the most evenly spread, mainly because most are
joint ventures and operate in a multiplicity of
activities.
   There is no obvious relationship between the
degree of foreign ownership of an industry
(table 4.6) and its productivity (table 4.5, value
added per worker) or profitability (table 4.5, the
obverse of remuneration to value added). However it
is likely that the level of dis-aggregation is
insufficient; and investment companies (numerically
the most important local-firm-dominated industry)
are among the least productive and profitable
industries. Further, it is worth noting that
financial institutions are generally more productive
than manufacturing concerns and pay higher average
wages and salaries. (Compare table 4.5 with
table 3.9.)

Commercial Banks

Commercial banking in Singapore dates back to the
1840s when the country was established as a centre
for entrepot trade by the British. During the
nineteenth century a number of foreign banks
invested locally in order to finance and facilitate
regional and international trade. The three most
important early foreign banks, all British, were the
Mercantile Bank, the Chartered Bank and the Hong
Kong and Shanghai Bank. (14) A US bank, CitiCorp,
began its Singaporean operations in 1902. These
western banks represented a financial "division of
labour" whereby international banks serviced foreign
trade and payments and domestic (Chinese) banks

Table 4.6 Financial Institutions: Breakdown of Paid-Up-Capital by Country of Origin, 1980

Industry	Paid Up Capital (US$ mn)	Country of Origin (%)								
		Singapore	USA	Hong Kong	Canada	UK	Malaysia	Japan	Others	Total
Commercial Banks a	1,955	24	21	8	14	5	3	2	23	100
Discount Houses	10	68	11	5	-	10	1	-	5	100
Merchant Banks a	155	13	15	18	8	11	-	3	32	100
Insurance Companies	236	33	1	38	-	18	1	2	7	100
Finance Companies	112	86	Neg	4	Neg	2	6	-	2	100
Investment Companies	904	82	Neg	4	Neg	3	7	1	3	100

cont.

Table 4.6 Financial Institutions: Breakdown of Paid-Up-Capital by
Country of Origin, 1980. Continued.

Industry	Paid Up Capital (US$ mn)	Country of Origin (%)								
		Singapore	USA	Hong Kong	Canada	UK	Malaysia	Japan	Others	Total
Brokers	31	99	Neg	Neg	-	Neg	Neg	-	-	100
Representative Offices	2	-	-	-	-	-	-	-	100	100
Others	56	88	1	2	-	Neg	6	Neg	3	100

Source: Singapore Department of Statistics (1982), Report on the Survey of
Services 1980.

Notes: a - includes Asian Currency Units.

Neg - negligible.

catered to the local populace. The earliest
domestic Chinese bank, the Kwong Yip Bank, was
established in 1903, but soon floundered and was
liquidated in 1918. Other banks prospered, however,
and three of the four largest local banks - the
Overseas Chinese Banking Corp., the United Overseas
Bank Ltd., and the Overseas Union Bank - trace their
origins to the early twentieth century. (15) Quite
a few banks, many foreign, were established just
before and after the second world war, but their
growth was curtailed by the stagnation of the
Singapore economy until the mid-1960s.

With the expansion of foreign investment, the
consequent growth of the manufacturing sector, the
inducements offered by the MAS and, later, the need
to recycle the oil surpluses during a global
economic depression, banking in Singapore again
became a profitable prospect. The rapid
proliferation of foreign banks, especially offshore
banks (which can only transact international
business), is shown by table 4.4. There is a wide
distribution by source-country, although banks from
the US, Japan (nearby Pacific-rim countries,
especially laden with petrodollars) and the UK
dominate numerically. (Table 4.7) Developing
countries' banks are well represented and even banks
from the USSR, the People's Republic of China and
Yugoslavia have local branches. Despite strong
participation in commercial banking by local banks
(table 4.8), foreign banks still account for over 80
percent of all assets.

Table 4.8 outlines various characteristics and
dimensions of the 15 largest banks operating in
Singapore. It is evident that the major
international banks are active on the island with
their local assets typically 3-6% of global assets.
US, Japanese and French banks are particularly
evident, with the Chartered Bank and the Hong Kong
and Shanghai bank representing old colonial
ties. (16) The "big four" local banks rank among
the top 15 in Singapore, but are all very small on a
world-wide comparison of assets. This suggests that
the major international banks will continue to have
a preponderant influence on Singapore's development
into an international financial centre. It is
difficult to compare profitability in Singapore with
each bank's global profitability because the
Singapore figure refers to net earnings and the
world-wide figure to pre-tax earnings. Further, the
periods differ and 1981 was a particularly bad year

Table 4.7   Foreign Banks in Singapore by Country
            of Origin.

	Number			
Country of Incorporation	Full License	Restricted License	Offshore License	Total
Asia	17[a]	6	20	43
- Japan	2	2	11	15
North America	4	1	22	27
- USA	4	1	17	22
- Canada	-	-	5	5
Europe	3	7	20[b]	30
- UK	1	1	6	8
- Netherlands	1	-	1	2
- Germany	-	2	1	3
- Switzerland	-	1	2	3
- France	-	1	5	6
Elsewhere	-	-	8	8
Total	24	14	70	108

Source: Ministry of Culture, Singapore 1984.

Notes: a - Includes banks from Malaysia,
              Indonesia, India, Thailand etc.

          b - Includes Moscow Narodny Bank Ltd.

for banks as a result of the international debt
crisis.   Nevertheless the profitability of
Singapore-based operations seems to be at least as
great as elsewhere; and the good showing of
domestically oriented banks (DBS, UOB, OCBC, HSBC,
OUB and CB) illustrates the underlying strength of
the local economy.
    Table 4.9 shows the assets and liabilities of
commercial banks in Singapore, excluding the
assets/liabilities of Asian Currency Units (ACUs).
Offshore banks and international transactions are
thus also largely excluded (but see next subsection)
and most figures refer to the domestic Singaporean
economy. (17) The assets of the commercial banking
sector have increased an enormous seventeen-fold
(eight-fold in real terms) in just over a decade.

Table 4.8 Singapore's Major Commercial Banks

Bank	Country of Origin	Status[a]	Size of Assets[b] (US$ billion)		Rank		Profitability[c] (%)	
			Singapore (1981)	World-wide (1983)	Singapore	World-wide	Singapore (Net, 1981)	World-wide (pre-tax, 1983)
DBS[d]	Singapore	Full	5.2	5.7	1	273	0.9	2.0
Bank of America	USA	Full	4.7	115.4	2	2	0.3	0.4
CitiCorp	USA	Full	4.1	130.0	3	1	0.4	1.3
B. of Tokyo	Japan	Full	3.9	65.0	4	21	0.1	0.4
UOB[e]	Singapore	Full	3.2	4.9	5	310	1.4	N.A.
Credit Lyonnais	France	Offshore	3.1	88.1	6	11	Neg	N.A.
OCBC[f]	Singapore	Full	2.7	3.4	7	420	1.5	N.A.
Fuji Bank	Japan	Offshore	2.6	103.5	8	4	0.1	0.6
BNP[g]	France	Restricted	2.4	101.0	9	6	0.4	0.3
HSBC[h]	Hong Kong	Full	2.3	58.0	10	27	1.2	N.A.
CMB[i]	USA	Full	2.3	75.3	11	16	0.7	0.9
Tokai	Japan	Offshore	2.2	63.3	12	22	Neg	0.4
Mitsubishi	Japan	Restricted	2.2	98.0	13	7	0.1	0.5
OUB[j]	Singapore	Full	2.1	3.0	14	456	1.0	1.5
CBK	UK	Full	2.0	N.A.	15	N.A.	1.2	N.A.

cont.

Table 4.8   Singapore's Major Commercial Banks

Sources: The Banker, June 1984; Times Directories (Pte) (1983), Singapore Banking, Finance and Insurance 1984.

Notes:
a – Type of license awarded by the MAS.
b – Includes ACU assets.
c – Earnings divided by Assets.
d – Development Bank of Singapore.
e – United Overseas Bank Ltd.
f – Oversea Chinese Bank Corp.
g – Banque Nationale de Paris.
h – Hong Kong and Shanghai Banking Corp.
i – Chase Manhattan Bank.
j – Overseas Union Bank.
k – Chartered Bank.

135

The Role of Multinational Companies in Banking,
Finance and the Services

The customer distribution of assets has not altered
greatly during this period with loans to non-bank
customers accounting for about 60 percent of assets
and claims on other banks accounting for a further
20 percent. However there has been an increase in
lending to banks/branches outside Singapore. The
loans to non-bank customers are fairly evenly
divided between sectors, with commerce receiving 25
percent of loans, manufacturing 18 percent,
construction 17 percent, financial institutions 15
percent and professionals/private individuals 11
percent. (18) The major effect of the entry of
foreign banks can be seen in the breakdown of
liabilities: the role of non-bank deposits as a
souce of bank funding has decreased and that of the
international inter-bank market has increased.
Local branches of foreign banks, especially those
with restricted licenses, borrow funds from banks
and branches overseas. Thus amounts due to banks
outside Singapore now constitute 26.4 percent of
liabilities of commercial banks, as opposed to only
8.9 percent in 1970. Such an influx of
international funds is even more important in the
Asiadollar market to which we now turn.

Asian Currency Units and the Asiacurrency Market

The Asiacurrency market (formerly the
Asiadollar market [19]) is a short-term
international money market equivalent to the much
larger Eurocurrency market. The distinction between
the two is purely geographical and is fading as new
technology allows a rapid shift of funds between
globally separate financial centres. Park and Zwick
(20) define Eurocurrencies (or Asiacurrencies) as,
'bank deposit liabilities denominated in a currency
other than the monetary unit of the country in which
the bank is physically (and legally) located ....'.
The Asiacurrency market is primarily located in
Singapore and Hong Kong and international bank
lending by banks based in these countries is mainly
in Asiacurrencies such as the US dollar, the pound
sterling and the Yen, although the MAS has recently
had to take action against attempts to
internationalise the Singapore dollar.
The Eurocurrency market originated in the
1950s, but the Asiacurrency market was established
more recently in 1968 when the Bank of America
inaugurated the first Asia Currency Unit (ACU) in
Singapore. (See page 124) As table 4.10 shows, the

Table 4.9 Assets and Liabilities of Commercial Banks, 1970-1983

| YEAR | Breakdown of Assets[a] (%) | | | | | Total Assets/ Liabilities (US$ bn) | Breakdown of Liabilities[a] (%) | | | |
| | Cash | Loans[b] | Amount due from Banks | | Other[d] | | Non-Bank Deposits | Amounts due to Banks | | Other |
			In Sgpr	O/S Sgpr				In Sgpr	O/S Sgpr[c]	
1970	0.9	62.9	12.3	9.3	14.6	1.6	63.4	11.9	8.9	15.8
1975	0.7	54.3	10.3	10.9	23.9	6.1	52.8	10.5	15.1	21.6
1980	0.8	60.7	8.2	12.4	17.9	15.6	48.0	8.7	21.3	22.0
1983	0.5	60.2	6.5	14.5	18.3	26.9	46.5	6.9	26.4	20.2

Sources: Singapore Department of Statistics, Economic and Social Statistics, 1960-1982 and Monthly Digest of Statistics, May 1984.

Notes: a - These items add up to 100%. b - Includes a small proportion of bills financed. c - Including some ACU transactions. d - Money on call, investments etc. Sgpr = Singapore. O/S = Outside.

market at this stage was very small and most funds
came from non-bank customers such as MNCs operating
locally, East Asia businesses and government
agencies. These funds were then channelled through
the inter-bank market for use in other regions,
essentially through the Eurocurrency market. Table
4.10 further shows that with the influx of foreign
banks (virtually all ACUs are operated by commercial
or merchant banks) the Asiacurrency market's assets
in Singapore have expanded massively from a mere
$9.9 million to $52.5 billion. Singapore remains a
major conduit of international inter-bank funds,
but, with the rapid expansion of East Asia and the
surplus petrodollars elsewhere, its role has been
reversed: funds are channelled in from Europe, the
Middle East and elsewhere and then lent out
regionally. Thus the 1983 breakdown of liabilities
shows that non-bank depositers accounted for only
18.4 percent of liabilities, while international
inter-bank liabilities funded 74.2 percent of the
requirements of Singapore-based ACUs. The Asset
breakdown shows that 27.2 percent of 1983 Assets
were loans to non-bank customers (up from only 4.6
percent in 1968). Some of these were domestic
customers, but most were based in other East Asian
countries, especially the ASEAN economies, South
Korea and Taiwan. Most of the remaining assets,
then and now, are inter-bank loans which are used by
borrowing banks or branches as funds for
"second-tier" lending to non-bank customers.
International credit is thus further channelled to
the above-mentioned countries as well as a number of
others, including the Peoples' Republic of China and
Hong Kong. Some of these inter-bank loans
(probably a hefty proportion) are used by the
branches of major banks based in Hong Kong for
syndicated international bank lending, especially to
sovereign borrowers (21) (see page 152).

Table 4.11 confirms Singapore's growing
importance as an international financial centre when
compared to other significant developing countries'
offshore financial centres and the major
industrialised countries. In 1970 UK based banks
were the most active in international banking,
accounting for 27.8 percent of all foreign assets;
Singapore with a share of 0.4 percent was
overshadowed by the Bahamas, a major tax-haven, with
5.4 percent. Since then the situation has changed
completely. The UK remains the largest
international financial centre on a stock basis, but

Table 4.10 Assets and Liabilities of Asian currency units, 1968–1983

| YEAR | Breakdown of Assets (%)[a] | | | | Total Assets/Liabilities (US$ bn) | Breakdown of Liabilities (%)[a] | | | |
	Loans to Non-Banks	Inter-Bank Funds In Sgpr	Inter-Bank Funds O/S Sgpr	Other Assets		Deposits of Non-Banks	Inter-Bank Funds In Sgpr	Inter-Bank Funds O/S Sgpr	Other Liabilities
1968	4.6	(95.1)		0.3	Neg.[b]	58.4	(41.3)		0.3
1975	27.7	2.3	70.0	1.6	5.3	16.7	4.6	77.0	0.7
1980	22.8	2.0	70.6	4.6	25.4	17.1	2.3	72.8	0.8
1983	27.2	2.5	64.1	6.2	52.5	18.4	1.6	74.2	5.8

Source: As table.
Notes: a – These items sum to 100% b – $9.9 million. Sgpr = Singapore. O/S=Outside

139

only accounted for 22.2 percent of new international
banking activity during 1980-1983 (table 4.11) - as
opposed to the USA's 39.6 percent. This impressive
performance by US-based banks (the United States'
share of international banking increased from 8.9
percent to 18.4 percent over 1970 to 1983) has also
encouraged the expansion of international banking in
other centres, for example Singapore, because of the
local presence of US banks. Singapore's share of
international banking activity has leapt from 0.4
percent to 3.8 percent (1970-1983) on a stock basis,
while the Bahamas' share increased sharply until
1975 and has fallen steeply since. Hong Kong,
Singapore's chief rival in East Asia, has also
recorded a rise in its share of international
banking, but lags behind at 2.9 percent.
Singapore's achievement is even more impressive if
its share of the 1980-83 increase in global loans
and assets in considered. Its 7.6 percent share is
the third largest after the US and the UK - and
equal to Japan's. Moreover this level of
international financial activity is equal to about
30 percent of such activity emanating from all
developing countries (22); and except for Hong Kong
this predominance is unlikely to be challenged in
the near future.

Merchant Banks and the Asiabond Market.

     In 1983 there were 50 merchant banks operating
in Singapore (table 4.4) with about 40 percent of
the assets of commercial banks. The expansion of
the former is even more spectacular than that of the
latter because until the 1970s merchant banks were
virtually unknown in Singapore. In under a decade
their assets have increased from $0.6 to $11.
billion (table 4.12) and because nearly all have
ACUs they represent a major force in the
Asiacurrency market.
     Because of their novelty most are foreign in
origin and predominantly joint ventures, often
between local-foreign companies. Table 4.1
indicates the country of origin of the controlling
shareholder (23) for each company, but this is an
over-simplification of some very complex ownership
patterns. For example Inter-Alpha Asia Ltd is owned
by seven banks each with a 14 percent share. (24)
Similarly, there is no separate entry for Japan in
table 4.13 bacause Japanese parent companies
normally own a minority share. (25) Nevertheless

Table 4.11 Singapore's Role in International Banking Activity, 1970-1983

Source Country	Share of all Foreign Loans and Assets[a] Outstanding				Share of the net increase in Foreign Loans and Assets Outstanding 1980-83[b]
	1970	1975	1980	1983	
Singapore	0.4	1.9	2.5	3.8	7.6
Hong Kong	0.9	1.6	2.2	2.9	5.2
Bahrain	Neg.	0.4	1.8	2.3	4.1
Bahamas	5.4	9.8	7.2	5.8	1.6
Cayman Is.	Neg.	1.2	1.9	2.1	2.8
United States[c]	8.9	9.7	11.6	18.6	39.6
France	7.6	7.4	8.3	6.0	-0.7
Germany	10.7	6.8	4.9	3.2	-1.8
Japan	5.0	3.6	3.7	4.7	7.6
UK	27.8	22.4	20.3	20.8	22.2
Switzerland	22.5[d]	8.5	8.0	7.0	4.0
Developing Countries	11.4	20.3	22.6	23.5	26.6
Industrial Countries	88.6	79.7	77.4	76.5	73.4
Total Amount All Countries (US$ bn)	133.1	561.5	1,754.2	2,324.7	570.5

cont.

Table 4.11 Singapore's Role in International Banking Activity, 1970-1983)   cont.

Source: International Monetary Fund, International Financial Statistics Yearbook, 1984.

Notes: a – Effectively a stock concept. The share for each country is derived by dividing the foreign assets (e.g. loans, inter-bank claims) of banks based in each country by total (foreign) assets of all banks each year. b – This indicates the distribution of the change in foreign bank loans and assets in recent years. (i.e. A flow concept.) The derivation is as above. c – US banks also account for much of the increase in activity of banks (including the local branches of foreign banks) based in other countries. This applies particularly to offshore banking centres such as Singapore, the Bahamas and Hong Kong. d – An estimate.

the table does suggest that to need to share
knowledge and risk promotes a relatively wide
distribution of source countries, although merchant
banks controlled by UK and US concerns are most
prominent.

Most merchant bank funds are raised on the
international inter-bank market and channelled
through Singapore to the East Asia region. About 15
percent of assets are held in Singapore and 85
percent in the surrounding region (26), chiefly as
loans to non-bank customers. (Table 4.12).
Merchant banks are highly profitable (Table 4.6)
because of their wide range of activities. These
are briefly outlined below (27):

Syndicated loans. Because commercial banks tend to
give only short-term loans to large borrowers,
merchant banks have carved out a niche for large
long-term loans which they undertake on a syndicate
basis in order to reduce risks. The tendency to
syndicate probably also explains the prevalence of
joint ventures.

Corporate services. These include the underwriting
of new equity share issues; advice to clients on the
money or capital markets; and the co-ordination of
client's merger and acquisition activities.

Investment Management. Many charities, small
companies and individuals take advantage of the
economies of scale inherent in merchant banks
managing joint investment portfolios, pension funds
etc.

Asiacurrency Market and Asiabond Market. As
mentioned earlier nearly all merchant banks operate
an ACU and are active in the Asiacurrency market
which is geared towards short-term credit. Merchant
banks are also the prime movers in the burgeoning
Asiabond market which finances large long-term
loans. There are few statistics indicating its
size, but the Asiabond market is substantial
(perhaps $16 billion - worth in 1984). The
International bond market is also of considerable
size and represents about 25 percent of all
international lending. (28).

Other Services. These include factoring, agencies
for government bond issues and a wide variety of
advisory services.

Table 4.12 Assets and Liabilities of Merchant Banks, 1974-1983

YEAR	Breakdown of Assets (%)[a]				Total Assets/ Liabilities (US$ bn)	Breakdown of Liabilities (%)[a]			
	Loans to Non-Banks	Amounts Due From Banks		Others		Borrowings from Non-banks	Amounts Owing to Banks		Others
		In Sgpr	O/S Sgpr[b]				In Sgpr	O/S Sgpr[b]	
1974	64.9	0.5	29.8	4.8	0.6	9.0	2.3	77.4	11.3
1980	53.0	0.5	42.6	3.9	6.2	7.9	1.4	83.9	6.8
1983	52.9	0.8	39.0	7.3	11.2	10.2	2.1	78.8	8.9

Source: Singapore Department of Statistics, Economic and Social Statistics,
1960-1982 and Monthly Digest of Statistics, May 1984.

Notes: a - These items sum to 100%. b - Includes ACU transactions.
Sgpr = Singapore. O/S = Outside.

The Role of Multinational Companies in Banking,
Finance and the Services

Table 4.13 Ownership of Merchant Banks, 1983

Country of Controlling Shareholder	Number
UK	12
USA	9
Canada	5
West Germany	3
Other European Countries	10
Asian and Pacific Countries	5
Local/Foreign Joint Ventures	4
Local	2
	50

Source: Peat, Marwick, Mitchell and Co., (1983)
Banking in Singapore.

Insurance Companies

Insurance companies are the third set of institutions dominated by foreign concerns. This is confirmed by table 4.14 which shows that 52 insurance companies out of 80 (and certainly many of the largest ones [29]) are foreign in origin. Old colonial ties explain the large number of companies from the UK, Hong Kong, India and Malaysia. UK companies have been established in Singapore since the nineteenth century both to insure domestic traders, but also to service the region. Because of the colony's prosperity firms from other parts of the British Empire commenced operations in the early twentieth century. The presence of US and Japanese insurance companies is no surprise. What is interesting is the investments by companies from countries such as Italy and the People's Republic of China.

The Role of Multinational Companies in Banking,
Finance and the Services

Table 4.14 Number of Registered Insurers By Country
of Origin, 1982.

Country	Number of Insurers Registered to Transact			
	Life Business Only	General Business Only	Life and General Business	Total
Direct Insurers				
Singapore	3	16	4	23
Australia	-	1	-	1
China	2	2	-	4
France	-	1	-	1
Holland	-	1	-	1
Hong Kong	1	3	2	6
India	-	4	-	4
Japan	-	4	-	4
Malaysia	-	3	1	4
New Zealand	-	2	-	2
Phillippines	-	1	-	1
United Kingdom	-	8	4	9
United States of America	-	5	1	5
Subtotal	6	51	8	65
Professional Reinsurers				
Singapore	-	5	-	5
France	-	1	-	1
Germany	-	1	1	2
Italy	-	1	-	1
Korea	-	1	-	1
Sweden	-	1	-	1
United Kingdom	-	3	-	3
United States of America	-	-	1	1
Subtotal	-	13	2	15
Total	6	64	10	80

Source: The Insurance Commissioner, Annual Report, 1982

The Role of Multinational Companies in Banking,
Finance and the Services

Life insurance is dominated by local firms,
while general insurance (covering risks such as
fire, marine, aviation, transit, construction and
motoring) is dominated by foreign companies. (30)
Table 4.15 shows that there has been fairly rapid
growth in both nominal and real terms in the general
insurance business (as measured by premiums).
Further, international (or offshore) business is
growing twice as rapidly as domestic business.
Future prospects for insurance companies based in
Singapore look bright given the rapid growth of
business in the East Asia region. Even during the
recent recession, insurance companies managed to
achieve a growth rate of 7.7 percent in 1982 (down
from 20 percent in 1981), although fortunes were
mixed in terms of different types of risk. (31).

The Interbank Market and SIMEX

Given the dominance of foreign banks and other
institutions in Singapore it is not surprising that
these institutions actively participate in all local
financial markets. These markets include: (i) the
money market which consists of the discount market
(dominated by domestic companies - see table 4.6)
and the interbank market (see below); the capital
market which includes the foreign dominated
Asiacurrency and Asiabond markets; the foreign
exchange market; the small stock market which
depends on foreign investors for about a third of
its liquidity (32); and the financial futures market
(SIMEX). International companies have been most
active in the Asiacurrency, the Asiabond, the
interbank and financial futures markets and it is
the global orientation of these markets which has
promoted Singapore's integration into the world
financial community. The Asiacurrency and Asiabond
markets have been previously mentioned: the latter
two will be discussed below.

The growth of the Singapore interbank market is
a direct consequence of the expansion of the
Asiacurrency and Asiabond markets which themselves
were spurred by the influx of foreign commercial and
merchant banks. This is readily demonstrated by
tables 4.9, 4.10 and 4.12 which are analysed in the
related text. In effect Singapore is the regional
nexus of the international interbank market which
consists of over a thousand banks from fifty
countries. The Bank for International Settlements
(BIS) estimates that the market's size is

The Role of Multinational Companies in Banking,
Finance and the Services

Table 4.15   Growth and Distribution of General
Insurance Premiums, 1978-82

US $ Millions

| Year | Gross Premiums | | | Net Premiums | | |
	Domestic (A)	Inter-national (B)	(B)/(A) (%)	Domestic (C)	Inter-national (D)	(D)/(C) (%)
1978	143	29	20	104	25	24
1979	174	55	32	127	36	28
1980	219	80	37	159	41	26
1981	267	112	42	186	53	28
1982	283	117	41	204	59	29
Nominal Increase 1978-82 (%)	198	403		196	236	
Real Increase (%)	156	318		155	194	

Source: The Insurance Commissioner, Annual Report,
          1982.

approaching   two   thirds   of   all international
interbank claims which in 1981 stood at a massive
$953 billion. (33)   The Singapore market plays a
pivotal   role   by   channelling   surplus   funds from
other parts   of   the   globe and harnessing these
resources for   use   in   the burgeoning East Asian
region.   The importance   of this position can be
gauged by the fact that   the Singapore interbank
 offered   rate (SIBOR: the   interest   rate
 pertaining in the interbank market) is as widely
quoted   as   the London interbank offered rate
 (LIBOR),   its   only   major   international
equivalent.
      The   Singapore International Monetary Exchange
(SIMEX) began operations on July 5, 1984 and like
other financial futures markets is chiefly used as a
hedge   against movements in interest rates and
exchange rates - and for speculation. Initially
trading   was confined to futures contracts in gold,

148

but since then trading has commenced in
Deutsche Marks, Yen and Eurodollars. At present
SIMEX appears to be operating successfully and an
expansion into oil futures contracts ('to underline
the country's position as a major trader, after
Houston and Rotterdam, in crude oil' [34]) is being
explored. (35) SIMEX is linked to the Chicago
Mercantile Exchange (CME) through a unique "mutual
offset" system which allows CME traders to operate
on SIMEX and vice versa. (36) In addition to
facilitating the expansion of the futures market in
Asia, the SIMEX-CME link-up goes a long way towards
realising the goal of 24-hour trading which would
allow traders to react instantly to any event world-
wide. At the moment, SIMEX and CME operate in
entirely separate time zones and the "mutual offset"
system therefore allows traders in each exchange to
extend their operations to the other exchange while
their own is closed. This allows Chicago traders,
for example, to extend their operations by 7 hours.
In addition Singapore's advantageous time-zone
location allows SIMEX to operate simultaneously with
exchanges in London, Zurich, Tokyo, Hong Kong and
Sydney at various times of the day, thereby
extending traders' operations and options even
further. (37) The advantages of SIMEX are obvious
and this explains the great interest of foreign
institutions; an interest which will be kindled even
further if the mooted adoption of a Japanese stock
index occurs (because the home-grown Stock Exchange
of Singapore stock index is not well-known).
Already many foreign institutions are trading in
SIMEX and their numbers will soon be swollen by
Chicago market makers (especially in the winter!)
and major Japanese banks such as Mitsubishi Bank,
Mitsui Bank, Dai-Ichi Kangyo Bank and the Bank of
Tokyo. (Japanese banks have local branches but no
subsidiaries; and only a Singapore incorporated
company is allowed to operate in SIMEX.)

SINGAPORE AS AN INTERNATIONAL FINANCIAL CENTRE:
THE COMPETITORS

The previous section has shown that Singapore is
firmly on the map as an international financial
centre, although it can never aspire to the primary
status of centres such as London, New York, Zurich
or (potentially) Tokyo. Instead the MAS recognises
the need to promote the island as a regional
financial supermarket; and is therefore constantly

The Role of Multinational Companies in Banking,
Finance and the Services

introducing new services and attempting to stave off
competition from other countries. Tokyo and Hong
Kong are undoubtedly Singapore's main competitors,
but in recent years Manila, Sydney and Taipei have
all attempted to enter the fray. These countries
are discussed below. There is also potential
competition from a number of other cities/countries,
especially Seoul, but the headstart enjoyed by
Singapore, Hong Kong and Tokyo is likely to prevent
them making any short term overtures to
international financial institutions.

Manila, Sydney and Taipei

     The cities of Manila, Sydney and Taipei each
host a fledgling offshore banking centre, but the
likelihood of their mounting an individual or
collective challenge to Singapore is remote. Manila
has one of the earliest East Asia financial centres
and its good geographical location, coupled with the
Philippines' long-standing political and economic
ties with the United States, should have stood it in
good stead. However, the social and political
turmoil engendered by the heavy-handed and now
beleaguered Marcos regime has prevented the
establishment of the stable environment much-beloved
by international financial institutions.
     Sydney's immediate prospects look good.
Australia is an industrialised country with an
adequate communications network and a strong
domestic financial community. It has a time-zone
advantage inasmuch as it bridges the trading hours
of the financial markets in the western United
States and East Asia; and 1984 saw the move towards
a tie-up between the Sydney Futures Exchange (SFE)
and the New York Commodity Exchange (COMEX) - a step
precipitated by Singapore's establishment of SIMEX,
but which will benefit Sydney by improving its links
with international financial markets. (38) However,
though geographical isolation should not cause too
much of a problem, further developments are likely
to be restrained by the sceptical attitude of
Australian political and business leaders. In the
final analysis the decisive factor may well be the
yawning lead already established by Hong Kong and
Singapore.
     Taipei's challenge dates from July 1984 when
the Taiwanese government introduced legislation
liberalising international financial flows. (39) In
order to attract international banks and promote the
local offshore banking centre a variety of tax

incentives were offered along with a reduction in
financial controls. Thus, for example, offshore
banking branches are now exempt from corporate
income tax, stamp duty and witholding tax. However,
Taipei is unlikely to pose any threat of
consequence to Singapore. Although Taiwan
is a newly industrialising country its
telecommunications and infrastructural facilities
are under-developed and its existing financial and
services industry small. Perhaps most important is
the fact that Taiwan, like Hong Kong, is claimed
by the People's Republic of China and for this
reason its future stability is not assured.

Tokyo

It is generally recognised that in the medium
and long term Singapore must fend off the challenge
from Tokyo if it is to retain its position as a
major East Asian international financial centre. As
the capital of Japan, the world's second largest
capitalist economy, Tokyo has all the hallmarks of a
primary centre for international activity. This
burgeoning city of 12 million people is the focus of
all Japanese domestic and international activity; it
has excellent, highly-developed communications and
financial networks; houses the powerful Japanese
banking and financial community; and is the
bridgehead for multinational companies entering the
gigantic Japanese market. The Japanese government
did not initiate a process to liberalise the
country's financial markets until the late
seventies; and even then under foreign pressure.
Japan's reluctance to establish itself as a major
international financial centre (a policy viewed with
relief in Singapore and Hong Kong) owes much to the
perceived disadvantages of such a move. In the
first place there is a very close relationship
between industrial companies and Japanese banks
which has resulted in the former maintaining very
high loan to equity ratios. (40) This policy for
relying on loans for investment and other activities
has been further fostered by low interest rates - a
benefit which would be lost if Japanese financial
markets were totally liberalised and the much higher
international interest rates were to come to
prevail. Further:

> 'Japanese bureaucrats have been horrified
> by America's experience of deregulation,
> with bank failures, volatile interest

The Role of Multinational Companies in Banking,
Finance and the Services

> rates and sudden surges of funds from one
> house to another. And the motive that is
> firing Britain's rapid financial
> reformation - a fear that London banks and
> brokers might be unable to compete in a
> global marketplace - is missing in Japan.
> Japanese banks and brokers are big and
> tough outside Japan and rank with the most
> muscular American firms.' (41)

It is likely, therefore, that Tokyo's evolution into
an international financial centre will be gradual
and this will allow Singapore to adapt
appropriately. In the short run, at least, Japanese
financial markets will remain relatively protected,
although Japanese banks are likely to play a major
role in London, New York, Singapore and elsewhere.
Singapore can take advantage of this and try to
initiate some sort of financial division of labour
between Tokyo (which will, of course, also have a
global outlook), Singapore and (perhaps) Hong Kong
in the East Asian region.

Hong Kong

Hong Kong and Singapore are presently the prime East
Asian international financial centres with an
approximately equal level of activity (table 4.11).
Both can trace this success back to an entrepot past
within the British Empire which helped establish
excellent infrastructural/communications facilities,
promoted a professional class (including financiers,
lawyers and accountants) and encouraged English as
the language of business. Like Singapore, Hong Kong
benefitted from the global trends which resulted in
the internationalisation of banks and other
financial institutions (see page 124), but until
recently there has been little head-on competition
between the two because of the specialisation in
services which occurred during the 1970s.
Singapore's time-zone advantage and MAS incentives
secured it the Asiacurrency and Asiabond markets;
Hong Kong, on the other hand, became the pre-eminent
East Asia centre for fund management (42) and loan
syndication (43), activities fostered by its
proximity to major international borrowers such as
China, Japan, South Korea, the Philippines and
Taiwan as well as its liberal attitude towards the
entry of foreign professionals. (44) This cosy co-
existence has been brought to an end by the climate
of competition created by a slow-growth world

economy. Hong Kong has attempted to expand its
Asiacurrency and Asiabond operations, while
Singapore is encouraging local fund management and
loan syndication. Both have inaugurated markets in
financial futures, but Singapore's SIMEX got a headstart and is likely to be more successful. (45)

At the moment Hong Kong is beset by two major
problems which will probably allow its rival
Singapore to become the premier East Asian financial
centre (barring Tokyo, perhaps). First, though the
British-Chinese agreement signed in December 1984
has resolved Hong Kong's future and guaranteed a
fifty year post-1997 "capitalistic" period, jitters
are likely as Hong Kong citizens and MNCs re-assess
the Peking treaty and realise that only twelve years
remain before the Chinese takeover. Secondly, the
slow growth in the private sector resulting from the
1997 question has meant that the public sector has
had to take up much of the economic slack. This
expenditure has however had to be paid for by an
increase in revenue, but unfortunately:

> Hong Kong's tax increases also took place
> at a time when its arch-rival, Singapore,
> did the opposite. In Singapore's Budget
> delivered on 2 March, a series of tax
> incentives and tax cuts was announced:
> extension of accelerated depreciation to
> all new equipment, investment allowances
> of up to 50% to local companies, extension
> of existing tax exemptions for offshore
> syndicated loans to other syndications of
> guarantees, performance bonds, etc.,
> granting of a 5 year tax holiday to the
> proposed financial futures market, a 10%
> tax rebate to individuals in the year of
> assessment 1984, and tax cuts ranging
> between 8.4% to 13.5% for various income
> brackets in the year of assessment 1985.
> (46)

These tax changes are generally regarded as having
affected Hong Kong adversely. One estimate, for
example, indicated that the economy lost $1.4
billion in funds under management as a result. (47)
There is no denying Hong Kong's resilience as an
economy and financial centre, but though Singapore
will continue to face hefty competition its rival
sister-city's difficulties will undoubtedly rebound
in its favour.

OTHER PRODUCER SERVICES

Since the late seventies, when the Singapore
government began to unveil its "plan for the
eighties", a variety of incentives have been made
available to companies operating services other than
banking or finance. Some of these incentives are
illustrated by table 4.16 which also indicates the
type of producer and distributive services most
welcomed by the authorities. Even before the
state's patent interest, however, foreign producer
services firms were operating in Singapore, as is
demonstrated by table 4.17. It is highly likely
that the level of foreign activity has increased
markedly since 1980.

Though foreign concerns apparently only account
for 16 percent of all paid-up-capital in non-
financial producer services (table 4.17), this is a
misleading figure resulting from real
estate/housing's 90 percent proportion of all
producer paid-up-capital. Given the shortage of
land in Singapore, it is not surprising that the
government prefers domestic control of this vital
resource; and consequently foreign companies have a
mere 11 percent participation in real estate and
housing development services. (State-owned
enterprises play a major role in this industry, as
table 3.12 [E] suggests.)

In well established professional services, such
as law, accounting and data processing, Singaporean
citizens are well established with a 55 percent
share of paid-up-capital. Moreover 34 percent of
the foreign share is accounted for by UK firms, many
presumably established to service Singapore's
historical entrepot trade. However, increased
foreign participation is likely given Singapore's
intention of upgrading its services and moving into
areas such as loan syndication which requires
sophisticated legal expertise; and the authorities
have recently removed barriers to foreign
professionals practising in Singapore. Foreign
participation is similarly increasing in business
and consulting services (note the special incentives
in table 4.16), but as in other areas what is being
promoted most is "offshore" business.

In technical services and marketing, fields
relatively new to Singapore, foreign participation
stood at 70 percent and 78 percent respectively even
in 1980 and these dominant shares are likely to
increase under present policies. The paucity of

154

Table 4.16 Economic Expansion Incentives Provided by the 1979 Relief from Income Tax (Amendment) Act.

	International trading company	Warehousing & servicing company	International consultancy firm	Investment allowances
Conditions for approval generally	i) Sale of S'pore manufactured goods and/or domestic produce of at least S$10m. p.a. ii) Sale of qualifying commodities (non-traditional commodities) of at least S$20m. p.a.	i) Fixed capital expenditure (excl. land) of at least S$2m. ii) Establishment or improvement of warehouse facilities wholly or mainly for the storage and distribution of manufactured goods.	Providing consultancy services in connection with overseas projects and gross revenue must exceed S$1m.	Approved project for the manufacture or increased manufacture of any product or for the provision of specialised engineering and technical services.

cont.

Table 4.16 Economic Expansion Incentives Provided by the 1979 Relief from Income Tax (Amendment) Act.

	International trading company	Warehousing & servicing company	International consultancy firm	Investment allowances
Conditions for approval generally cont.		iii) Providing technical or engineering services wholly or mainly to persons outside Singapore		
Formula for computing exempt income	$\left(\dfrac{\text{Export}-\text{Export Base}}{\text{Sales Value}}\right)$ Total XIncome 50% ———— (Total Sales)	$\left(\dfrac{\text{Export}-\text{Export Base}}{\text{Earnings Earnings}}\right)$ Total XIncome 50% ———— (Total Earnings)	$\left(\dfrac{\text{Export}-\text{Export Base}}{\text{Earnings Earnings}}\right)$ Total XIncome ———— (Total Earnings)	)Same as)ware-)housing) Exemption is limited to a maximum of 50% of the capital expenditure

cont.

156

Table 4.16   Economic Expansion Incentives Provided by the 1979 Relief from Income Tax (Amendment) Act.

	International trading company	Warehousing & servicing company	International consultancy firm	Investment allowances
Qualifying period 5 years from:	commencement day	commencement day	commencement day	investment day
Dividends paid out of exempt income	free of tax in hands of shareholders	free of tax in hands of shareholders	free of tax in hands of shareholders	free of tax in hands of shareholders

Source: Peat, Marwick, Mitchell and Co. (1983), Taxation in Singapore, Singapore.

Table 4.17   Producer Services[a]: Breakdown of Paid-Up-Capital by Country of Origin, 1980.

Service Industry	Number of Establishments	Employment (thousands)	Turnover (US$bn)	Total Paid-Up-Capital (US$)	Breakdown of Paid-Up-Capital by Country of Origin (%)						
					S'pore	USA	Hong Kong	UK	Malay-sia	Japan	Others
All Producer Services	6,516	59.7	2.2	1,293	84.3	2.7	4.2	0.7	2.7	2.6	2.8
Real Estate & Housing Development	1,832	19.7	1.4	1,183	88.6	1.6	4.4	0.2	2.5	1.7	1.0
Legal, Accounting, Data Processing	731	8.0	0.1	7	55.1	4.1	1.4	34.0	-	neg	5.4
Engineering, Architectural & Technical	770	9.1	0.3	20	29.6	32.1	1.6	4.6	0.1	17.4	14.6[b]

cont.

Table 4.17 Producer Services^a: Breakdown of Paid-Up-Capital by Country of Origin, 1980.

Service Industry	Number of Establishments	Employment (thousands)	Turnover (US$bn)	Total Paid-Up-Capital (US$)	Breakdown of Paid-up-Capital by Country of Origin (%)						
					S'pore	USA	Hong Kong	UK	Malay-sia	Japan	Others
Advertising/ Market Research	1,087	6.0	0.3	20	22.1	31.9	4.9	14.2	4.4	14.5	8.0
Business & Management Consultancy	434	3.3	0.1	21	71.4	5.7	2.2	0.7	4.2	7.7	8.1
Others	1,662	13.7	0.2	42	30.4	5.6	0.4	0.3	6.9	12.4	44.0

Source: Singapore Department of Statistics, Report on the Survey of Services, 1980.

Notes: a - Excluding banking and finance. b - of which 6.7% of the Paid-Up Capital belongs to Dutch concerns.

domestic competition can be explained by a lack of
local expertise and the fact that these services are
often provided to MNCs and therefore need to be
relatively sophisticated. Not unexpectedly most
foreign companies are US or Japanese in origin; and
the high share of UK, Hong Kong and Malaysian firms
is partly due to old colonial ties. The greatest
foreign participation in "other" services is in the
leasing of machinery and office equipment (including
computers) and US and Japanese firms are again
dominant.

Table 4.18 indicates the type of technical
services offered by foreign companies established in
Singapore. (There are also services offered to,
say, the electronics industry, but these are less
important.) The reasons why specific technical
service industries are sited in Singapore are
complex, deserving further study, but in the case of
the petroleum industry and related services three
facts are pertinent: (i) the potential of the
continental shelf beneath the South China sea and
nearby waters is considerable; (ii) Singapore
possesses a good infrastructure (including deep
water ports and support facilities) in an ideal
location and (iii) the island-economy also offers
manufacturing back-up, especially in related
industries such as shipbuilding. Oil companies,
especially the US Majors, are deeply involved in
East Asian oil exploration and production.
Companies servicing these activities, necessarily
foreign, have followed in their wake. Similarly,
Singapore has developed into a major transit and
communications centre and this has also aided the
manufacture and service of transport equipment such
as aircraft.

Another vital industry growing rapidly is
computer vending which provides many important
services, including contract programming, bureau
services and time sharing. (Table 4.19) Much
importance is attached to these services by the
state because computerisation is necessary if
Singapore is to acquire information technology and
expand into more advanced industries. The state and
state-owned enterprises are heavily involved in this
industry and related services, though foreign
participation is vital (most vendors in table 4.19
have at least some foreign ownership). CAD/CAM
(Computer Aided Design/Computer Aided Manufacture)
is being promoted in co-operation with Grunman
Corporation, a US company experienced in CAD/CAM
applications (48), and other foreign concerns

Table 4.18 Major International Companies Offering
Technical Services to the Transport Equipment,
Process Engineering and Offshore Petroleum
Industries.

Parent Company	Singapore Company	Services
USA		
Baker Marine Corp	Baker Marine Pte Ltd	Offshore platform elevating systems
Combustion Engineering	Gray Service Co	Warehousing & repair of oilfield wellhead equipment
Core Laboratories Inc	Core Laboratories Intl Ltd	Well logging & core analysis services
Dow Chemical of USA	Dowell Schlumberger Intl Inc[a]	Core analysis; drill-stem testing; cementing stimulation services
Geosource Inc	Geosource Petty - Ray Seismic Data Processing Centre	Seismic data acquisition & processing
Halliburton Ltd	Brown & Root (Singapore) Pte Ltd	Design engineering services for offshore oil/gas industry
Litton Industries	Western Geophysical Co of America	Seismic data acquisition & processing

cont.

Table 4.18 Major International Companies Offering
Technical Services to the Transport Equipment,
Process Engineering and Offshore Petroleum
Industries.   cont.

Parent Company	Singapore Company	Services
McDermott Inc	McDermott Engineering Pte Ltd	Design engineering services for offshore oil/gas industry
Petrolane, Inc	Eastman Whipstock Inc	Servicing & repair of oil-field directional drilling equipment
Smith International Inc	Sii Smith Tool	Warehousing & servicing of drill bits
Tri-State Oil Tools (Subsidiary of Baker Int. Corp)	Tri-State Oil Tools (S'pore) Pte Ltd	Oil field equipment
Texas Instrument Inc	Geophysical Service Inc.	Seismic data acquisition & processing
Aero Systems Inc	Aero Systems Pte Ltd	Repair & overhaul of avionics & instruments
Garrett Corp	Garrett Singapore Pte Ltd	Overhaul, repair & manufacture of aircraft components

cont.

Table 4.18 Major International Companies Offering
Technical Services to the Transport Equipment,
Process Engineering and Offshore Petroleum
Industries.   cont.

Parent Company	Singapore Company	Services
EUROPE		
Aerospatiale (France)	Samaero Co Pte Ltd	Servicing, maintenance & overhaul of Aerospatiale's helicopters & fixed wing aircraft
Anglo Thai Corp (UK)	FAS-Orient (Pte) Ltd	Overhaul & repair of aircraft hydraulic equipment
	Heli Orient Pte Ltd	Servicing, maintenance & overhaul of fixed wing & rotary wing aircraft
Chris-Marine AB (Sweden)	Chris-Marine (Singapore) Pte Ltd	Maintenance of marine equipment
Dunlop Ltd (UK)	Dunlop Aviation SEA Pte Ltd	Repair & overhaul of aircraft pneumatic & hydraulic components

cont.

Table 4.18 Major International Companies Offering Technical Services to the Transport Equipment, Process Engineering and Offshore Petroleum Industries. cont.

Parent Company	Singapore Company	Services
Indivers Group-Interturbine Division (Netherlands)	Interturbine Singapore Pte Ltd	Overhaul & repair of hot sections of aircraft engines
Kone (Finland)	Kone-FELS Cranes Pte Ltd	Shipyard/harbour cranes
M.A.N.-B&W (West Germany)	M.A.N.-GHH (Singapore) Pte Ltd	Diesel engine assembly & servicing
M.T.U. Moteren-und Turbinen-Union Friedrichshafen GmbH (W Germany)	M.T.U. Singapore Pte Ltd	Diesel engine assembly & servicing
Det Norske Veritas (Norway)	Det Norske Veritas Singapore (Pte) Ltd	Ship classification & certification; structural analysis & other offshore-engineering services
Matthew Hall (UK)	Matthew Hall Engineering (SEA) Pte Ltd	Process plant engineering services
Protech International (Netherlands)	Protech Int'l Pte Ltd	Process plant engineering services

cont.

The Role of Multinational Companies in Banking, Finance and the Services

Table 4.18 Major International Companies Offering Technical Services to the Transport Equipment, Process Engineering and Offshore Petroleum Industries.   cont.

Parent Company	Singapore Company	Services
Schlumberger (France)	Dowell Schlumberger Intl Inc[a]	Core analysis; drill-stem testing; cementing stimulation services
	Flopetrol Int'l SA	Well-testing, measurement & interpretation
	Transitrex Research & Development Corp	Test laboratory for oilfield wire-logging equipment
JAPAN		
Chiyoda Chemical Engineering	Chiyoda Singapore (Pte) Ltd	Process plant engineering services
AUSTRALIA		
Hawker De Havilland Australia Pty Ltd	Hawker Pacific Pte Ltd	Repair & overhaul of aero-engines & related components

Source: Singapore Economic Development Board (1983), Leading International Companies Manufacturing and Providing Technical Services in Singapore, Singapore.

Note: a - Joint Venture.

165

(page 68); 500 new computer professionals entered the labour market in 1984 and 600-700 new personnel will become available from 1985 onwards (49); and robotisation is being spurred by Robot Leasing and Consultancy Pte. Ltd. which is a tripartite venture between two state-owned enterprises (Singapore Automotive Leasing Pte. Ltd and the Economic Development Board) and Japan Robot Leasing Co. Ltd (50). Computer services are a logical extension for overseas computer and electronics companies manufacturing in Singapore and much of the expansion evident in table 4.19 can be explained by MNC diversification.

DISTRIBUTIVE SERVICES

As table 4.20 shows the distributive services, as a whole, are only 30 percent foreign owned. This is unsurprising since much transportation and trade is domestically oriented; and telecommunications are a state monopoly. Because of the importance of exports, mainly by MNCs manufacturing in Singapore, wholesale trade and sea transport are the two services with the greatest foreign participation (35 percent and 20 percent respectively). In addition the importance of Hong Kong, Malaysian and Indonesian investors is due to the extensive role played by the overseas Chinese community in the distributive services. As an entrepot and internationally-oriented economy, Singapore needs to expand constantly its distributive services and the policies of the PSA, JTC and other government boards are geared to this effort (pages 84 ff). The role of MNCs and state-owned enterprises is likely to grow at the expense of private domestic firms in the forseeable future. An interesting new growth area, inaugurated by Bell Helicopters' establishment of a regional product support facility in Singapore on July 12, 1984, is likely to be in regional air services. (51) (See also table 4.18)

SOCIAL AND PERSONAL SERVICES

Perhaps unexpectedly, table 4.21 indicates that foreign concerns are quite important in social and personal services. In the case of social services the answer is straight forward: the paid-up-capital figure excludes state sector services and this implies that the 56 percent foreign share mainly

Table 4.19   Computer Vendors in Singapore.

	Number	%
TOTAL NO. OF COMPUTER VENDOR COMPANIES	114	100.0
1. No. Of Computer Companies Established In The Following Years:		
Before 1980	36	31.6
1980	19	16.7
1981	29	25.4
1982	30	26.3
2. No. Of Computer Companies Whose Capital Ownership Is:		
Wholly Local	54	47.4
More Than Half Local	10	8.8
More Than Half Foreign	10	8.8
Wholly Foreign	40	35.1
3. No. Of Computer Companies Which Provide:		
Software Sales	84	73.7
Hardware Sales	72	63.2
Professional Consultancy	54	47.4
Turnkey Project	54	47.4
OEM Distributor	38	33.3
Contract Programming	38	33.3
Training/Education	37	32.5
Bureau Services	30	26.3
Time Sharing	21	18.4
Facilities Management	19	16.7

cont.

Table 4.19   Computer Vendors in Singapore.

	Number	%
4. Total No. of Mainframes/Mini Computers Sold Locally In The Following Years:	612	100.0
1977	34	5.5
1978	58	9.5
1979	94	15.4
1980	162	26.5
1981	264	43.1
5. Value of Mainframes/Mini-computers Sold Locally In The Following Years: ($ million)		
1977	3.1	
1978	7.1	
1979	13.7	
1980	22.7	
1981	37.5	
6. Total No. Of Microcomputers Sold Locally In The Following Years:		
1979	356	
1980	855	
1981	2568	
7. Value of Microcomputers Sold Locally In The Following Years: ($ million)		
1979	0.6	
1980	1.7	
1981	5.9	

cont.

Table 4.19 Computer Vendors in Singapore.

	Number	%

8. Total Value Of Software Services/Packages Sold Locally In The Following Years: ($ million)

Year	Number
1977	0.7
1978	0.9
1979	2.5
1980	4.5
1981	14.4

9. Total Value Of Software Services/Packages Exported In The Following Years: ($ million)

Year	Number
1977	0.2
1978	0.2
1979	2.1
1980	2.7
1981	3.2

10. Total Payment Of Royalties/ Foreign Consultancy Fees In The Following Year: ($ million)

Year	Number
1979	0.2
1980	0.3
1981	0.7

Source: National Computer Board (1983), Singapore Computer Industry Survey, Singapore.

represents international private medical companies, chiefly those from developed countries. Even the high share for Hong Kong is probably due to the regional operations of locally based US and European firms. (Ciba-Geigy, the Swiss firm, transferred its regional medical facilities from Hong Kong to Singapore in 1984.) The high foreign share of foreign companies in personal and household services

Table 4.20 Distributive Services: Breakdown of Paid-Up-Capital by Country of Origin, 1980/81

Service Industry	Number of Establishments	Employment (Thousands)	Turnover (US$bn)	Total Paid-up Capital (US$bn)	Paid-up-Capital by Country of Origin (%)	
					Singapore	Malaysia
All Distributive Services	40,954	304.2	34.1	2.0	70.6	6.1
Land Transport	3,195	25.2	0.3	Neg.	97.4	1.6
Sea Transport	733	23.1	1.3	0.1	80.1	1.5
Air Transport	3	12.7	1.2	0.1	99.7	-
Transport-related	1,711	17.6	0.9	0.1	74.5	1.3

Table 4.20 Distributive Services: Breakdown of Paid-Up-Capital by
Country of Origin, 1980/81

Service Industry	Number of Establishments	Employment (Thousands)	Turnover (US$bn)	Total Paid-up Capital (US$bn)	Paid-up-Capital by Country of Origin (%)	
					Singapore	Malaysia
Storage/ Warehousing	60	0.8	Neg.	(0.1 (		
Telecommuni- cations	1	10.0	0.3	((	88.5	–
Wholesale Trade	18,794	107.3	26.1	1.3	65.4	6.5
Retail Trade	16,457	65.5	3.9	0.2	74.7	13.8

Table 4.20 Distributive Services: Breakdown of Paid-Up-Capital by Country of Origin, 1980/81

Service Industry	Paid-Up-Capital by Country of Origin (%)						
	Hong Kong	USA	Japan	UK	Indonesia	Netherlands	Others
All Distributive Services	5.9	4.7	2.9	1.8	1.0	1.2	5.8
Land Transport	0.7	–	0.3	–	–	–	–
Sea Transport	9.8	0.1	0.3	0.2	N.A.	4.8	3.2
Air Transport	–	–	–	–	–	–	0.3
Transport-related	5.6	2.7	1.5	1.3	N.A.	1.3	11.8

Table 4.20 Distributive Services: Breakdown of Paid-Up-Capital by
Country of Origin, 1980/81

Service Industry	Paid-Up-Capital by Country of Origin (%)						
	Hong Kong	USA	Japan	UK	Indonesia	Netherlands	Others
Storage/ Warehousing)) Telecommuni-) cations)	3.6	4.5	3.5	-	-	-	-
Wholesale Trade	6.1	6.6	3.7	2.5	1.5	1.1	6.6
Retail Trade	6.3	Neg.	1.9	0.7	0.3	-	2.3

Sources: Singapore Department of Statistics: (i) Report on the Survey of Wholesale
and Retail Trades, Restaurants and Hotels 1981; (ii) Report on the Survey of
Services 1980.

Notes: N.A. - Not Available. Neg. - Negligible.

Table 4.21 Social^a and Personal Services: Breakdown of Paid-Up-Capital by Country of Origin, 1980/81.

Service Industry	Number of Establishments	Employment (Thousands)	Turnover (US$bn)	Total Paid-up Capital (US$bn)	Breakdown of Paid-Up-Capital by Country of Origin (%)	
					Singapore	USA
Social Services[b]	2,453	15.2	152	17	44.1	5.3
Recreational & Cultural	420	7.7	154	36	91.6	0.1
Personal & Household	5,289	17.2	192	8	48.0	0.3
Restaurants & Hotels	2,986	42.5	814	343	86.7	1.0

Table 4.21 Social[a] and Personal Services: Break down of
Paid-up-Capital by Country of Origin, 1980/81.

Service Industry	Break down of Paid-Up-Capital by Country of Origin (%)				
	Hong Kong	UK	Malaysia	Japan	Others
Social Services[b]	21.2[c]	0.6	Neg.	2.1	26.7
Recreational & Cultural	1.9	3.2	0.6	2.1	0.5
Personal & Household	Neg.	42.8[d]	2.3	–	6.6
Restaurants & Hotels	5.0	Neg.	4.1	2.1	1.1

Source: As table 4.20

Notes: a – Excluding Government Social Services (but including those of state owned enterprises). b – Education, medical services etc, mainly the latter. c – Entirely in medical services. d – Mainly laundry and repair of domestic equipment.

The Role of Multinational Companies in Banking,
Finance and the Services

Table 4.22 Major International Hotel chains with
Hotels in Singapore.

Comfort Hotels (UK)
Golden Tulip (Netherlands)
Hilton (USA)
Holiday Inns (USA)
HRI (USA)
Hyatt Hotels Co. (USA)
International Hotels (USA)
JAL Hotel System (Japan)
Mandarin International (Hong Kong)
Merlin Hotels (Malaysia)
Sheraton Hotels (USA)
Sofital (France)
SRS Hotels (West Germany)
South Pacific Hotel Corp. Ltd. (Australia)
Trust House Forte (UK)
Westin Hotels (USA)

Source: Financial Times (1983), World Hotel
          Directory, 1983/84, Longman.

is nearly entirely accounted for by a few UK
companies   involved   in   laundries   and   domestic
equipment repair.
     As expected, only 8 percent of recreational and
cultural   services   are   foreign   owned, but the 13
percent foreign ownership of restaurants and hotels
is probably an understatement. International hotel
chains (table 4.22) and other MNCs have rushed to
take   advantage   of   Singapore's   "tourism" industry
which   "contributes   16   percent   ($1   billion)   of
foreign exchange earnings and 6 percent of gross
domestic   product".   (52)   (The foreign ownership in
restaurants   and   hotels   is   low   because   of
franchising: in any case the share will undoubtedly
rise   as   the   spate   of new international hotels is
completed and the number of rooms increases manifold
[53].) Singapore's tourists, though short stay, net
about 30-40 percent of all tourist receipts in ASEAN
countries.   (54)   These   tourists   consist of: (i)
transit   passengers   taking advantage of Singapore's
shopping facilities and easy access to other South
East Asian countries; (ii) "shoppers" from nearby
Indonesia   and   Malaysia;   (iii)   international
businessmen (because of the large contingent of
locally   operating   MNCs);   (iv) expatriates such as
engineers working on offshore oil fields; and (v)
conference   participants.   (55)   Despite   a   drop in

tourism receipts in 1983, tourism earnings have
resumed an upward trend since 1984 and under such
circumstances the inrush of foreign tourism oriented
companies is likely to continue.

CONCLUDING REMARKS

For many years the services sector has been
moored in the backwaters of economic theory and its
potential contribution to the development process
has been overlooked. More recent studies, however,
stress the role of services as a prerequisite to
growth and development. Thus, according to UNCTAD:

> The overall efficiency of an economy
> depends to an ever-increasing extent upon
> the interlinkages which are established
> among the different productive activities
> themselves. Services are interlinked with
> the rest of the economy in numerous ways.
> Transportation, telecommunications and
> radio and public utilities, for example,
> are a key part of the general
> infrastructure. Legal services,
> advertising and accounting play an
> important role in the vertical integration
> of corporate activities.
> Telecommunications and telematics have
> helped the international finance industry
> to expand into other service activities,
> such as real estate and insurance. (56)

Because of historical conditions the Singapore
government recognised the importance of services at
an early stage and embarked upon a strategy of
expansion in the services sector. The state has
been involved both directly and indirectly and
services have been regulated and promoted by boards
and enterprises such as the MAS, the Singapore
tourism promotion board and the Development Bank of
Singapore (DBS). The role of these bodies cannot be
understated and the DBS, for example, has played a
major role in encouraging new financial services.
According to Professor Tan Chwee Huat:

> It has granted loans and participated in
> equity share holding in merchant banks,
> finance companies, discount houses,
> leasing, factoring, insurance and
> reinsurance companies. For example,

during the early years of banking, it was instrumental in promoting the market by participating in the share-holding of two merchant banks (DBS Daiwa Securities International Ltd. and Singapore Nomura Merchant Bank) which have been very active. Among the four discount houses in Singapore, the DBS has 45 percent holding in the National Discount Company while the government-owned Post Office Savings Bank has a 40 percent share in the Discount Company of Singapore. For familiar reasons, the DBS went into joint ventures in the leasing business with Orient Leasing of Japan to form a local leasing company. Similarly, factoring activities were introduced into Singapore with the formation of its joint venture with Heller Factoring of Hong Kong and Walter Heller Overseas Corporation. (57)

Other state-owned enterprises also participate in the service sector and, as with manufacturing, these are present in all the major service industries, including banking and finance, distribution, communication, business services, tourism and real estate. (See table 3.12) The last few years has seen yet a further push into the services sector by major state-owned enterprises such as Singapore Airlines (which has expanded into finance) and Keppel Shipyards (presently involved in retail banking, international finance and insurance); and recent changes in Singapore legislation will mean that even the MAS could assume a commercial as well as a regulatory role. (58)

Despite the state's major stake in services and many grumbles about "conservative regulations" (e.g. the MAS's rules preventing the internationalisation of the Singapore dollar [59]) foreign service companies are a potent force in Singapore and their numbers are increasing annually. In fact most hue and cry is raised by private domestic service companies because of their fear that they are being squeezed out by state enterprises and MNCs, both powerful interests in their own right. It is certainly true that key, lucrative, internationally-oriented service industries such as banking and technical services are dominated by foreign companies whose domination is likely to continue because of their control of resources, technology and expertise. In their rush to foster a

international service sector the Singapore
authorities have paid little heed to this problem,
but it is one which will have to be faced sooner or
later.

In any case the service sector is likely to
maintain its prominence and importance in ensuing
years. Table 4.23 shows how the sector has always
employed 60 percent or more of the Singaporean
workforce (despite a structural decline, 1957-1980)
and that the proportion employed is on the increase.
All forecasts predict that only service industries
such as banking, consultancy and distribution can
generate the employment required by future
generations, especially because of the global
effects of rapid technological change. Under these
circumstances the island's political masters have
concluded that the economy must maintain its
regional and international service capabilities and
competitiveness - dependent as these are on foreign
capital - and have acted accordingly.

Table 4.23 Employment by Industry, 1957 - 1983

Industry	Percent				
	1957	1970	1975	1980	1983
Agriculture	8.5	3.5	2.1	1.6	1.0
Manufacturing	14.5	22.3	27.7	30.2	27.8
Utilities	1.2	1.2	1.3	0.8	0.7
Construction	5.2	6.6	4.7	6.7	7.2
Services	70.2	66.3	65.1	60.7	62.9
- Trade	24.2	23.4	22.9	21.3	22.7
- Transport	10.7	12.1	11.7	11.1	11.3
- Finance & Business	4.6	4.0	6.1	7.4	8.1
- Other	30.7	26.8	24.4	20.9	20.8
Others	0.4	0.1	0.3	Neg.	0.1
Total Number Employed	100.0	100.0	100.0	100.0	100.0

cont.

The Role of Multinational Companies in Banking, Finance and the Services

Table 4.23 Employment by Industry, 1957 - 1983
cont.

	Percent				
Industry	1957	1970	1975	1980	1983
(Thousands of persons)	471.9	650.9	833.5	1,077.1	1,169.6

Source: Singapore Department of Statistics, Economic and Social Statistics, 1960-1982 and Monthly Digest of Statistics, May 1984.

NOTES

1.   Services here include Trade, Transport, Finance and Other Services less imputed bank charges.

2.   Greece's service-orientation is, of course, towards international tourism.

3.   The UK, the US and other industrialised countries have large domestically orientated service sectors because of their (arguably) post-industrial stature.   Hong Kong and Singapore have large internationally oriented service sectors because of their small size and entrepot past.

4.   Singapore Investment News, April 1984: Dr. Tony Tan's Address to the 31st Meeting of the Asia Pacific Council of the American Chamber of Commerce, March 30.

5.   For further discussion of these divisions see J. Singlemann (1978), From Agriculture to Services: The Transformation of Industrial Employment, Sage Publishers.

6.   Or at least in the rate of increase of demand for loans.

7.   Tan Chwee Huat, "The Role of Government in Developing Singapore as a Financial Center: Lessons for other Developing Countries", AISEC Business Executive, Vol 2, 1983, page 7.

8.   Factoring is a financial instrument in which the factoring company purchases debts from a client and uses its world-wide connections to collect this debt.   The client also receives a number of other services simultaneously. At present only Heller Factoring (Singapore) Ltd operates in

180

NOTES continued

Singapore: for further details see Kwan Kuen-Chor
and Ong Biauw Kiat (1982), "Factoring in Singapore",
in Phillip D. Grub et al, East Asia: Dimensions of
International Business, Practice/Hall International.
See also C.O. Livijn, "Export Factoring", in C.J.
Gmur and N. Budd, Trade Financing, Euromoney
Publications, 1984.

9. For a discussion of the MAS and Singaporean
financial institutions see Tan Chwee Huat (1981),
Financial Institutions in Singapore, Singapore
University Press; Robert Effros (1982), Emerging
Financial Centres, International Monetary Fund,
Washington; and Bowman Brown (1982), International
Banking Centres, Euromoney Publications.

10. That is activity in regional or
international markets by Singapore based
institutions.

11. The Asiadollar market is the Asian
equivalent of the Eurodollar and is essentially an
international money and capital market where United
States dollars and other foreign currencies are
pooled for on-lending, mainly to countries in Asia.
(The Monetary Authority of Singapore [1980], The
Financial Structure of Singapore, Singapore, page
6.)

12. An ACU is an integral department of a
financial institution, but is maintained as a
separate accounting body for the purpose of its
reports to the MAS and the Inland Revenue. Any
financial institution wishing to operate an ACU
needs to obtain a license from the MAS.

13. International Monetary Fund, Financial
Statistics Yearbook 1984, page 57.

14. The Hong Kong and Shanghai Bank was, of
course, until recently domiciled in Hong Kong.

15. For further details see Patrick Smith and
Frieda Koh, "Roots in a migrant past", Far Eastern
Economic Review, August 20, 1982; Peat Marwick
(1983), Banking in Singapore, Singapore; and Tan
Chwee Huat (1981), Financial Institutions in
Singapore, Singapore University Press.

16. There are also a large number of Canadian
banks active, but these all have lower assets. The
Bank of Montreal is largest with assets amounting to
$2.0 billion.

17. Though no breakdown is available it is
probable that many regional asset/liability
movements (especially to/from Malaysia) are included

NOTES continued

in table 4.9.

18. The remainder of the loans are accounted for by transportation, communication, agriculture, housing and "other" sectors.

19. Lending by the Eurocurrency and Asiacurrency markets was originally in dollars, but other currencies, especially the UK pound, the Yen and the German Mark have come into increasing usage.

20. Yoon S. Park and Jack Zwick (1985), International Banking in Theory and Practice, Addison-Wesley, page 10.

21. Important sovereign borrowers are the governments of China, South Korea and Indonesia.

22. It is worth mentioning that developing countries as a whole are also increasing their share of international bank lending.

23. The sole owner, of course, in the case of a 100 percent owned subsidiary.

24. Banco Ambrosiano (Italy), Berliner Handel-Und Frankfurter (Germany), Credit Commercial de France (France), Kredit Bank NV (Belgium), Nederlandsche Middenstandbank (Netherlands), Privatbanken (Denmark) and William and Glyns Bank (UK).

25. For example DBS-Daiwa Securities International Ltd. is owned by three banks with the following shareholding: Development Bank of Singapore (50 percent), Daiwa Securities Ltd. (40 percent) and Sumitomo Bank (10 percent). The latter two banks are both Japanese.

26. Financial Times Survey, Singapore, December 12 1984, page iv.

27. For further details see Tan Chwee Huat, (1981), Financial Institutions in Singapore, Singapore University press and Michael T. Skully (1981), Merchant Banking in ASEAN, Oxford University Press.

28. Bank for International Settlements, 54th, Annual Report; World Financial Markets, April, 1985

29. For example, Prudential, Taisho Marine and Fire and General Accident.

30. This is similar to the local-foreign division in commercial banking.

31. For example marine, aviation and transit insurance did badly because of the slump in international trade. See V.G. Kulkarni, "a policy of caution", Far Eastern Economic Review,

NOTES continued

July 7, 1983.

32. See, "The Institutions role is big and it could turn active" in Far Eastern Economic Review, April 12, 1984.

33. Park and Zwick (1985), op.cit., pages 130-132.

34. Joyce Quek, "Will SIMEX become the missing link?", Euromoney, October 1984, page 347.

35. Ibid. See also "Flurry on a quiet day in the Eurodollar pit", Financial Times, December 12, 1984.

36. The System is a little more complicated than this and is explained further in Lincoln Kaye/Robert Manning, "Its an early bird ...", Far Eastern Economic Review, September 6 1984, page 130. See also Quek (1984) and Financial Times (1984), op.cit. Also Joyce Quek, "Will Singapore do things the American way?", The Banker, July 1984.

37. A link-up with London, presently being considered, would make the 24 hour trading concept a reality.

38. See Peter Starr, "Sydney's all-clear", Far Eastern Economic Review, July 12, 1984.

39. See I-Shuan Sun, "Taiwan: prospects of the Taipei offshore banking centre", Bulletin For International Fiscal Documentation, 1984, vol 38 part 6; and Andrew Tanzer, "Not drowning, waving", Far Eastern Economic Review, July 26, 1984.

40. See Raymond W. Goldsmith (1983), The Financial Development of Japan, Yale University Press.

41. The Economist, "Limbering up: a survey of Japanese finance and banking", December 8, 1984, page 5.

42. Fund Management refers to the investment in securities and other long-term assets carried out by institutions such as pension funds, insurance companies, unit trusts and investment trusts.

43. Loan syndication refers to the process whereby a number of banks and other financial institutions co-operate in securing a customer's request for large scale funds. The "syndicated product" is necessary because such large loans are impossible for a single institution (however large) to undertake and requires considerable financial and legal expertise in arranging. Sovereign loans are usually arranged through syndication.

44. See Yoon S. Park, "A comparison of Hong

NOTES continued

Kong and Singapore as Asian Financial Centres" in
Phillip D. Grub et al (1982), East Asia: Dimensions
of International Business, Prentice Hall
International.

45. See "Hong Kong's Uncertain Future",
Euromoney, October, 1984. It is worth mentioning
that at the moment there is no direct competition
between SIMEX and the Hong Kong Futures Exchange
because different items are being traded.

46. Y.C. Jao, "Hong Kong's New Revenue
Proposals and Their Implications", Bulletin for
International Fiscal Documentation, 1984, Vol 38,
page 301.

47. "Tax reform leads to HK$13bn outflow",
Financial Times, December 12, 1984.

48. Singapore Investment News, October 1984,
page 1.

49. Singapore Investment News, August 1984,
page 1.

50. Singapore Investment News, July 1984,
page 2.

51. Ibid., page 2.

52. Financial Times, "Tourism in Singapore",
December 12, 1984, page 7.

53. It is estimated that the number of rooms in
hotels will increase from 15,000 in 1981 to 31,000
in 1987. See The Singapore Tourism Promotion Board,
Annual Statistical Report on Visitor Arrivals to
Singapore, 1982, page 36, table 31.

54. World Tourism Organisation (1984), Economic
Review of World Tourism, Madrid.

55. Many of the new hotels are being built in
anticipation of a rise in conferences and similar
events.

56. UNCTAD Bulletin, November 1984, page 2.
UNCTAD stands for the United Nations Conference on
Trade and Development.

57. Tan Chwee Huat (1983), "The Role of
Government in Developing Singapore as a Financial
Centre", op cit., page 10.

58. See, for example, Catherine Ong, "Keppel
Sets Sail for America", Euromoney, July, 1983;
Lincoln Kaye, "The State goes banking", Far Eastern
Economic Review, August 16, 1984; Kathryn Davies,
"Keeping an eye on Hong Kong", The Banker, July,
1983; and Catherine Ong. "Money Management even
other Airlines talk about", Euromoney, July 1983.

59. In 1982 the MAS expelled a number of

NOTES continued

expatriate bankers who attempted to internationalise Singapore by a process known as "round-tripping" (whereby banks booked Singapore dollar deposits in one of their overseas branches and repatriated them as capital). For this and other tensions between the MAS and bankers see, Basil Caplan, "Singapore's ruffled feathers", The Banker, May 1984 and Lincoln Kaye, "Bankers' discomfiture", Far Eastern Economic Review, February 9, 1984.

Table 4.24   A List of Major Financial Institutions in Singapore.

Commercial Banks
Full Banks

1. Algemene Bank Nederland NV
2. Asia Commercial Bank Limited
3. Ban Hin Lee Bank Berhad
4. Bangkok Bank Limited
5. Bank Negara Indonesia 1946
6. Bank of America NT & SA
7. The Bank of Canton Limited
8. Bank of China
9. The Bank of East Asia Limited
10. Bank of India
11. Bank of Singapore Limited
12. The Bank of Tokyo Limited
13. Banque Indosuez
14. The Chartered Bank
15. The Chase Manhattan Bank NA
16. Chung Khiaw Bank Limited
17. Citibank NA
18. The Development Bank of Singapore Limited
19. Far Eastern Bank Limited
20. The First National Bank of Chicago
21. Four Seas Communications Bank Limited
22. The Hongkong and Shanghai Banking Corporation
23. Indian Bank
24. Indian Overseas Bank
25. Industrial & Commercial Bank Limited
26. International Bank of Singapore Limited
27. The Kwangtung Provincial Bank
28. Lee Wah Bank Limited
29. Malayan Banking Berhad
30. Malayan United Bank Berhad

The Role of Multinational Companies in Banking,
Finance and the Services

Commercial Banks continued
Full Banks continued

31. The Mitsui Bank Limited
32. Oversea-Chinese Banking Corporation Limited
33. Overseas Union Bank Limited
34. Tat Lee Bank Limited
35. United Commercial Bank
36. United Malayan Banking Corporation Berhad
37. United Overseas Bank Limited

Restricted Banks

1. American Express International Banking
   Corporation
2. Banca Commerciale Italiana
3. Banque Nationale de Paris
4. Bayerische Landesbank Girozentrale
5. Credit Suisse
6. Dresdner Bank AG
7. European Asian Bank
8. First Commercial Bank
9. Habib Bank Limited
10. Korea Exchange Bank
11. The Mitsubishi Bank Limited
12. Moscow Narodny Bank Limited
13. The Sumitomo Bank Limited

Offshore Banks

1. Amsterdam-Rotterdam Bank NV
2. Arab Banking Corporation
3. Australia and New Zealand Banking Group
   Limited
4. Banco do Brasil SA
5. Banco do Estado de Sao Paulo SA
6. Banco Urquijo SA
7. Bank Bumiputra Malaysia Berhad
8. Bank of Montreal
9. The Bank of New York
10. Bank of New Zealand
11. The Bank of Nova Scotia
12. Bankers Trust Company
13. Banque Bruxelles Lambert SA
14. Banque Francaise du Commerce Exterieur
15. Banque Paribas
16. Barclays Bank International Limited
17. Canadian Imperial Bank of Commerce
18. Chemical Bank
19. The Commercial Bank of Korea Limited

Offshore Banks continued

20. Commonwealth Trading Bank of Australia
21. Continental Illinois National Bank and Trust
    Company of Chicago
22. Credit Lyonnais
23. The Dai-Ichi Kangyo Bank Limited
24. The Daiwa Bank Limited
25. Den Danske Bank af 1871 Aktieselskab
26. Deutsche Genossenschaftsbank
27. First City National Bank of Houston
28. First Interstate Bank of California
29. The First National Bank of Boston
30. The Fuji Bank Limited
31. Grindlays Bank PLC
32. Harris Trust and Savings Bank
33. The Industrial Bank of Japan Limited
34. Inter First Bank Dallas NA
35. Irving Trust Company
36. Kuwait Asia Bank EC
37. Lloyds Bank International Limited
38. The Long-Term Credit Bank of Japan Limited
39. Manufacturers Hanover Trust Company
40. Marine Midland Bank NA
41. Midland Bank PLC
42. The Mitsui Trust and Banking Company Limited
43. Morgan Guaranty Trust Company of New York
44. Multibanco Commermex SA
45. National Bank of Abu Dhabi
46. National Commercial Banking Corporation of
    Australia Limited
47. National Westminster Bank PLC
48. Nordic Bank PLC
49. Philippine National Bank
50. Rainier National Bank
51. Republic Bank Dallas NA
52. The Royal Bank of Canada
53. The Saitama Bank Limited
54. The Sanwa Bank Limited
55. Security Pacific National Bank
56. Societe Generale
57. Societe generale de Banque
58. State Bank of India
59. The Sumitomo Trust & Banking Company Limited
60. Swiss Bank Corporation
61. The Taiyo Kobe Bank Limited
62. The Tokai Bank Limited
63. The Toronto Dominion Bank
64. Union Bank of Switzerland
65. Union de Banques Arabes et Francaises

The Role of Multinational Companies in Banking,
Finance and the Services

Offshore Banks continued

66. Wells Fargo Bank NA
67. Westpac Banking Corporation

Merchant Banks

1. Amro Bank (Asia) Limited
2. Arbuthnot Latham Asia Limited
3. Armco Pacific Limited
4. Asia Pacific Capital Corporation
5. Asian-American Merchant Bank Limited
6. Associated Merchant Bank Private Limited
7. Bank of Montreal Asia Limited
8. The Bank of Nova Scotia Asia Limited
9. Bankers Trust International (Asia) Limited
10. Banque Internationale a Luxembourg Bil (Asia)
    Limited
11. Banque Nationale de Paris (South East Asia)
    Limited
12. Baring Brothers Asia Limited
13. Bergen Bank Asia Limited
14. Canadian Imperial Bank of Commerce (Asia)
    Limited
15. Citicorp International (Singapore) Limited
16. Commerzbank (South East Asia) Limited
17. Credit Suisse First Boston (Asia) Limited
18. DBS-Daiwa Securities International Limited
19. Deutsche Bank (Asia Credit) Limited
20. Dresdner (South East Asia) Limited
21. First Chicago Asia Merchant Bank Limited
22. Guinness Mahon (Asia) Limited
23. Haw Par Merchant Bankers Limited
24. Indosuez Asia (Singapore) Limited
25. Inter-Alpha Asia (Singapore) Limited
26. Jardine Fleming (Singapore) Pte Limited
27. KDB International (Singapore) Limited
28. Lloyds International Merchant Bank (SEA)
    Limited
29. Marac Merchant Bank (S E Asia) Limited
30. Merrill Lynch International (Asia) & Company
31. Midland Bank (Singapore) Limited
32. Morgan Grenfell (Asia) Limited
33. Morgan Guaranty Pacific Limited
34. P K Christiania Bank (South East Asia) Limited
35. Rothschild N M & Sons (Singapore) Limited
36. Republic National Bank of New York (Singapore)
    Limited
37. The Royal Bank of Canada (Asia) Limited
38. Samuel Montagu & Company Limited

Merchant Banks continued

39. Singapore International Merchant Bankers
    Limited
40. Singapore Nomura Merchant Banking Limited
41. Singapore-Japan Merchant Bank Limited
42. Skandinaviska Enskilda Bankers (South East
    Asia) Limited
43. Standard Chartered Merchant Bank Asia Limited
44. Temenggong Merchant Bankers Limited
45. The Toronto Dominion (South East Asia) Limited
46. Union Bank of Finland (Singapore) Limited
47. United Merchant Bank Limited
48. Wardley Limited
49. Wells Fargo Asia Limited

Discount Houses

1. Commercial Discount Company Limited
2. The Discount Company of Singapore Limited
3. International Discount Company Limited
4. National Discount Company Limited

Money Brokers

1. Astley & Pearce (Pte) Limited
2. Charles Fulton (Singapore) 1982 Limited
3. Degani, Tullett & Riley (S) Private Limited
4. Harlow, Sassoon (Singapore) Private Limited
5. Hung Chue Pedder Martin Private Limited
6. K-T Forex (Private) Limited
7. Marshalls (Singapore) Private Limited
8. Ong Tradition Singapore (Private) Limited
9. Tan Swee Hee - Butler Private Limited

Source: Ministry of Culture, Singapore 1983.

Chapter Five

SINGAPORE AND THE EMERGING INTERNATIONAL ECONOMIC
ORDER

Singapore's pivotal role as a regional and
international business centre (1) can only be
understood in the context of an ongoing global redistribution of manufacturing and service
industries. The post-war era can be characterised
by (i) a massive global expansion in output and
international trade (2); (ii) an unprecedented
internationalisation of nearly all economies (table
5.1); and (iii) the emergence of a "new"
international division of labour (NIDL) as part of
the redistribution process. (3) The "old" division
of labour was created during the colonial era and
entailed a specialisation in international
production and exchange whereby industrialised
countries produced and exported manufactured goods,
while developing countries produced and exported
agricultural goods and raw materials
("commodities"). Though this trade structure still
predominates, it has been modified by the rapid
expansion of manufacturing and service exports from
developing countries. In 1981, for example, 11
percent of developing country visible exports
consisted of manufactured goods, although 85 percent
of this trade was accounted for by just ten
countries (including Singapore). (4) The term "new"
international division of labour therefore refers to
a system of international trade in which there is
intra-industry, intra-services specialisation
between industrialised and developing countries.
Despite the gradual shift of production and
trade in favour of developing countries (table 5.2),
there has been a variety of constraints on their
growth and development. In particular, commodities
(still the preponderant export items) are prone to
price instability and sluggish productivity growth;
and financial, technological and related resources,
necessary for the expansion of manufacturing and

Table 5.1 Share of Exports in GDP

Percent

| Year | Industrialised Countries | | | | Socialist Countries[a] | Developing Countries | World |
	Total	OECD	USA	Japan			
1950	10.1	9.9	4.5	9.8	N.A.	12.8	10.6
1960	11.7	11.5	5.1	10.8	5.3[b]	15.6	11.1
1970	13.7	13.5	5.7	10.8	5.8	15.9	12.5
1975	17.6	17.4	8.5	12.8	8.0	24.2	16.9
1980	20.6	20.2	10.2	14.0	8.9	26.8	19.6

Source: UNCTAD (1984), Trade and Development Report, Geneva.

Notes: a – Socialist countries exclude China in 1960 and 1980.
        b – Ratio excludes countries with missing export or GDP data.

service industries, are largely controlled by MNCs from industrialised countries. Thus, in order to encourage the development process, developing countries have called for a New International Economic Order (NIEO). This is an 'economic and political concept, variously interpreted, which encapsulates the developing countries' demands for a greater access to the world's economic, financial and technological resources'. (5) The NIEO is too lengthy a topic to discuss here, but it is pertinent that some fundamental NIEO proposals (e.g. multilateral aid, reform of the IMF and the World Bank, untied technology transfer and control of MNCs) strike at the very core of the industrialised countries' economic and political dominance over the international system. (6) With their privileged status at stake it is unsurprising that the western capitalist economies have conceded little during the NIEO negotiations in fora such as UNCTAD and UNIDO. (7,8) Instead they have responded by encouraging a specific NIDL which delineates an emerging international economic order (EIEO) in which some technologies, industries and services are transferred to some developing countries, often with a degree of MNC control. (9) The EIEO is not a product of chance: it has been forged by economic necessity and political will (10); but its stability is, as yet, difficult to gauge. Singapore's position in this new world regime will be analysed in the following pages, with particular attention to the country's role in ASEAN and the Pacific Community.

PERIPHERAL INTERMEDIATION AND THE EMERGING INTERNATIONAL ECONOMIC ORDER

Map 5.1 illustrates the phenomenon of peripheral intermediation. (11) The world economic system is dominated by a group of capitalist industrialised countries (North America, Western Europe, Japan and Australasia - the metropole) which are surrounded by a large number of "peripheral" (mainly developing) countries whose chief international economic and political interactions are preponderantly with this capitalist "core". (12) However, metropole-periphery economic relations have been transformed over the last decade (13) by the advent of a peripheral sub-group of countries which can be referred to as intermediate economies (IE). (14) This small group of countries is involved in

Table 5.2 Estimated Shares in World Manufacturing Value Added
By Country Groupings and Illustrative Sub-Groups

Percent

	1938	1948	1953	1963		1970	1975	1980	1982	2000
Developed Market Economies of which:	61.0	72.2	72.0	64.8	77.3	73.4	67.5	65.2	64.0	58.0
Mature Market Economies[b]	41.0	58.7	55.2	44.5	46.1	39.6	35.7	33.4	N.A.	N.A.
Late Industrializing Market Economies[c]	13.8	6.5	10.4	14.0	22.9	25.8	24.2	24.3	N.A.	N.A.
Others	6.2	7.0	6.4	6.3	8.3	8.0	7.6	7.5	N.A.	N.A.
Centrally Planned Economies	34.5	22.1	23.2	28.5	14.6	17.8	22.5	23.8	25.0	21.0
Developing Countries of which:	4.5	5.7	4.8	6.6	8.1	8.8	10.0	11.0	11.0	21.0
Semi-industrialized Countries[d]	3.3	4.0	3.2	4.4	5.5	6.5	7.0	7.7	N.A.	N.A.

cont.

193

Table 5.2   Estimated Shares in World Manufacturing Value Added   Page 2 of 2
By Country Groupings and Illustrative Sub-Groups

Sources: UNIDO (1983), Industrial Strategies and Policies for Developing Countries, Vienna; UNIDO (1984), World Industrial Restructuring and Redeployment, Fourth General Conference of UNIDO, II Jan, item 5(e), Vienna; UNCTAD (1984), Review and appraisal of the basic targets of the International Development Strategy, Report by the UNCTAD Secretariat, Geneva, TD/B/AC.36/2.

Notes: Data for the years 1938 - 1963 are in current prices. There is a double column in 1963 because of a change in the basis of calculation. Figures for 1938 - 1963 were derived from data compiled according to industrial census concepts. Figures for the years 1963 - 1980 were compiled from national accounts sources for manufacturing value added expressed in US dollars at 1975 prices.

a - UNCTAD estimate.
b - Mature market economies were defined to include Belgium, France, Luxembourg, Netherlands, Norway, Sweden, United Kingdom of Great Britain and Northern Ireland and the United States of America.
c - Late industrializing market economies are the Federal Republic of Germany, Greece, Ireland, Israel, Italy, Japan, Portugal and Spain.
d - Semi-industrialized developing countries and territories include Argentina, Brazil, Colombia, Egypt, Hong Kong, India, Malaysia, Mexico, Philippines, Republic of Korea, Singapore, Thailand and Turkey.
N.A. - Not available.

a process of (peripheral) intermediation which can be defined as, "the production of goods and services in a given country, predominantly utilising inputs (15) from abroad for the principal purpose of export to other countries". This intermediation activity can be conducted by both indigenous firms and (Western) MNCs, but the latter predominate in most intermediate economies. (16) Intermediate activity can be both entrepot (e.g. Singapore acts as a distribution centre for commodities and manufactures regionally and globally; it also reroutes excess funds between regions because it is the East Asian centre for the inter-bank market) and productive (e.g. Singapore's oil refining; Hong Kong's loan syndication and fund management). Finally, it is important to recognise that while some countries are almost entirely intermediators (Singapore, Hong Kong, the Bahamas), others are only partial intermediators (Brazil, India, South Korea) and it is necessary in these cases to determine the appropriate activity and the extent of intermediation. (17)

Peripheral intermediation is most marked in manufacturing activity and partly explains the developing countries' share of world manufacturing value added (table 5.2: the share is up from 4.5 percent in 1938 or 8.1 percent in 1963 to 11.0 percent in 1982; and possibly 21.0 percent by the year 2000) and global trade (table 5.3: the 1970s saw the recovery of non-oil developing countries' trade after a long period of structural decline; manufacturing oriented Asian countries led the way by boosting their share of world trade from 5.0 percent in 1970 to 8.2 percent in 1983). Much of this intermediation has arisen as a result of activity by MNCs attracted by cheap labour, rapidly growing regional markets and other factors (see chapter three and next section). Intermediate activity generated by MNCs can take the form of exports to the source country or third countries or inputs into export-oriented industries in the host country (all three forms prevail in Singapore). (18,19) Further, the trade engendered by intermediation can be inter-industry (e.g. textiles exported by IEs in return for high technology manufactures), intra-industry (radios and black and white TVs in return for colour television) or intra-product (IE subsidiaries of MNCs or indigenous firms are involved in part of a global production process [20]). Again all three types prevail in Singapore. The net result of manufacturing peripheral

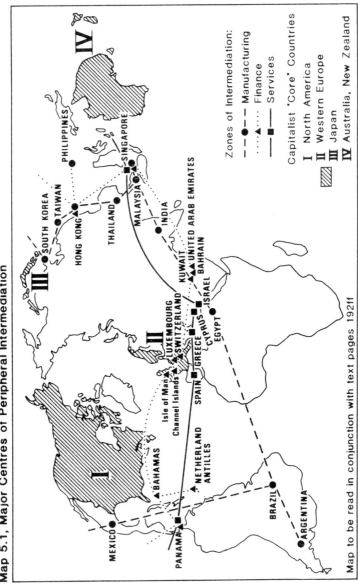

Map 5.1, Major Centres of Peripheral Intermediation

Map to be read in conjunction with text pages 192ff

Zones of Intermediation:
● ------ Manufacturing
▲ .... Finance
■ —— Services

Capitalist 'Core' Countries
I   North America
II Western Europe
III Japan
IV Australia, New Zealand

IV
III
II
I

PHILIPPINES
SINGAPORE
SOUTH KOREA
TAIWAN
HONG KONG
THAILAND
MALAYSIA
INDIA
UNITED ARAB EMIRATES
KUWAIT
BAHRAIN
ISRAEL
EGYPT
CYPRUS
GREECE
SWITZERLAND
LUXEMBOURG
Isle of Man
Channel Islands
SPAIN
BAHAMAS
NETHERLAND ANTILLES
MEXICO
PANAMA
BRAZIL
ARGENTINA

intermediation is indicated by tables 5.4, 5.5 and 5.6. Table 5.4 shows that though the network of world manufacturing trade is still dominated by industrialised countries, developing countries are increasing their share: in 1970 they accounted for 5 percent of international manufacturing exports; by 1980 this figure had risen to 10 percent and is rising. What is particularly interesting is the increase of manufacturing trade between developing countries (up from 2 to 4 percent) which is chiefly intra-IE or IE-developing countries in scope. (See figure 5.1.) Table 5.5 shows that a large share of metropole imports now come from the periphery and that the share of Asian countries and Singapore is significant. Excluding commodities, the peripheral share of imports is high in chemicals, machinery, transport equipment, clothing and basic manufactures. The high import penetration in basic manufactures and clothing indicates that technology transfer from industrialised countries to intermediate economies (whether via FDI, licensing or other channels) continues to be in the

Table 5.3 Developing Countries' Share of World Trade[a],[b], 1951-1983.

| | Percent | | | | | |
	1951	1960	1970	1975	1980	1983
Oil-Exporters	6.6	6.3	5.9	13.7	15.8	10.6
Non-Oil Exporters	27.4	20.3	16.9	15.5	17.1	19.4
(Asia)[c]	(10.2)	(6.1)	(5.0)	(5.2)	(6.5)	(8.2)
Total	34.0	26.6	22.8	29.2	32.9	30.0

Source: IMF, International Financial Statistics Yearbook, 1984, Washington.

Notes: a - excluding most East European countries.
b - developing countries share of World Exports.
c - excluding oil exporters and the Middle East.

Table 5.4   Network of World Trade in Manufacturing, 1970 - 1982

US$ billions

Exports from	Exports to			
	Industrialised Countries	Developing Countries	Socialist Countries	World
Industrialised Countries				
1970	121.3(64)a	32.8(17)	6.3(3)	161.4(85)
1982	564.1(54)	235.6(23)	36.9(4)	844.1(81)
Developing Countries				
1970	5.8(3)	3.4(2)	0.5(-)	9.5(5)
1982	63.6(6)	40.3(4)	3.6(-)	108.7(10)
Socialist Countries				
1970	2.8(1)	2.9(2)	13.4(7)	19.1(10)
1982	16.2(2)	20.3(2)	53.4(5)	90.8(9)
World				
1970	129.9(68)	39.1(21)	20.1(11)	190.0(100)
1982	643.9(62)	296.2(28)	93.9(9)	1,043.6(100)

Source: UNCTAD (1984), Protectionism and Structural Adjustment in the World Economy, Part II, TD/B/981, Geneva.

Note: a - Figues in brackets indicate the proportion of each element to total world trade. (In percent).

intermediate and low technology range. Finally,
table 5.6 illustrates that manufacturing peripheral
intermediation is concentrated in a small number of
developing countries: the top five exporters account
for 62.9 percent of the total, while the top ten
account for 82.1 percent. (Singapore is the fifth
largest exporter.) Furthermore MNCs are very active
in all countries, excepting Yugoslavia and India.
(21)

Table 5.5 Imports of the USA, Japan and the EC from
Developing Countries, 1981.

	Percent		
Selected Industries and Exporting Country/Area	Developing Country imports as a Proportion of all imports in each industry (%)		
	USA	Japan	European Community [a]
All Industries [b]			
- Developing Countries	45	62	41
- Asia	13	23	6
- Singapore	1	3	1
Food/Beverages/Tobacco			
- Developing Countries	55	30	47
- Asia	10	21	8
Chemicals			
- Developing Countries	14	26	8
- Asia	3	20	1
Machinery and Transport Equipment			
- Developing Countries	13	14	8
- Asia	11	13	5
Basic and Miscellaneous Manufactures			
- Developing Countries	32	42	25
- Asia	27	33	17
Clothing			
- Developing Countries	82	65	59
- Asia	79	65	49

cont.

Table 5.5   Imports of the USA, Japan and the EC from
             Developing Countries, 1981.   cont.

Source: Calculated from source in table 5.6.

Notes: a - Figures for the EC have been revised to
          exclude the effect of intra-EC trade.
          b - Primary and manufacturing sectors.

Table 5.6   Leading Developing Country Exporters of
             Manufactured Goods to twenty
             Industrialised Countries, 1981.

Country	Value of Exports (US$bn)	Proportion of all Developing Country Exports (%)
Korea	10.9	19.9
Hong Kong	10.2	18.6
Brazil	5.0	9.2
Mexico	5.0	9.0
Singapore	3.4	6.2
Top Five	34.5	62.9
Yugoslavia	2.5	4.6
Malaysia	2.4	4.5
Philippines	2.4	4.3
India	2.1	3.8
Thailand	1.1	2.0
Top Ten[b]	45.0	82.1
Top Twenty	50.2	91.4
Top Forty	53.5	97.4
All Others[a]	1.4	2.6
All Developing Countries	54.9	100.0

Source: UNCTAD (1983), Trade in Manufactures and
         Semi-Manufactures of developing countries:
         1980-81 Review, Geneva.

Notes: a - About 100 countries.
          b - Statistics for Taiwan are not available,
          but it would undoubtedly figure as one of
          the Top Ten if they were.

Major financial peripheral intermediation mainly dates from the early to the mid-seventies (for reasons explained in chapter four) and is also restricted to a small number of countries. Excluding the European Centres (22), the major centres are Panama, the Bahamas, the Netherland Antilles, Kuwait, Bahrain, the Philippines and especially Hong Kong and Singapore. Singapore is a major intermediary in the interbank market, Asiacurrency loans, Asiabonds, financial futures, insurance etc. It is also attempting to expand into loan syndication and fund management (23) in which it is relatively weak. For an excellent account of international financial intermediation see R.A. John's, Tax Havens and Offshore Finance. (24) Peripheral intermediation in other services (e.g. technical services, computer and data services and medical services) is a very recent phenomenon and there are few relevant statistics. Nevertheless the statistics in tables 4.2 and 4.3 indicate that peripheral intermediation in the services is very important for Singapore and, in all likelihood, for a number of other developing countries. This is confirmed by a number of recent UNCTAD reports concerning the role of services in developing countries. (25)

Peripheral intermediation is obviously related to the new international division of labour (NIDL), but only partly. The NIDL also encompasses a transfer of technology, industry and services to the periphery for purposes other than intermediation (e.g. the establishment of refineries in OPEC countries). Peripheral intermediation is a vital aspect of the emerging international economic order (EIEO) as figure 5.1 illustrates. Intermediate countries such as Singapore help maintain a world system dominated by industrialised countries: they (i) create a buffer zone between the metropole and the periphery; (ii) permit some flexibility in global industrial restructuring; (iii) offer high growth economies with profitable opportunities for MNCs and indigenous enterprise during a period of world stagnation; and (iv) enable industrialised countries to provide a facade of resource transfer to the periphery when in reality most transfers are concentrated in a few sympathetic regimes. (26) However, there is no certitude that the EIEO depicted in figure 5.1 will remain stable, especially during an era of global instability, protectionism and international debt crises. Moreover, while peripheral intermediation may offer a ray of hope to industrialised countries faced with demands for a New International Economic Order (NIEO), it may also represent the thin edge of the wedge. (27, 28)

Figure 5.1   A Diagrammatic Representation of the Emerging International Economic Order

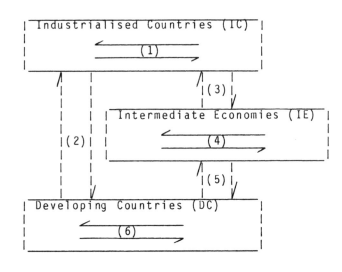

Key:
(1)   Intra-industry trade in high technology manufactures and higher value added services (including banking and finance). Constitutes the bulk of international trade.
(2)   Trade along the lines of the old international division of labour: manufactures exported by industrialised countries; commodities exported by developing countries. Financial flows from ICs to DCs include FDI (in raw materials) and "aid".
(3)   Trade along the lines of the new international division of labour (NIDL). ICs export high technology/high value added goods and services and IEs export intermediate technology/ intermediate value added goods and services. Much of the production of goods and services in IEs is undertaken by MNCs to take advantage of local opportunities (e.g. low wages, rapidly

growing markets), but some technology transfer to indigenous firms does occur. Most MNC production in IEs is exported back to ICs, including semi-finished, semi-processed and assembled goods.

(4)   Intra-IE trade in intermediate technology/ intermediate value added goods and services. MNCs prominent e.g. international banks established in Singapore to make loans to rapidly growing East Asia. However indigenous firms have larger share of intra-IE than IC-IE trade, especially in certain market niches.

(5)   Trade along the lines of the NIDL with IEs exporting intermediate technology/intermediate value added goods and services in return for low technology/low value added goods and services -and for raw materials. Indigenous IE firms are prominent, perhaps as foreign investors in DCs.

(6)   Intra-DC trade in low technology manufactures and commodities. IC MNCs prominent in certain commodities; IE MNCs prominent in some low technology industries.

SINGAPORE AS AN INTERMEDIATE ECONOMY

Intermediation is not a new phenomenon from Singapore's point of view. Since the mid-nineteenth century the island has been a centre for entrepot trade and ancillary services, linking resource-rich South East Asia with the industrialised countries; and intermediation remains the island's raison d'etre. What is new, however, is that its intermediary role has been extended extensively into a wide range of manufacturing and service industries. To be sure, some of the output of these industries is sold locally, but most is oriented towards export markets, as chapters three and four showed. Furthermore, Singapore is the only peripheral economy (29) which intermediates across the entire range of manufacturing, financial and other service activities (map 5.1) and is therefore a vital component of the emerging international economic order. (30)

The rest of this section discusses Singapore's intermediary role both geographically (within ASEAN and the Pacific Community) and industrially (petroleum, shipbuilding and electronics), but it is first worth addressing the question: why Singapore?

Mention has already been made of factors such as state support, investment climate, location, incentives etc. as spurs to Singapore's success; and GSP, US tariff items 807 and 806.30, and other (31) industrialised country regulations promoting exports by developing countries, could also be referred to; but these do not explain why Singapore is relatively more successful in attracting foreign capital and technology. This question can perhaps best be answered by comparing Singapore with Asia's three other newly industrialising countries. Table 5.7 shows that the "gang of four" have much in common. All have right wing, authoritarian regimes; few raw materials; are industrially diversified; and possess cheap, skilled, responsive work forces whose power is controlled by tight trade union legislation. Singapore's manifest advantages over the other three countries are a high level of inducements (see especially table 3.2), excellent infrastructure and a massive acreage made over to export processing zones (with all their advantages). (32) These benefits especially attract MNCs involved in manufacturing peripheral intermediation. Service MNCs are also attracted by Singapore's lack of restrictions, low taxes (especially for offshore activity) and the experience, skills and communication networks developed during its entrepot past. (33) In fact historical factors are probably the most important determinants of each country's development strategy. Hong Kong and Singapore developed as distribution centres within a world-wide British Empire whose economic pre-eminence was dependent upon free, unhindered international trade and investment: hence the reliance on MNCs and a liberal trade policy. The policies of South Korea and Taiwan, on the other hand, are undoubtedly conditioned by their background as ex-colonies of an inward-looking, protection-dependent Japanese Empire. (See table 5.7, note a.) Interestingly, as a consequence, South Korean and Taiwanese indigenous companies are larger and more powerful than those from Singapore and Hong Kong; moreover the latter are highly dependent on foreign technology. (table 5.7)

A recent comparison of Singapore and other ASEAN countries revealed that motivations such as market penetration, raw material procurement and cheap labour were the primary determinants of country choice by multinationals. (34) However for export-oriented manufactures (and services) Singapore was the preferred site: factors such as

Table 5.7   A Comparison of the Four East Asian Newly
             Industrialising Countries

Item	South Korea	Hong Kong	Singapore	Taiwan
Regime	Right Wing, Authoritarian	Right Wing, Authoritarian	Right Wing, Authoritarian	Right Wing, Authoritarian
Former Colonial Power	Japan[a] (US links)	Britain (until 1997)	Britain	Japan[a] (US links)
Raw Materials	Few	None	None	Few
Market Size	Large	Small (but China?)	Small (but ASEAN?)	Medium
Labour Situation	Cheap, skilled, "docile"	Cheap, skilled, "docile"	Cheap, skilled, "docile"	Cheap, skilled, "docile"
Restrictions	Many[b]	None	Few	Few
Inducements	Some	None	Many	Some

cont.

205

Table 5.7 A Comparison of the Four East Asian Newly Industrialising Countries

Item	South Korea	Hong Kong	Singapore	Taiwan
Infra-structure	Good	Good	Excellent	Good
EPZs[c]	277 acres	None[d]	17,300 acres[d]	168 acres
Industrial Diversific-ation	Yes	Yes	Yes	Yes
Role of MNCs	Small[e]	High	Dominant[f]	Some
Largest Local Firms[g] (US$ bn)	Hyundai (9.1)[h] Samsung (7.2)[h] Lucky (7.2)[h] Sunkyong (6.2)[h]	World Wide Shipping (1.2)[i] China Light and Power (0.7)[i]	Singapore Airlines (1.3)[i] Straits Trading Co (0.5)[i] Neptune Orient Lines (0.4)[i]	Chinese Petroleum (5.3)[h] Taiwan Power (2.7)[i] Formosa Plastics (1.7)

cont.

Table 5.7   A Comparison of the Four East Asian Newly
            Industrialising Countries

Item	South Korea	Hong Kong	Singapore	Taiwan
Techno-logical Independence	Yes	Some	Little	Yes
Role of Government	Great	Little	Great	Great

Notes: a – Both South Korea and Taiwan were greatly industrialised through Japanese foreign investments before the second world war. This probably explains the greater role of indigenous enterprises in these two countries as opposed to other NICs – all former Japanese properties were expropriated and little FDI was allowed after 1945.

b – The restrictions on FDI in South Korea were reduced somewhat in 1984.

c – "Industrial zones located outside custom barriers" offering foreign investors duty-free movement and other inducements (page 84). The acreage refers to the size of export processing zones (EPZs) in operation in the early eighties.

cont.

Table 5.7   A Comparison of the Four East Asian Newly
            Industrialising Countries

Notes: continued

d – Both Singapore and Hong Kong are free ports with a range of entrepot and
supporting activities e.g. free trade zones and offshore banking. (see pages
83–84)

e – Because of former Japanese tutelage Korea has developed industrial
groupings known as Caebol (e.g. Hyundai) which are large, powerful and
similar to Japanese industrial groups, the Zaibatsu or Keiretsu.

f – In no other country are MNCs so preponderant.

g – The largest local firms as appearing in the Fortune International
Industrial 500 or the South 500. The South Korean and Taiwanese firms are
much more powerful than their Singaporean or Hong Kong counterparts.
Hyundai, for example, is 37th in the Fortune list and as large as Toshiba, a
little smaller than ICI and larger than Rio Tinto-Zinc.

h – 1983 figure.
i – 1982 figure.

good infrastructure, skilled labour, pacific industrial relations and political stability offset the disadvantageous lack of cheap labour or raw materials (which were the benefits offered by other ASEAN countries, especially Indonesia and Malaysia).

ASEAN

As discussed in chapter two (pages 43 ff.) ASEAN was founded in 1967 as a means of diffusing political conflict among its member states (Indonesia, Malaysia, Thailand, the Philippines, Singapore; and now Brunei). Since then economic objectives have come to the fore and economic cooperation and integration are major issues for discussion on any ASEAN agenda.

Singapore plays a pivotal role in the organisation and table 5.8 shows that the island's trade with fellow ASEAN countries accounts for between 20-30 percent of its total trade. (The exact proportion depends on whether Singaporean or Malaysian/Indonesian statistics are used.) More significantly, it is possible to calculate from table 5.9 that Singapore accounts for 85 percent of intra-ASEAN trade, 21 percent of ASEANs trade with the Pacific rim countries and 36 percent of ASEANs exports world-wide. Thus, though all ASEAN states have considerable trade with other countries, Singapore's share of trade is totally out of proportion to its size; and its intermediary role is clear. Table 5.12 shows that the main ASEAN exports to Singapore are petroleum and rubber; and the main imports from Singapore are chemicals, petroleum products, industrial machinery, electrical/ electronic machinery and transport equipment. Most petroleum products and rubber products (largely manufactured using ASEAN raw materials) are exported to the USA, Japan and the "rest of the world" (e.g. Hong Kong for petroleum products); and entrepot trade involving ASEAN is also high. (Entrepot trade in table 5.12 appears as "change in in-transit goods" in part B.) In specific services Singapore is also a pivot (e.g. in the 1970s Singapore-based banks and MNCs supplied 45 percent of the loans to related companies in Thailand; and these received 51 percent of Thai financial outflows [35]); and MNCs operating in ASEAN tend to establish their headquarters in Singapore and co-ordinate their South East Asian activities from there. Much "Singaporean" investment in ASEAN in fact results

from the South East Asian operations of
multinational subsidiaries based in Singapore. (36)
However, though ASEAN is dependent on Singapore, the
reverse also applies. In 1983, for example,
Singapore's trade with its ASEAN partners was 26
percent of its total trade and 50 percent of its
trade with developing countries. (37) The PAP must
therefore tread very carefully in its relations with
ASEAN if it is not to jeopardise its attractiveness
to foreign investors involved in Singapore's
intermediation between ASEAN and the rest of the
world.

A variety of schemes have been adopted over the
last decade aimed at increasing ASEAN co-operation.
The most important are listed below:

ASEAN Industrial Projects (AIP). This scheme aims
to promote large-scale industrial plants in ASEAN by
dividing projects between member countries, thereby
avoiding duplication and taking advantage of
economies of scale. This scheme has so far only
started two sets of projects and has been hindered
by political difficulties and the question of how to
trade-off efficiency and equity. (38) The first
scheme, approved in 1976, divided five projects
thus: urea (two projects, Indonesia and Malaysia),
diesel engines (Singapore), super-phosphate (the
Philippines) and soda-ash (Thailand).

ASEAN Industrial Complementation (AIC). Established
in 1980 this scheme is intended to promote
complementarity among existing ASEAN industries by
offering incentives to private companies:
application is through the various Chambers of
Commerce, but companies from at least four countries
must participate. Few AIC proposals have however
been approved to date because approval depends on
periodic meetings of Ministers. (39) The first AIC
project began at the end of 1980 after a delay
because the companies concerned wanted exclusive
production rights, thus forestalling competition;
ironically it was the various states which resisted
this demand. The project involves the manufacture
of motor parts and is largely MNC dominated: Elgi
Mark a (Japanese joint venture), Ambali Engineering
(UK joint venture) and Malaysia Roller Chains
(Honda/ Nippon Cable) are involved in Malaysia;
Bosma Indra (state owned enterprise) is involved in
Indonesia; Ensite (Ford) is involved in the
Philippines; Repco (an Australian company) is
involved in Singapore; and Toyota Auto Body, Isuzu

Table 5.8   Singapore's Major Trading Partners, 1983

Territory or Country	Share of Each Country or Territory			
	Exports[a]		Imports	
USA	18.3		15.2	
Japan	9.2		18.1	
European Community	9.2		10.3	
– Germany		2.3		2.7
– UK		2.3		2.8
Australia	2.8		1.8	
Other Industrialised Countries	2.7		2.3	
ASEAN	25.0[b]	32.7[b]	16.0[b]	25.5[b]
– Indonesia		16.1[b]		11.1[b]
– Malaysia		9.2[b]		11.5[b]
– Thailand		4.3		1.8
– Philippines		2.0		0.5
– Brunei		1.1		0.6
Hong Kong	6.9		2.1	
South Korea	2.3		1.5	
India	2.0		1.2	
China, P.R.	0.9		2.9	
OPEC[c]	6.0		19.5	
Other Developing Countries	12.4		6.1	
Comecon	1.1		0.4	
Total – Percent	98.8[d]		97.2[d]	
– Amount (US$ bn)	21.8		28.2	

Source: IMF, Direction of Trade Statistics Yearbook, 1984, Washington.

Notes: a – Exports from Singapore.
b – Singapore statistics do not separate Indonesia and Malaysia. When Indonesian and Malaysian sources are used their statistics do not accord with those of Singapore. Singapore claims to export $3.8 billion to Indonesia/Malaysia and import $4.1 billion. Indonesian and Malaysia statistics record $5.5 billion worth of exports to Indonesia/Malaysia and $6.4

Table 5.8 Singapore's Major Trading Partners, 1983

Notes: continued.

> billion imports. These are considerable
> differences - only partly explained by the
> complications of Singapore's entrepot trade
> (cf. the row over trade with Vietnam as
> recorded in chapter two) - and this
> explains the difference between the two
> estimates given for ASEAN's share of
> Singapore's exports (25 percent and 32.7
> percent) and imports (16.0 percent and 25.5
> percent). Indonesia and Malaysia's share
> (as shown in this table) is derived from
> the statistics of these two countries.
> c - Excluding Indonesia.
> d - The shares of all countries do not sum
> to 100 percent because of incomplete
> statistics.

Auto Body, Siam Motors (Nissan) and Thai Rung Union
(indigenous private company) are involved in
Thailand. (40) This project has been called into
question recently by Odaka. (41)

ASEAN Industrial Joint Ventures (AIJV). This
scheme, still being finalised in 1984, is intended
to create industrial co-operation between investors
from at least two ASEAN countries. Non-ASEAN
participation of up to 49 percent will however be
allowed. (42)

ASEAN Preferential Trading Arrangements (PTA). This
scheme was established in 1977 and went some way
towards liberalising trade between ASEAN countries.
However tariff and non-tariff barriers were not
completely removed and there appear to have been few
positive effects on intra-ASEAN trade. (43)

In addition to the above there are many arrangements
or schemes in operation, or under consideration, in
areas such as investment promotion and co-operation
in banking and services. Interestingly Japan has
played a major role in promoting ASEAN co-operation;
Japan is, after all, the largest foreign investor
(44) in ASEAN and depends heavily on the grouping
for raw materials, markets and cheap labour exports.
A number of Japan-ASEAN schemes are in operation
including: (i) The ASEAN Promotion Centre on Trade,

Investment and Tourism (since 1981 in Tokyo: Japan contributes 90 percent of the budget); (ii) a preferential tariff system for ASEAN exports to Japan; and (iii) Japan-ASEAN Human Resources Development Projects in which a number of centres have been established: vocational/service training (Indonesia), advanced skill training (Malaysia), productivity development (Singapore), human resources development (the Philippines), primary health care (Thailand) and productivity research and training (Okinawa). The Japan Economic Research Institute recently promoted the idea that intra-Asian trade (including Japan-Asian and intra-ASEAN trade) should be expanded through a division of labour in particular industries and technologies. This semi-official body (supported by the four major business organisations) is normally heeded by the Japanese government and the business community and this suggests that new proposals are in the offing. (45)

Though co-operation between the ASEAN countries is on the increase, moves towards greater integration continue to flounder on a tide of rivalries and mutual mistrust (46); and it is interesting that many of the pressures towards integration emanate from external sources, such as Japan. The PAP must be painfully aware that these external pressures work in Singapore's favour: the intra-ASEAN division of labour created by foreign investors (47) maintains the city-state as the advanced nexus of a relatively under-developed region. A recent analysis of ASEANs trade with the European Community by Schmitt-Rink (48) illustrates this point well. The relevant conclusions are these: (i) Singapore's share of all ASEAN-EC trade is 23 percent; (ii) intra-industry trade (essentially in manufactures i.e. along the NIDL) accounts for one sixth of ASEAN-EC trade; (iii) Singapore's share of intra-industry trade is 55 percent; and (iv) "Without Singapore the commodity composition of ASEAN's trade with the EC would be similar to that of LDC. (sic) In other words: Thailand's, Indonesia's, Malaysia's and the Philippines' trade with the EC still follows the colonial and post-colonial pattern of international specialisation, namely exchange of raw materials for manufactured products." (The old division of labour.) (49) The benefits of peripheral intermediation in such a context obviously create strains between a highly industrialised/developed Singapore and its ASEAN co-members; and the government needs to tread warily in its foreign relations.

The Pacific Community

The countries of the Pacific region range from a multitude of tiny island states (many still colonies) in the Pacific basin to the power-houses of the Pacific rim. The USA, Canada, Mexico, Colombia, Peru, Ecuador and Chile are the largest countries on the Pacific's eastern rim; while the western rim consists of Japan, South Korea, Taiwan, Hong Kong, the ASEAN countries, Australia and New Zealand - as well as four socialist countries, the USSR, China, North Korea and Vietnam. (Map 2.1) Characterised by cultural diversity, economic disparity and major political rifts, these countries are united solely by their shared geography - and economic dynamism. (50) In 1984, as the figures below suggest, the major Pacific countries grew more rapidly than countries in other regions. (51)

	Growth rate of GDP, 1984 (%)
USA	6.7
Japan	5.5
Canada	4.7
(Industrialised Countries' average)	4.7
Singapore	8.9
South Korea	7.9
Taiwan	10.3
Hong Kong	8.1
China	7.9
Malaysia	6.7
Thailand	6.2
Indonesia	4.4
Philippines	-4.8
(Developing Countries' average)	3.2

Table 5.9 shows that international commodity trade is the main integrating force in the Pacific region. The majority of exports from each country (or country group) go to another country on the Pacific rim; and total intra-pacific exports ($459.9 bn in 1983) amount to about 30 percent of world exports. (52) The USA and Japan are the twin loci of this activity with 24 percent and 20 percent of Pacific exports respectively. Their mutual exports alone amount to 14 percent of Pacific exports; but, significantly, Japan has a balance of trade surplus ($26.8 bn), while the USA has a deficit

(-$53.4 bn). (53) ASEAN is the third largest trading bloc on the Pacific rim with the export of oil and raw materials (from Indonesia, Malaysia and Brunei) being most important. Singapore, an exporter of manufactured goods, also has a significant 3.4 percent share of intra-Pacific exports (thrice its share of world exports), of which two thirds go to non-ASEAN countries. Though the Singapore authorities seek to maintain diversified export markets (like the USA, the city-state's exports are only 55 percent intra-Pacific), potential trade opportunities arising from increased intra-Pacific collaboration are not likely to be spurned. (54)

The concept of Pacific economic and political co-operation - indeed, of a Pacific Community - can be traced back to 1960 when the Japanese politician Morinosuke Kajima suggested the creation of a Pan-Pacific organisation. (55) Kajima's concept was nebulous and received little attention, but the efforts of Saburo Okita and Kiyoshi Kojima (both leading economists) were more fruitful. The establishment of the Japan Economic Research Centre (JERC) in 1962 provided a powerful forum (56) for promoting the Pacific Community concept: JERCs first report in 1963 (written under Okita's auspices) was entitled, "Economic Co-operation in the Pacific Area" and led to the establishment of the Pacific Basin Economic Council. In 1965 Kojima used a JERC international conference to air his proposal for a Pacific Free Trade Area (PAFTA) which paved the way to the more general Pacific Trade and Development Conferences (PAFTAD). The first PAFTAD conference took place in 1968 and there had been fourteen by 1984. Participants are drawn from a wide range of countries (the USA, Japan, Australia, Mexico, Chile, South Korea, ASEAN etc.) and topics discussed are mainly economic in orientation; for example, free trade zones, foreign direct investment, technology transfer, trade and employment and mineral resources. PAFTAD is only one of an expanding set of fora established since 1968 (57) and three professional groups have been most active in promoting the idea: academics, politicians and businessmen (the last through, for example, the 400 member Pacific Basin Economic Council). (58) Though the level of intra-Pacific interaction and interdependence is increasing as the result of a variety of economic forces (chiefly MNCs, FDI, international loans and international trade in goods and services), many countries remain wary of the Pacific Community concept. The main reason for this

215

Table 5.9   The Pacific Rim Trade[a] Matrix, 1983

US$mn

EXPORTS FROM	EXPORTS TO							
	USA	Japan	ASEAN	(Singapore)	Hong Kong[b] and South Korea	South America	Canada Australia New Zealand	PRC[c]	Total
USA	-	21.9	9.9	3.8	8.5	22.9	42.8	2.2	112.0 (56)[d]
Japan	43.3	-	15.1	4.4	11.3	5.5	8.8	4.9	93.3 (63)
ASEAN	13.1	18.7	15.3	7.1	4.4	1.7	2.1	0.6	63.0 (81)
(Sing-apore)	4.0	2.0	5.9	-	2.0	0.5	1.0	0.2	15.6 (55)
Hong Kong & South Korea	15.1	4.4	4.6	1.4	1.1	0.7	2.2	2.6	32.1 (67)

cont.

Table 5.9   The Pacific Rim Trade^a Matrix, 1983

US$mn

EXPORTS FROM	EXPORTS TO							
	USA	Japan	ASEAN (Singapore)	Hong Kong^b and South Korea	South America	Canada Australia New Zealand	PRCC	Total
South America	31.6	4.6	0.6	0.1	0.8	9.9	1.7	1.2	50.5 (61)
Canada/ Australia/ N. Zealand	56.6	10.4	2.8	0.8	1.8	2.0	2.7	1.7	78.8 (89)
PRC^c	1.7	4.5	1.2	0.6	5.8	0.4	0.4	–	14.6 (66)
Total	165.4	66.5	55.4	18.2	35.7	43.6	61.7	13.4	459.9e (66)

Source: IMF, Direction of Trade Yearbook, 1984, Washington.
Notes: a – Excluding the USSR, North Korea, Vietnam, other Indo-Chinese countries
         and many Pacific islands. South America also includes a few countries not
         in the Pacific, notably Brazil. b – Figures for Taiwan, the fourth East
         Asian NIC are not available. c – Peoples' Republic of China. d – Figures
         in brackets denote each country/region's exports to the Pacific Rim region
         as a proportion of that country/region's total exports. e – Double-counting
         Singapore.

wariness is the central role that Japan would play, whatever the membership of any prospective Pacific grouping. Japan is the economic super-power of the Pacific (the USA also has an Atlantic orientation) and most countries are relatively dependent on its trade and investment. Trade-wise imports from Japan are seldom less than 15 percent of any country's regional imports (China, 37 percent, Singapore 39 percent), but few countries' exports account for more than 7-8 percent of Japan's imports (China, 7 percent, Singapore 3 percent). (Table 5.9) Japan's FDI is concentrated in the Pacific region, as table 5.10 shows, and though the absolute total is smaller than the USA's Pacific FDI, it is more concentrated in ASEAN and the Asian NICs. In addition Japan is the source of large-scale aid and other financial flows to a great number of Pacific countries. Many East Asians in fact see the Pacific Community concept as simply a post-war version of Japan's pre-war "Greater East Asian Co-Prosperity Sphere" and Oborne and Fourt sum up these fears well:

> When notions of a shared destiny among the nations of the rim have been promoted in the past as a means of securing greater economic benefits for the area, they have been perceived by many of the non-industrial nations of the Pacific as basically political structures, and not economic ones created for the mutual benefit of the nations in the region. The history of failures of regional co-operation efforts in the area has left markedly sceptical attitudes on the part of South East Asian nations in particular. Moreover, some critics even see plans to integrate the Pacific area as an effort to generate strategic and political structures rather than purely economic ones. (60)

ASEAN's general position towards a Pacific Community is lukewarm and its position was made clear in a conference held in Bangkok on Pan-Pacific Co-operation: (i) ASEAN must not be weakened nor its existence and prosperity jeopardised; (ii) ASEAN must perceive clear benefits from regional co-operation which in totality far exceed the costs; (iii) the concept must not be perceived as a western, neo-colonial proposal devised for western neo-colonial purposes; (iv) the concept must not compromise the non-aligned status of the ASEAN

218

Table 5.10   Foreign Direct Investment[a] by Japan,
             the USA and the Asian NICs[b] :
             Breakdown by Destination, 1982.

Destination	Percent		
	Source Country/ies		
	Japan	USA	Asian NICs[c]
Pacific Region	70.6	40.4	91
Of Which:			
- USA	26.3	-	-
- Japan	-	3.1	-
- Canada	2.4	20.1	-
- Australia	5.4	3.9	-
- New Zealand	0.4	0.3	-
- ASEAN (excluding Singapore)	17.7	2.4	56
- Indonesia	13.7	1.1	-
- Singapore	2.6	0.8	-
- South Korea	2.5	0.4	-
- Taiwan	0.9	0.3	-
- Hong Kong	3.4	1.4	-
- Asian NICs	9.4	2.9	15
- South America[d]	8.2	7.6	8
- Others	0.8	0.1	-
Europe	11.6	45.1	3
Rest of World	17.8	14.5	6
Total Amount (US$ bn)	53.1	221.3	2.2

Source: US Dept. of Commerce; Japanese Ministry of
          Finance; United Nations Centre for
          Transnational Corporations.

Notes: a - Stock of FDI at yearend.
          b - Singapore, South Korea, Hong Kong and
          Taiwan.
          c - 1980 figures.
          d - Only countries on the Pacific Coast.

states nor enmesh them in political entanglements
which they seek to avoid; and (v) it is important
for the ASEAN states to feel that they are not being
rushed into anything.   (61)   Quite evidently the

ASEAN countries do not wish to become enmeshed in an unnecessary arrangement which would simply institutionalise the existing international economic order. Within ASEAN, Thailand is most favourably disposed towards Pacific co-operation, Indonesia is sceptical and Singapore's position is ambiguous. From the PAPs viewpoint the following are among the benefits and costs which need to be assessed: (i) increased trade and investment (including foreign investment by Singaporean companies - see table 5.9 for example and the concentration of FDI by Asian NICs) against greater dependence on external sources; (ii) the benefits of increased peripheral intermediation against the disruption of peripheral intermediation in Singapore by other countries (e.g. in a more stable environment Indonesia may be able to increase domestic processing of raw materials; or international banks may prefer a stable Hong Kong over Singapore); (iii) the political benefits resulting from the island's role as an anti-Communist regional bulkwark against costly involvement in great power rivalry; and (iv) a boost for Singapore's Japanisation programme against the possible turmoil arising from Japanese domination (bear in mind the atrocities committed against the Chinese by Japanese forces in East and South East Asia during the 1930s and 1940s.)

In July 1984 Indonesian Foreign Minister Mochtar Kasumaatmadja proposed a very loose level of Pacific co-operation which was accepted by ASEAN and representatives of the USA, Canada, Japan, Australia and New Zealand. In effect:

> The 11 countries agreed that while there should be no form of Pacific club, with a membership, there should be a loose gathering of the countries concerned on a regular basis to discuss economic trends in the most economically vibrant area in the world. To cement this relationship, it was agreed at Mochtar's suggestion that one project - a plan to develop human resources, by integrating training in such fields as food processing and agricultural development - should start the ball rolling. (62)

However, the pressures for more formalised political and economic arrangements will persist and this is likely to increase discord within ASEAN. In particular, an institutionalisation of the emerging international economic order (within the Pacific region) is generally to the benefit of intermediate economies such as Singapore, but unwelcome from the viewpoint of developing countries such as Indonesia and Malaysia.

Intermediation in Selected Industries

This section deals only with intermediation in manufacturing industries: intermediation in finance and the services was dealt with in chapter four. The structure of Singapore's international trade is largely the result of its role as an intermediate economy. Thus, compared to selected NICs, developing countries and industrialised countries raw materials are a very low proportion of its imports (table 5.11, part A). This is chiefly because in the existing division of labour Singapore is used by MNCs to (further) process industrial supplies, fuels and machine parts. Accordingly the bulk of its imports consist of these items and capital equipment. Its entrepot activity shows up in table 5.11 also and, like Hong Kong, consumer goods are a larger share of its imports than other NICs or developing countries. Export-wise (table 5.11, part B) Singapore differs from other NICs by not exporting a great deal of textiles: instead the bulk of its exports are chemicals (including petrochemicals) and machinery (both areas in which MNCs dominate). As an intermediate economy it also differs from Malaysia and India whose exports are dominated by primary products and which broadly still trade on the basis of the old division of labour. In some ways Singapore's export structure resembles that of the UK.

Table 5.12 illustrates Singapore's intermediation in a number of ways. In petrochemicals, for example, value added is a mere 12 percent: crude petroleum is imported from the Middle East, Malaysia and Indonesia, processed and then exported to countries such as Indonesia, Hong Kong, Australia, Japan and Malaysia (table 5.13). Significantly Singapore only uses 13 percent of the output of its petroleum products industry and most exports are destined for intermediate use elsewhere. In industrial, electrical and electronic machinery the value added is rather higher, but otherwise the process is the same. Parts are imported into Singapore (from the USA, Japan or Europe) or produced locally (by MNCs); processed/utilised; and the final output is largely exported overseas (most

Table 5.11   Trade Structure of Singapore and Selected Countries, 1982   Page 1 of 2

Part A : Imports

Country	Percent				
	Economic Category				
	Food and Beverages	Raw Materials	Processed Industrial Supplies	Fuels	Capital Equipment
Singapore	6.0	3.8	19.8	33.6	13.2
Hong Kong	12.0	6.7	33.2	8.0	9.8
South Korea	9.7	13.5	21.9	29.7	12.2
Malaysia	11.0	4.6	23.8	17.1	15.7
India	8.8	6.8	24.7	44.6	7.2
USA	7.4	3.0	17.4	26.5	9.1
UK	11.8	6.3	24.6	12.9	13.0
Japan	10.5	13.9	13.5	50.2	3.8

Table 5.11 Trade Structure of Singapore and Selected Countries, 1982 Page 2 of 2

Part A : Imports

Country	Economic Category Percent			
	Machine Parts	Transport Equipment	Consumer Goods	Total[a]
Singapore	7.3	6.7	8.7	100
Hong Kong	5.2	4.5	20.2	100
South Korea	3.8	7.1	1.8	100
Malaysia	10.4	10.6	6.2	100
India	2.3	4.4	1.1	100
USA	3.5	16.1	14.7	100
UK	3.5	12.2	13.8	100
Japan	1.3	1.6	4.5	100

Source: United Nations (1984), Yearbook of International Trade Statistics, 1982, New York.
Note: a - Includes other goods.

Table 5.11   Trade Structure of Singapore and Selected Countries, 1982   Page 1 of 2

Part B : Exports

Country	Primary Industry[a]	Percent			
		Industrial Breakdown			
				Manufacturing	
		Food	Textiles	Wood and Paper	Chemicals
Singapore	9.4[b]	4.4	4.0	2.6	36.8[c]
Hong Kong	1.0	1.1	43.2	1.5	3.2
South Korea	5.6	2.2	36.1	3.1	7.5
Malaysia	51.5	14.8	2.8	6.1	2.5
India	40.1	7.8	29.5	0.5	5.2
USA	18.8	5.3	2.2	3.5	14.4
UK	20.9	5.6	4.5	2.1	17.3
Japan	0.5	0.9	4.4	0.9	7.5

Table 5.11   Trade Structure of Singapore and Selected Countries, 1982   Page 2 of 2

Part B : Exports

| Country | Percent Industrial Breakdown | | | | |
	Mineral Products	Basic Metal	Manufacturing Machinery	Other	Total
Singapore	0.7	3.3	29.5^d	9.4	100
Hong Kong	0.3	0.3	32.4	17.0	100
South Korea	2.7	9.2	30.3	3.2	100
Malaysia	0.2	8.2	13.2	0.8	100
India	0.7	1.4	12.1	2.7	100
USA	0.8	2.3	50.5	2.3	100
UK	1.2	4.8	40.3	3.5	100
Japan	1.4	12.2	69.6	2.7	100

Source: As table 5.11, Part A.
Notes: a – Agriculture and mining. b – Mainly live animals. c – Mainly petroleum products. d – The whole range of machinery, but especially: general industrial machinery, machines for specialised industries, telecommunication and sound equipment, ships and aircraft, and parts for electrical/electronic machinery.

demand in Singapore is, in fact, intermediate). A similar analysis applies to most other industries and table 5.12 is worth studying further. It also shows the importance of entrepot trade ("change in in-transit goods") and indicates that MNCs are encouraged to produce locally because of low import duties.

Table 5.13 indicates (i) that some Singaporean industries and products are significant in world trade; and (ii) that most of Singapore's trade is intra-industry, intra-product, i.e. along the lines of the NIDL. As mentioned before, intermediation is most important in petroleum products, machinery and some marine industries. The origin and destination of imports and exports depends on the product in question. Thus, in the case of petroleum products, imports come mainly from the Middle East and South East Asia and exports are directed to East Asia and Australia; with ships and boats imports derive from industrialised economies and exports go to developing countries; and with televisions imports originate in Japan and Germany (which have a comparative advantage) and locally produced televisions are exported to a great number of countries. Trade in radios and transistors is interesting. The former are at the end of their product life-cycle and therefore most imports are from other NICs and exports are destined for industrialised countries in Europe and North America. The latter shows a division of labour in East Asian countries: Singapore imports certain transistors/valves from nearby countries and exports yet others to these countries - it is not possible, however, to indicate the basis of this specialisation. The rest of this section analyses three key industries in Singapore.

Petroleum Products. This industry accounts for 40 percent of current FDI in manufacturing, one-sixth of the sector's value added and over 30 percent of exports. (Chapter three; table 5.11.) As table 5.14 shows, the industry is almost entirely controlled by foreign concerns. Shell first established an oil bunkering and distribution service in Singapore in 1892 and was naturally the first company to establish a refinery in 1961. The main reason for establishment was the central position of Singapore in South East Asia and the country's strategic location between the Middle East and the growing Japanese economy; soon other oil MNCs followed suit. The proximity of Vietnam during

Table 5.12   International Input-Output Structure of Key Industries
in Singapore, 1975.

Part A : Inputs

Percent

Inputs From:	Textiles	Chemicals	Petroleum Products	Rubber Products	Industrial Machinery
USA	2	5 (5)	-	-	8 (9)
JAPAN	3	8 (M)	-	-	8
ASEAN	3	4	16 (I:16)	48 (I,M)	4
SINGAPORE	40 (9,14)	41 (5,14)	3 (14,15)	34 (7,14)	29 (14)
REST OF THE WORLD	3 (9)	21 (5)	69 (A:16)	-	14
VALUE ADDED (S'pore)	38	19	12	17	36
FREIGHT/INSURANCE	1	2	0	1	1
DUTIES	0	0	0	0	0
TOTAL - PERCENT	100	100	100	100	100
- AMOUNT (US$ mn)	546	356	2,018	325	279

cont.

Table 5.12   International Input-Output Structure of Key Industries in Singapore, 1975.

Part A : Inputs

Inputs From:	Percent				
	Electrical Machinery	Transport Equipment	Construction	Trade and Transport	Services
USA	10 (10)	5 (17)	5	1	1
JAPAN	7 (10)	18 (17)	9 (17)	1	1
ASEAN	-	1 (K)	1	2	1
SINGAPORE	37 (10,14)	22 (14,17)	43 (14,9, 8,3)	35 (15)	29 (15)
REST OF THE WORLD	11 (14)	8 (17)	8	9 (6)	7
VALUE ADDED (S'pore)	31	44	33	51	60
FREIGHT/INSURANCE	1	2	1	1	0
DUTIES	3	0	0	0	0
TOTAL - PERCENT	100	100	100	100	100
- AMOUNT (US$ mn)	930	540	848	2,300	2,129

cont.

Table 5.12   International Input-Output Structure of Key Industries
in Singapore, 1975.

Part A : Inputs

Source: Calculated from the Institute of Developing Economies, International Input-
Output Table for ASEAN Countries, 1975, Tokyo.

Notes: (i) Electrical Machinery includes Electronic Instruments. (ii) ASEAN
includes South Korea. (iii) Numbers in brackets refer to the most important
input industry(ies). Thus, for example, 18 percent of inputs into
Singapore's transport equipment industry come from Japan; most of these
imports are metal parts (i.e. industry coded 17). Key to code: 3 – Lumber
products; 5 – Chemicals; 6 – Petroleum Products; 7 – Rubber; 8 – Mineral
Products; 9 – Industrial Machinery; 10 – Electrical/Electronic Machinery; 14
– Trade and Transport; 15 – Services; 16 – Crude Petroleum; 17 – Metal
Parts. (iv) Letters in brackets refer to the country(ies) in ASEAN or the
rest of the world which provide an important input. Thus, for Petroleum
Products both Indonesia (I) and the Middle East (A) are important sources of
inputs. For Rubber Products, Indonesia (I) and Malaysia (M) are most
important. K – South Korea (v) – = negligible.

Table 5.12 International Input-Output Structure of Key Industries in Singapore, 1975.

Part B : Outputs

Outputs To:	Textiles	Chemicals	Petroleum Products	Rubber Products	Industrial Machinery
Intermediate Demand					
USA	2	-	3	7	9[a]
JAPAN	-	9	13	1	3
ASEAN	1	12[c]	12[d]	1	6[e]
SINGAPORE	18	42	6	64	4
Final Demand					
USA	3	-	1	2	3
JAPAN	-	-	3	-	3
ASEAN	1	-	5	-	11[e]
SINGAPORE	54	5	7	2	36
Demand from Rest of the World	15	18	50	5	21
Change in In-Transit Goods[h]	5	14	3	18	2
Total - Percent	100	100	100	100	100
- Amount (US$ mn)	546	356	2,018	325	279

cont.

Table 5.12   International Input-Output Structure of Key Industries in Singapore, 1975.

Part B : Outputs

Outputs To:	Electrical Machinery	Transport Equipment	Construction	Trade and Transport	Services
Intermediate Demand					
USA	12b	-	-	-	-
JAPAN	-	-	-	2	1
ASEAN	2	2	-	3	1
SINGAPORE	31	20	9	48	40
Final Demand					
USA	16	-	-	2	-
JAPAN	-	-	-	-	-
ASEAN	3f	69	-	-	1
SINGAPORE	19	52	85	30	34
Demand from Rest of the World	14	8	-	-	-
Change in In-Transit Goodsh	3	10	6	13	23
Total - Percent	100	100	100	100	100
- Amount (US$ mn)	930	540	848	2,300	2,129

cont.

231

Table 5.12   International Input-Output Structure of Key Industries   Page 3 of 3
              in Singapore, 1975.

Part B : Outputs

Source: As table 5.12, Part A.

Notes: See table 5.12, Part A. Also: a,b – Semi-processed parts for further
         processing in the USA. c – Indonesia, the Philippines and Malaysia. d –
         Especially Indonesia and Malaysia. e – Especially Indonesia. f –
         Especially Malaysia. g – Especially Thailand. h – Presumably increase in
         value due to entrepot trade.

Table 5.13   Trade in Key Manufacturing Industries and Products, 1982

	Industry or Product			
	Petroleum Products		Televisions	Radios
	Refined	Residual		
Imports as a Proportion of World Trade (%)	2.2	2.5	2.2	2.6
Main Source Countries of Imports into Singapore	Bahrain Other Middle East USA Indonesia	Bahrain Other Middle East Indonesia	Japan Germany	Japan Hong Kong Korea Malaysia
Exports as a Proportion of World Trade (%)	7.0	22.0	6.2	8.7
Main Destination Countries of Singapore Exports	Indonesia Hong Kong Malaysia Japan Australia	Japan Indonesia Australia Netherlands	France UK USA Netherlands Hong Kong Australia	USA France Germany UK Netherlands Italy

cont.

233

Table 5.13   Trade in Key Manufacturing Industries and Products, 1982   Page 2 of 2

	Industry or Product		
	Industrial Machinery	Transistors	Ships and Boats
Imports as a Proportion of World Trade (%)	1.4	8.6	6.5
Main Source Countries of Imports into Singapore	Japan Germany USA UK Netherlands	USA Japan Malaysia Hong Kong Germany Philippines	Japan Norway Germany Sweden UK USA
Exports as a Proportion of World Trade (%)	2.6	7.4	2.3
Main Destination Countries of Singapore Exports	USA Germany France Italy Australia	USA Malaysia Germany Hong Kong UK Italy	Indonesia Saudi Arabia Australia Liberia

Source: United Nations, Yearbook of International Trade Statistics, 1982, New York.

a period of heavy US involvement also played a role in the industry's expansion. Singapore is now the world's third largest refining centre after Houston and Rotterdam with 1.3 percent of world refining capacity. As demand for some petrol products began to drop in the 1970s, many companies diversified into the production of specialised fuels, oils, lubricants and basic petrochemicals, such as ethylene, butadiene and benzene. With intense over capacity in the petrochemicals industry world wide exports of these products have also begun to falter; and Singapore based companies are presently upgrading their activities to manufacture thermoplastics, synthetic fibres and synthetic rubbers. (See table 5.14, note a, for the diversified activities of the Singapore Petrochemical Complex.) Further competition is likely to be generated by the Indonesian, Malaysian, Thai and Philippine petrochemical complexes planned for the near future. (63)

Petrochemicals is therefore an intermediate industry with problems, but these are not insoluble. First, diversification can proceed much further and Exxon (for example) has invested in petrochemical chemical additives through its subsidiary Exxon Chemical Singapore (Pte) Ltd. Secondly, the burgeoning offshore oil and gas industry of East and South East Asia continues to provide opportunities for Singapore's petroleum related industries. The island can provide: (i) storage and distribution facilities (hence the recent inauguration of the Dutch/Singaporean Van Ommeren storage terminal in 1983); (ii) support services and oil rig construction (see table 4.18 and related text); and (iii) integrated petroleum related facilities (thus the establishment of the Jurong Marine Base). Finally, considerable Arab, Chinese and international finance is available for projects such as the International Petroleum Centre. (64)

Petroleum products and related industries are a good example of peripheral intermediation and Singapore's chief benefits derive from the employment generated, employee remuneration and some linkages established with other industries e.g. shipbuilding and repair. There are, however, large costs associated with maintaining this capital intensive, infrastructurally expensive and volatile industry. Furthermore, foreign domination is likely to continue and there has been little technology transfer to indigenous firms - though Chong has shown that there has been the transfer of managerial knowhow and other skills through Esso Singapore. (65)

Electrical and Electronic Products. These two related industries are vital to Singapore and have played a major role in the country's vigorous diversification into more advanced technologies. Their share of the manufacturing sector is large and in 1982 they accounted for 24 percent of output (of which electronic products constitute 17 percent), 20 percent of value added (16 percent), 27 percent of employment (22 percent) and 24 percent of direct exports (21 percent). (66) The two industries are foreign dominated in terms of paid-up-capital (page 104) and the number and size of firms (table 5.15). Both industries were insignificant until the 1970s when US MNCs led a wave of foreign companies intent on establishing manufacturing operations in Singapore. The two earliest firms of note were in fact indigenous and were set up in 1965 (Setron) and 1966 (Roxy) to manufacture monochrome televisions. In 1969 Philips (of the Netherlands) and a number of US companies established labour-intensive, export-oriented plants in Singapore to assemble semiconductor components. Since then the number of establishments (table 5.15), employment and output (table 3.8) has leapt enormously.

The structure of production has also changed with shifts in Singapore's comparative advantage (which itself altered as a consequence of the government's high-wage policy) and table 5.15 shows that assembly of components is less important than the production of components, intermediate parts and final consumer goods. In the electronics industry, for example, the number of establishments has increased from 35 in 1970 to 195 in 1982, while output has soared from under $0.1 billion to $2.1 billion over the same period. Consumer electronics (such as televisions, radios, amplifiers, calculators and tape recorders) account for 40 percent of the 1982 output with electronic components (semiconductor devices, capacitors, cathode tubes etc.) making up a further 55 percent. The remaining 5 percent consists of industrial electronic equipment, including computers, peripheral equipment and telephones. There is a constant upgrading of technology with a move into, for example, the production of computers, robots and VLSI; and the introduction of computer aided design and manufacturing (CAD/CAM). (67)

Table 5.14   Companies Producing Petroleum Products
             in Singapore.

Company	Main Source(s) of Capital	Number of Workers (range)
1. BP Refinery Singapore (Pte) Ltd	UK	100 - 149
2. Caltex (Asia) Ltd	USA	50 - 99
3. Castrol (F.E.) Pte Ltd	UK	100 - 149
4. Esso Singapore (Pte) Ltd	USA	500 - 999
5. Highway International (Pte) Ltd	Singapore	50 - 99
6. MBP Singapore (Pte) Ltd	Malaysia	10 - 49
7. Mobil Oil Singapore (Pte) Ltd	USA	200 - 299
8. Resource Development Corp. (Pte) Ltd	Singapore	10 - 49
9. Shell Eastern Petroleum (Pte) Ltd	UK/ Netherlands	1000 and over
10. Shell Lubricants Blending(s) Pte Ltd	UK/ Netherlands	50 - 99
11. Singapore Petrochemical Complex[a]	Japan/ Singapore/ Others	n.a.
12. Singapore Refining Co (Pte) Ltd	Singapore/ UK/USA	300 - 499

Source: Dept. of Statistics, Singapore
          Manufacturers and Products Directory, 1982,
          Singapore.

Note: a - Consists of the Petrochemical
          Corporation of Singapore (a joint venture
          of Sumitomo Chemical, over 20 other
          Japanese companies, the Singapore
          government and DBS) producing ethylene,
          propylene xylene etc. from naphtha, LPG and
          low sulphur fuel oil; plus six downstream
          plants/companies producing products such as
          polyethylene, polypropylene, 2 ethyl
          hexanol and ethylene oxide/glycol.
          Phillips Petroleum and Shell are
          participating in these latter projects,
          though Japanese firms still dominate.

Table 5.15   Some Characteristics of Electrical and
             Electronic Machinery Establishments in
             Singapore.

A. Electrical Machinery

	Number of Establishments			
	Source of Capital			
	Singapore	Indust. Countries	Developing Countries	Total
Size of Establishment (No. of Employees)				
10 - 50	47	15	2	64
50 - 100	8	14	2	24
100 - 200	3	13	1	17
200 +	3	16	0	19
Activity				
Final Production[a]	12	13	0	25
Supportive[b]	49	42	5	91
Total	61	57	5	123

B. Electronic Machinery

	Number of Establishments			
	Source of Capital			
	Singapore	Indust. Countries	Developing Countries	Total
Size of Establishment (No. of Employees)				
10 - 50	36	14	5	55
50 - 100	14	20	7	41
100 - 200	12	18	3	33
200 +	9	53	4[e]	66
Activity				
Final Production[a]	36	36	8	80
Assembly[c]	13	7	2	22
Supportive[b]	29	72	10	111
Total[d]	71	105	19	195

Table 5.15   Some Characteristics of Electrical and
             Electronic Machinery Establishments in
             Singapore. continued.

Source: Calculated from Singapore Department of
          Statistics, Singapore Manufacturers and
          Products Directory, 1982.

Notes: a - Production of final consumer goods.
          b - Production of intermediate products,
          components and servicing.
          c - Assembly of components and kits into
          either final consumer goods or semi-
          finished products requiring further
          processing elsewhere.
          d - The totals for the size of
          establishment and activity differ because
          some establishments have more than one main
          activity.
          The "total" refers to the actual number of
          establishments.
          e - One of these companies has been
          established by the Hong Kong subsidiary of
          Fairchild (US).

        The electrical and electronics industries are
also good examples of peripheral intermediation and
were   established   in Singapore essentially for
offshore production. As elsewhere, these industries
are deployed as part of a strategy of world-wide
sourcing   by   MNCs   (in   search of cheap labour, low
taxes and incentives, as discussed elsewhere) and
initially only consisted of low technology products
and processes. More recently, however:

        ... computer-based automation is pervading
        practically   all   stages   of   the   design,
        application and maintenance of electronic
        hardware and complementary software   ...
        [and]   ...   the   internationalisation   of
        production and support services in the
        electronics industry is acquiring new forms
        and mechanisms. ...   The issue for the
        1980s is not so much the possibility of
        relocating industrial activities from
        [industrialised]   countries   to   the
        developing   countries   ...   Rather,   in
        consumer   electronics   and   in electronic
        components, both automation and industrial

> redeployment to developing countries are
> taking place as complementary processes,
> with automation coming to the fore as the
> driving force. (68)

Curiously then, despite automation, the electronics
industry (and, for similar reasons, electrical
manufacturing) is likely to expand in Singapore and
other developing countries, albeit in an altered
form and structure. Ironically this is because of
the shortage of skilled labour in industrialised
countries, combined with the availability of highly
skilled labour and engineers in countries such as
South Korea, Hong Kong, Singapore, India and Brazil.
(69) Singapore's present policy of expanding the
output of its scientific, engineering and technical
manpower is therefore likely to pay handsome
dividends. Two subsidiary reasons also contribute
to continuing peripheral intermediation in the
electrical and electronics industry. First, social
legislation is relatively lax in most developing
countries, thus making them attractive to MNCs keen
on maximizing the usage of costly equipment by
running multi-shift operations. Secondly,
incentives and low priced infrastructure (especially
EPZs and "science parks") are key elements in any
MNCs locational decisions. (70) Intermediate
economies should be wary, however, because, 'the
developmental benefits of offshore production to be
reaped by developing countries in terms of
employment generation, skill formation, forward and
backward inter-industrial integration and
technological spin-offs might become even smaller
and less viable than they are today.' (71) This is
a point of considerable concern to the Singapore
authorities because the benefits of existing
foreign investment can also be questioned. Pan Eng
Fong and Linda Lim (72), while acknowledging the
patent benefits of Singapore's MNC-dominated
electronics industry, also suggest four key
problems: (i) the industry is volatile (e.g. in 1982
it shed 10 thousand local workers); (ii) there is
little technology transfer (because of MNC
preponderance; the partial transfer of products and
processes; and a paucity of local R & D); (iii) few
inter-industry vertical linkages; and (iv) a
negative effect on the local competition. Kwan
Kuen-Chor and Lee Soo Ann agree on the third problem
and point out that Japanese electrical firms, such
as Matsushita, Sanyo and Hitachi have solved the
problem of industrial support by asking other

Japanese firms to set up in Singapore. (73) Table 5.15 indicates that this may apply generally with foreign "supportive" establishments outnumbering other establishments in both the electrical and electronics industry. (Of course many "supportive" establishments are themselves involved in offshore production.) As for the effect on local firms, the following is illustrative, although the beneficial effects on competition and linkages should not be discounted:

> While many local firms benefit from having multinational customers, and most are not in competition with the multinationals in Singapore but rather with small Hong Kong and Taiwan firms, there is a prevailing attitude of resentment against the multinationals. In the opinion of one of the largest local companies, the net benefits from having multinationals are probably less than what is generally assumed. Foreign companies borrow from local banks at lower interest rates and use local capital, land and labour - in competition with local manufacturers - to earn profits free of tax which are repatriated. Even without tax exemption they can use transfer pricing to avoid paying tax. (74)

Shipbuilding and Repair. Singapore's marine industry (i.e. shipbuilding and repairing, oil rig construction, marine engineering and related industries) is one of the country's largest, accounting for about 11 percent of employment and value added in the manufacturing sector in 1982. (see also page 109.) About half of the output is exported and this amounts to 5 percent of the economy's annual merchandise exports. (75) The industry is also significant in two other respects. First, it offers an important supportive and servicing facility to key industries, including (i) shipping and transport (UNCTAD recently declared that, 'there is a close relationship between the existence of shipping services and prospects for economic development' and Singapore is now the world's twelfth largest maritime power [76]); (ii) petroleum products and related industries (e.g. through port storage facilities and repair of tankers); (iii) the offshore petroleum extraction industry (through the construction of oil rigs and other equipment); and (iv) even the burgeoning aircraft construction/repair and air distribution services (because of some similarity in equipment and engineering requirements). (77) Secondly, unlike the other two industries discussed above, the marine industry is dominated by indigenous firms which wholly or majority own all but 40 of the 260 relevant establishments. (78) MNCs from the USA, Japan, Switzerland and the UK were the main foreign investors. An orientation towards local industries and the use of sizeable local talent by indigenous firms suggests that the marine industry is generally not involved in peripheral intermediation, although some sections are (e.g. oil rig construction); and the industries being supported are often themselves intermediate in nature.

Though some of the major local shipbuilding and repairing companies trace their origins back to the country's colonial past, many are recent establishments whose development owes much to joint ventures with foreign companies, especially Japanese shipbuilders. Three good examples are: Jurong shipyard founded as a joint venture between the Singapore government and Ishikawajima-Harima Heavy Industries (IHI) in 1963 and now employing over 2000 Workers (IHIs ownership share is only 11 percent); Mitsubishi Singapore Heavy Industries Ltd, a joint venture between the government and the Japanese concern of the same name founded in 1968 with nearly 1000 workers; and Hitachi Zosen Robin dockyard, a joint venture initiated by the private indigenous Robin Group with over 1000 workers. (79) (The number of employees is relevant because most establishments are very small and often vertically integrated, i.e. linked to larger concerns.) According to Yeow (80) the transfer of technology, skills and organisation was very complex and was chiefly achieved through seconded personnel from the Japanese parent company. In the case of Jurong Shipyard transfer took a lengthy period of time with a peak of 55 seconded personnel (including scientists, engineers, designers and other specialist staff) in 1965 tapering to the 1983 level of 4 Japanese staff. (81) Despite some tied imports from Japan, these joint ventures have successfully transferred technology to Singapore. However three additional points should be made. First, the government's initiative was vital and a number of other large firms in this industry are state owned enterprises (e.g. Keppel shipyard, Sembawang shipyard and Singapore Shipbuilding and

Engineering). Secondly, Singapore already possessed many skills and facilities required for marine industries in the 1960s when most joint ventures were inaugurated; (see page 32: the Winsemius mission recommended the establishment of shipbuilding and repairing). Such a state of affairs may now be prevalent in, say, the electronics industry, a point which the authorities should heed. Finally, the success of shipbuilding, repairing and other marine industries would have been impossible without excellent infrastructure and communications and a rapid expansion in related industries (shipping, petroleum, offshore oil etc.).

Singapore needs to remain abreast of current technologies, although this is not always possible. In the oil rig construction sub-sector (including drilling and processing equipment), for example, there are only 11 indigenous firms all of which are very small (10-100 workers each). Foreign firms (13 from the USA, 2 from Switzerland and one each from Indonesia and Malaysia) are mainly larger (300-1000 workers each) and tend to specialise in more advanced and lucrative technologies and products. Since this sub-sector accounted for 34 percent of the output of marine industries in 1981, the indigenous lag in the relevant technologies should be a point for concern. It is only fair to add, however, that most of the running in this offshore industry is being made by the local subsidiaries of US MNCs which have access to technologies developed in other parts of the globe. Interestingly, as a consequence of this activity by US MNCs, Singapore was the world's leading builder of jack-up oil rigs in 1981 and only the USA exceeded it in terms of total oil rig construction. (82)

This section has analysed Singapore's role as an intermediate economy by focussing on three key industries. It has shown that the establishment of each of these industries was determined by a varied constellation of factors, including location, incentives, government initiative and infrastructure. In addition each industry's impact on the Singapore economy was assessed and seen to differ considerably (e.g. the electronics industry created much employment and offered potential access to highly advanced technology; the marine industry was much more successful in transferring technology to Singapore and establishing linkages). The question of impact will be examined further in chapter six.

CONCLUDING REMARKS

This chapter has illustrated Singapore's role in the NIDL, peripheral intermediation and the emerging international economic order (EIEO). This role will probably be maintained, but its exact characteristics and dimensions depend not only on future economic trends, but also on political realities.

The world economic crisis, rapid technological change and global industrial restructuring (83) have all contributed to an international power struggle in which industrialised countries have been pitted against each other and against NICs and developing countries demanding a New International Economic Order (NIEO). (84) The EIEO will resolve this conflict (essentially in the interest of industrialised countries) by (i) reducing inter-industrialised country competition; and (ii) placing intermediate economies and developing countries in subordinate positions in a new global political and economic hierachy of alliances and inter-relationships. The chief impetus for this new world system comes, not unexpectedly, from elite groups such as the Trilateral Commission (TriCom) which is intent on recreating the liberal trade and investment regime of the 1944-1970 period. TriCom was established in 1973 as a "'private' initiative on matters of common concern" by David Rockefeller (of Chase Manhattan Bank fame), Zbigniew Brzezinski (former U.S. Secretary of Defence) and a large number (now about 300) of top businessmen, politicians, academics and even union leaders from the USA, Japan and Europe. (85) (These matters included the protectionist stance of the Nixon administration, the NIEO and inter-capitalist competition and strife.) Since then TriCom has conducted a lengthy internal dialogue, published a series of reports (including "The Reform of International Institutions" [1976], "Towards a Renovated International System" [1977], "Trade in Manufactured Products with Developing Countries: Reinforcing North-South Partnership" [1981] and "The Institutional Foundations for an independent World" [1985]) outlining a fairly specific, international economic order and promoted the group's ideas in national and international fora. A glance at the membership (86) indicates how influential the group is. It is significant that Saburo Okita, initiator of the <u>Pacific Community</u> idea, chairman of the Pacific <u>Basin Cooperation</u> study group and former

Japanese Minister of Foreign Affairs, is a member of TriCom's executive committee. (He is also a co-author of the recent TriCom publication, "Democracy Must Work". The other authors are Brzezinski and the UK's David Owen.) (87) ASEAN's fears of economic and political domination by Japan and other industrialised countries (see page 218) do, in fact, have a very real foundation.

However it must be recognised that TriCom is not an all-powerful agent of a monolithic international power structure. In industrialised countries, as in developing countries, elites are divided by their diverse opinions and conflicting political and economic interests. Attitudes vary from the arch-conservative (much of the Thatcher and Reagan administrations, perhaps Bilderberg) through the liberal (Council on Foreign relations, TriCom itself) to the relatively progressive (the Brandt Commission, the International Progress Organisation). Further, many international organisations (UNIDO, UNCTAD, UNESCO) are sympathetic to developing countries; and some of the latter (e.g. OPEC, China, India, even ASEAN) are not entirely powerless themselves. It is this profusion of interest groups and power relations which offer Singapore and other developing countries hope for a relatively just NIEO. (88)

NOTES

1. The term "international business centre" refers to the fact that Singapore is involved in international manufacture, finance and the services.

2. Between 1955 and 1970 world output grew at 5.1 percent per year on average; and between 1970 and 1980 at the rate of 3.8 percent per year. By historical standards these are unprecedented rates of economic growth. (Developing countries grew even faster.) For further details see The World Bank, The World Development Report 1984, Geneva.

3. Undoubtedly the three are related, but Riedel correctly cautions against assuming any necessary causal link between trade and growth in his excellent monograph, James Riedel (1984), Trade as an Engine of Growth in Developing Countries: A Reappraisal, World Bank staff working paper, number 555, Washington. For further details on post-war trends in world output and trade see, for example, UNCTAD, Trade and Development Report, 1984. Geneva, especially part II: "The Evolution of the Trade and

NOTES continued

Payments Systems"; and UNIDO, (1983), Industrial
Development Strategies and Policies for Developing
Countries, Vienna. Of particular interest is the
Bretton Woods Conference of 1944 which spawned
bodies such as the World Bank, the IMF and GATT
which have played an important part in maintaining a
"liberal", stable post-war international trading
regime, thereby facilitating economic expansion.
    4.   See UNCTAD (1983), Trade in manufactures
and semi-manufactures of developing countries: 1980-
81 review, Geneva.
    5.   Hafiz Mirza (1984), "The New International
Economic Order" in Michael Z. Brooke and Peter J.
Buckley (eds), Handbook of International Trade,
Kluwer.
    6.   For further information see Mirza (1984),
op.cit.   See also: Ervin Lazlo et al (1978), The
Objectives of the New International Economic Order,
Pergamon Press; The Brandt Commission, (1983),
Common Crisis, Pan Books; UNCTAD, Trade and
Development Report, 1984, Geneva; Commission of the
Churches Participation in Development (1979), For a
New International Economic Order, World Council of
Churches, Geneva; and OECD (1983), World Ecomomic
Interdependence and the enduring North - South
Relationship, Paris.
    7.   The Industrialised countries also seem to
be ignoring the advice of the Brandt Commission and
other commentators that pouring resources into the
developing world is in their own interest. Put
very simply this argument is one of global Keynesian
demand management: an expanding developing world
will prove to be an excellent market for western
products and services.
    8.   UNCTAD: United Nations Conference on Trade
and Development; UNIDO: United Nations Industrial
Development Organisation; IMF: International
Monetary Fund.
    9.   The reasons why some transfer of
industries and services is necessary are two-fold:
First, a "new" international division of labour is
emerging anyway as (i) MNCs (e.g. electronic firms,
banks and technical services) take advantage of
cheap labour, rapid growth rates and other
opportunities in developing countries; (ii) third
world firms become more competitive in certain
industries (e.g. textiles, shipbuilding); and (iii)
developing raw material producers encourage more
local processing and production. Secondly, the

developing countries - and especially OPEC and the NICs - are not entirely powerless and it is therefore politic to show a degree of response, however small. Nevertheless western governments and MNCs try to ensure that the type of resource flows that occur (e.g. foreign direct investment, licensing agreements and tied, bilateral aid) maintain their economic dominance. Thus the pace and form of resource transfers depends on national and international policies and institutions. In addition, more powerful developing countries (e.g. OPEC) or those with more amenable regimes and economic opportunities (most NICs) are likely to enjoy most favour in the emerging international economic order (EIEO).

10. See note 9; see also page 244 on the role of the Trilateral Commission.

11. The map is only tentative. For example, Spain and Greece are only included because of their major tourist activities - but there are problems in counting tourism as an intermediate activity.

12. Comecon countries and China are excluded from this scheme, though, in a sense, they share some of the characteristics of the metropole and the periphery.

13. Longer in some cases.

14. Intermediate is used here in both its normal sense, but also in the sense of "financial intermediary", e.g. a bank is a financial intermediary between savers and borrowers.

15. Raw materials, semi-finished products, capital goods etc.

16. South Korea, Taiwan and India are key exceptions.

17. Of course there is "intermediation" in industrialised countries (witness European financial intermediate economies in map. 5.1), but such activity is unlikely to affect these countries as much as peripheral countries (Ireland may be an exception).

18. The source country is the country of origin of the MNC/FDI; the host country is the country in which the investment takes place - the intermediate economy in this case; and third countries are all other countries.

19. Indigenous firms cannot, of course, export to a "source" country.

20. E.g. They may produce microchips, specialised chemicals or assemble parts while other

NOTES continued

activity pertaining to the final product occurs elsewhere.

21. For further discussion of the transformation of the international trade in manufactures see: UNCTAD (1983), Trade in Manufactures.... op.cit.; OECD (1983), World Economic Interdependence... op. cit.; UNCTAD (1984), Trade and Development Report ..., op. cit., UNIDO (1983) Industrial Development Strategies..., op.cit.; and Institute of Developing Economies (1983), Two Decades of Asian Development and outlook for the 1980s, Tokyo.

22. Not strictly peripheral anyway.

23. According to Fidelity International only 9 Trusts are based in Singapore, accounting for less than 1 percent of total Asian assets of $19.5bn. Hong Kong has a 50 percent share, South Korea 27 percent and India 15 percent. See Far Eastern Economic Review, "Managed Funds - the record and the prospects", January 10 1985".

24. R.A. John (1983) Tax Havens and Offshore Finance: A Study of Transnational Economic Development, Frances Pinter. See also UNCTAD (1984), Trade and Development Report... op.cit.; Y.S. Park and J. Zwick (1985), International Banking in Theory and Practice, Addison Wesley; and OECD (1984), International Trade in Services: Banking, Paris.

25. See, for example, UNCTAD (1984), Service and the Development Process, Geneva, TD/B/1008; UNCTAD (1984), Insurance in the context of services and the Development Process, Geneva, TD/B/1014; UNCTAD (1984), Technology in the Context of Services and the Development Process, Geneva TD/B/1012; and UNCTAD (1984), International Trade and Foreign Direct Investment in Data Services, Geneva, TD/B/1016.

26. The degree of concentration is quite amazing and suggests that strategic considerations are much more important than other criteria, particularly when the identity of resource recipients is considered. Thus, for example: (a) 10 countries (Malaysia, the Philippines, Singapore, Greece, Egypt, Argentina, Brazil, Chile, Columbia and Mexico) received 75 percent of all FDI to non-oil developing countries during 1980-82; (b) 10 countries (Korea, Malaysia, Portugal, Argentina, Brazil, Mexico, Panama, Indonesia, Venezuela and South Africa) accounted for 55 percent of all

NOTES continued

international loans outstanding of developing countries in 1983; (c) 7 countries (Mexico, Venezuela, India, Indonesia, Korea, Malaysia and Israel) accounted for 86 percent; of all Eurobond issues by developing countries in 1981-83 - Mexico alone accounted for 40 percent and (d) 11 countries (Turkey, Kenya, Martinique, Reunion, Tanzania, Israel, Bangladesh, India, Egypt, Indonesia and Pakistan) received 48% of all bilateral aid to developing countries from industrialised countries during 1980-82. These figures were calculated from the following sources: IMF, International Financial Statistics, October, 1984, Washington; IMF, Balance of Payments Statistics Yearbook, 1983, Part 2, Washington; Morgan Guaranty Trust, World Financial Markets, October/November 1984; OECD (1984) Geographical Distribution of Financial Flows to Developing Countries, Paris.

    27. For example, countries such as South Korea - or even Singapore - may progress to industrialised country status (emulating Japan), while some industrialised countries (the UK?) may regress to the IE level!

    28. See Carl Stone (1983), "Patterns of Insertion into the World Economy: Historical Profile and Contemparary Options", Social and Economic Studies, Vol 32, Number 3, for a general discussion of the role of the periphery in international trade and investment.

    29. Hong Kong being the only other possibility.

    30. This importance, of course, depends on the relative scale of Singapore's trade in goods and services. Tables 1.1 and 5.9 suggest that this trade is significant.

    31. GSP is the generalised system of preferences (developed on the basis of discussions at UNCTAD I in 1964) in which industrialised countries lower their tariffs on selected goods from specific developing countries. For a discussion of the systems effectiveness see, OECD (1983), The Generalised System of Preferences: Review of the First Decade, Paris. See also, C.R. MacPhee (1984), Evaluation of the Trade Effects of the Generalised System of Preferences, UNCTAD, TD/B/C.5/87, Geneva. Items 806 and 807.30 allow US companies to export parts, assemble these overseas and then re-import them to the USA, paying duty only on the value added in the foreign location.

NOTES continued

32. Singapore's role as a free port - with FTZs, EPZs and inducements for banks - is a major component of its success. For the effectiveness of such zones in general, and for Singapore in particular, see, Rudy Maex (1983), Employment and Multinationals in Asian Export Processing Zones, International Labour Office, Geneva; Dean Spinager (1984), "Objectives and Impact of Economic Activity Zones - Some Evidence from Asia", Weltwirtschaftliches Archive, Bd. CXX, Band 1; and The Sabre Foundation (1983), Free Zones in Developing Countries: Expanding Opportunities for the Private Sector, US Agency for International Development (AID).

33. Hong Kong, of course, largely shares these characteristics - hence the competition.

34. See Barry Wain (ed), (1979), The ASEAN Report, Don Jones Publishing Company, Hong Kong.

35. See UN, Centre on Transnational Corporations (1981), Transnational Banks: Operations, Strategies and their Effects in Developing Countries, New York, ST/CTC.16.

36. See Sueo Sekiguchi (1983) "Japanese Direct Foreign Investment and ASEAN - Japan Relations: A Synthesis" in Sueo Sekiguchi (ed.), ASEAN - Japan Relations : Investment, Institute of South East Asian Studies, Singapore. See also F. von Kirchbach (1982), "Transnational Corporations in the ASEAN Region: A survey of Major Issues", Economic Bulletin for Asia and the Pacific, Vol XXXIII. No 1, June 1982.

37. Calculated from IMF, Direction of Trade Yearbook 1983, Washington.

38. See F. Sercovich and E. White (1984), Enterprise to Enterprise Corporation among Developing Countries: Elements for a Global Strategy, UNIDO/PC. 99, Vienna, pages 59-60.

39. Ibid, pages 60-62.

40. See S. Awanohara, "Yours, Mine, Ours" in Far Eastern Economic Review, November 14, 1980.

41. Konosuke Odaka (1984), "The 'Becak' and the 'Jeepney' are best!", Euro - Asian Business Review, Vol 3 No. 3.

42. Sercovich and White (1984), op.cit., page 62.

43. See especially, Ooi Guat Tin (1981), The AESAN Preferential Trading Arrangements (PTA): An Analysis of Potential Effects on Inter-ASEAN Trade, ASEAN Economic Research Unit, Institute of South East Asian Studies, Singapore.

NOTES continued

44. Japan accounts for about 30 percent of the foreign investment in ASEAN, Hong Kong, South Korea and Taiwan.   It is the largest investor in South Korea and Thailand; the second largest in Indonesia, Hong Kong, Taiwan, the Philippines and Malaysia; and the third (or fourth) largest in Singapore. See, "Japanese Private Direct Investment in East and South East Asia", IFO - Digest, 1/1984.

45.   See Ministry of Foreign Affairs, (1984), ASEAN AND Japan, Tokyo; and Journal of Japanese Trade and Industry, January/February 1985, "Promoting Horizontal Trade with Asian Nations", page 74.

46. As illustrated, for example, by the bitter recriminations Singapore faced over the level of its trade with Vietnam (page 45).

47. And international trade in goods and services.

48. Gerhard Schmitt-Rink (1983), "The Relative Importance of Intra - and Inter-Industry trade in ASEAN-EC Trade, 1974-81", Third conference on ASEAN-EC Economic Relations, October 1983, Bangkok, held under the auspices of the Institute of Southeast Asian Studies, Singapore.

49. Ibid., page 29.

50. The USSR (probably best considered in a European context) and North Korea and Vietnam (with little economic contact with the other, mainly capitalist countries of the Pacific region) are excluded from the rest of the analysis in this section.

51. Figures from: Barclays Bank, International Economic Survey, December 1984; South, February 1985; Overseas Development Institute, Briefing Paper, December 1984; and IMF Survey, January 21, 1985. All figures are estimates or forecasts.

52. Calculated from the IMF, Financial Statistics Yearbook 1984, Washington: excluding Comecon.

53. On the other hand the USA has a very large balance of invisible trade surplus with Japan. See table 4.2.

54. For a further discussion of intra-pacific trade see Geoffrey C. Kiel and Carol Ann Howard (1984), "The Pacific Rim - Vision or Reality?", European Journal of Marketing, Vol 18, No 4.

55. For a history of the Pacific Community concept see, especially, Haki Soesastro and Han

NOTES continued

Sung-joo (eds.) (1983), Pacific Economic Cooperation: The Next Phase, Centre for Strategic and International Studies, Jakarta; Michael West Oborne and Nicolas Fourt (1983), Pacific Basin Economic Cooperation, OECD, Paris; and The Centre for Strategic and International Studies (1980), Asia-Pacific in the 1980s: Toward Greater Symmetry in Economic Interdependence, Jakarta.
    56. JERC is semi-governmental and funded by the four largest business organisations in Japan.
    57. See Oborne and Fourt (1983), op.cit., for a list of fora.
    58. Ibid., page 7.
    59. The Pacific basin island states, ASEAN and Australia have voiced the greatest concern.
    60. Oborne and Fourt (1983), op.cit., page 6. For more on Japan's role see also: Bruce McFarlane (1982), "Western Strategies in the Asian-Pacific Region", in E. Utrecht (ed), Transnational Corporations in South East Asia and the Pacific, Vol iv, Transnational Corporations Research Project, University of Sydney; David W. Edgington (1983), Japanese Transnational Corporations and the Economic Integration of Australia and the Asian-Pacific Region, Working Paper No 15, Transnational Corporations Research Project, University of Sydney; V. Chan Kim and Vern Terpstra (1984), "Intraregional Foreign Direct Investment in the Asian Pacific Region", Asia Pacific Journal of Management, September 1984; L.B. Krause and S. Sekiguchi (eds) (1980), Economic Interaction in the Pacific Basin, The Brookings Institute; and Miyohei Shinohara (1977), The Japanese Economy and Southeast Asia, Institute of Developing Economies, 1977.
    61. The five "imperatives" in Pacific Community Newsletter, Vol 2, No 2.
    62. Rodney Tasker (1984), "Enter the Pacific", Far Eastern Economic Review, July 26.
    63. For further details on Singapore's Petrochemical industry see, Process Plant EDC (1984), Selling to the Energy Industries in South East Asia: Singapore, National Economic Development Organisation, London; BP, Statistical Review of World Energy 1984, London; UNIDO (1984), World Industrial Restructuring and Redeployment, Vienna, ID/Conf. 5/3; K. Snitwangse and s. Paribatra (1984), The Invisible Nexus: Energy and ASEAN's Security, Executive Publications, Singapore; and

NOTES continued

Lim Joo-Jock et al. (1977), Foreign Investment in Singapore: Economic and Socio-Political Ramifications, Institute of South East Asian Studies.

64. The International Petroleum Centre will offer support facilities (e.g. training, engineering, computer and design services) and will also house Arab shipping, trading and insurance companies.

65. See Chong Li Choy (1983), Multinational Business and National Development: Transfer of Managerial Knowhow to Singapore, Maruzen Asia.

66. Figures derived from: Singapore Department of Statistics (1983), Report on the Census of Industrial Production 1982; and The Singapore Economic Development Board (1983), Annual Report, 1982/83.

67. For figures see the Singapore Economic Development Board (1983), Singapore Electronics Manufacturers Directory 1984. See also: Pang Eng Fong and Linda Lim (1977), The Electronics Industry in Singapore, Chopmen Enterprises, Singapore; and Andrew Tanzer (1983), "Asia Plugs into the Computer", Far Eastern Economic Review, July 21.

68. UNIDO (1984), World Industrial Restructuring and Redeployment, Vienna, ID/Conf. 5/3, pages 16-17.

69. According to the above report (page 18) 15 percent of electronics engineers in the USA are from developing countries; 5 percent are from Europe.

70. UNIDO (1984), World Industrial Restructuring ... op.cit., page 18.

71. Ibid, page 17.

72. Pang Eng Fong and Linda Lim (1977), The Electronics Industry in Singapore: Structure, Technology and Linkages, Chopmen Enterprises, Singapore.

73. Kwan Kuen-Chor and Lee Soo Ann (1983), "Japanese Direct Investment in ·Singapore Manufacturing Industry" in Sueo Sekiguchi (ed.) (1983), op.cit.

74. Pang and Lim (1977), op.cit., page 60.

75. Figures from the Singapore Economic Development Board (1983), Report on the Census of Industrial Production.

76. See UNCTAD (1984), Shipping in the Context of Services and the Development Process, Geneva and "Shipping '84" in Far Eastern Economic Review, 16 February 1984.

253

NOTES continued

77. See "Asia: Billions for Aerospace" a special advertising section in Aviation Week and Space Technology, January 16 1984.
78. The figures for the number of establishments in this section relate to 1982 and are taken from the Singapore Department of Statistics (1983), Singapore Manufacturers and Products Directory 1 82.
79. Ibid., pages 279 ff and T.H. Seow (1984), Shipbuilding and Shiprepairing Industry in Singapore, UNCTAD, ID/WG.413/14.
80. Ibid., pages 10 ff.
81. Ibid., pages 10 and 68.
82. Ibid., pages 7 and 64. Between 1970 and 1982, 108 oil rigs and related equipment were constructed in Singapore. The equivalent figure for jack-ups was 83.
83. Of course all these factors are related to each other and with other factors such as the demands for a NIEO.
84. It is not possible to explain all this in depth here. Readers are referred to Mirza (1984), op.cit.; UNCTAD, Trade and Development Report 1984, op.cit. especially part 1: "the continuing world economic crisis"; and Holly Sklar (1980), Trilateralism, South End Press. For some remarks on the effect of the East-West conflict on the North-South power struggle see R.G. Coyle (1984), "East and West and North and South: A preliminary model", Futures, December. See also the publications referred to in note 6.
85. Hence the Trilateral Commission.
86. It is only possible to list a few easily recognisable names here: (i) from the US: David Rockefeller, Zbigniew Brzezinski, Lane Kirkland, John Glenn, Henry Kissinger, Robert McNamara, Andrew Young and George Bush; (ii) from Europe: David Owen, Peter Shore, Rolf Rodenstock and Garrat Fitzgerald; and (iii) from Japan: Joji Itakura, Takeo Fukuda, Naohiro Amaya and Saburo Okita.
87. For further discussion on TriCom and its role in the OECD, the IMF and other international institutions see especially Sklar (1980). See also the other material in note 84. The Trilateral Commission though an elite group is not a conspiracy and information on its views and activities are readily available. TriCom's latest publication is: David Owen, Zbigniew Brzezinski and Saburo Okita (1984), Democracy Must Work: A

NOTES continued

Trilateral Agenda for the Decade, New York University Press.

88. See also, International Progress Organisation (1980), The New International Economic Order - Philosophical and Socio-Cultural Implications, Vienna; and Detlef Lorenz (1983), "International Division of Labour Versus Closer Co-operation? With special regard to ASEAN-EC economic relations", paper presented at the Third Conference on ASEAN-EC Economic Relations, Institute of Southeast Asian Studies.

Chapter Six

THE FUTURE OF SINGAPORE

The many benefits of Singapore's policy of
MNC-financed, internationally-oriented development
are plainly visible. This tiny, resourceless city-
state has achieved the second highest per capita
income in East Asia, and its inhabitants boast a
relatively high level of material welfare.
Moreover, critics of the regime are keenly aware
that during the long tenure of the PAP a mulitutde
of ills, including malnutrition, epidemics,
illiteracy and housing-shortage, have been banished
permanently from the island. Nevertheless it is
necessary to mention that these benefits have been
bought at considerable cost. This chapter will
examine some of these costs and a number of
obstacles the country is likely to face in the near
future. The key areas to be discussed are
Singapore's relationship with multinational
companies and industrialised countries; the PAPs
relationship with the populace (which is a direct
consequence of the state's policy of accommodating
MNCs); and the country's relationship with ASEAN.

SINGAPORE AND THE MULTINATIONALS

Singapore's expansion in manufacturing and
services over the last two decades has been
facilitated by a considerable influx of foreign
capital, technology and skills. (1) However,
foreign retention of control over these factors of
production means that the country is highly
dependent on multinational companies, international
and regional markets and the political intentions
of industrialised countries. (2) At present, of
course, the island provides MNCs with a stable,
profitable environment and their present commitment

need not be questioned; but in a swiftly altering,
crisis-torn, world economy this cannot be
guaranteed. Rapid technological change,
international industrial restructuring, an upswing
in protectionism in industrialised countries
(increasingly in high-tech goods and utilising non-
tariff barriers [3]) and continuing competitive
pressures from other developing countries are all
factors likely to affect greatly Singapore's trade
in goods and services. (4) Industries such as
petroleum products, electronics and financial
services (on whose exports the economy heavily
depends) are among those most susceptible to market
growth and stability, though the prospects for the
latter two seem reasonable for the moment. (5)
In any case continuing financial and
technological dependence calls into question the
PAPs development strategy. The considerable
employment and "multiplier" effects of MNC
involvement notwithstanding, these benefits are
merely those of a well-run "industrial estate" -
and bought at considerable expense. (The promotion
of foreign investment has meant the large-scale use
of resources towards infrastructure and input
provision, including the training of workers. The
cost of tax holidays and the like are incalculable.
[6]) The strategy has often failed in ensuring
technology transfer, foreign-indigenous industrial
linkages and stimulative competitive effects, all
of which would have boosted Singapore's self-
reliance.

Technology and Skill Transfer

Chapter five showed that there has been little
by way of technology transfer in two major
industries, petroleum products and electronics.
Fransman argues that the same applies for the
machinery industry (7) and Odaka indicates why
technology transfer may not occur:

> 'Technology transfer' is a fashionable
> term these days, but it is not always
> clear exactly what is meant by it. At the
> very least, it encompasses (i) production
> technology, (ii) production control, and
> (iii) product design. If 'transfer'
> implies only the transplanting of hardware
> (i), the matter is rather simple, since it
> can be boiled down to the problem of
> financing the purchase of given

> 'technology' (plant and/or equipment).
> But the transplantation of technology
> means much more than that. It entails not
> only the appropriate choice of products
> and of techniques, but also the formation
> of suitable institutional set-ups and the
> supply of qualified manpower. ... The
> most demanding task is the third: the
> development and design of new products.
> (8)

The lack of technology transfer (in Odaka's full
sense) to Singaporean firms is fully explicable if
the nature of foreign-dominated industries such as
petroleum products, machinery and electronics is
examined. Each is an offshore-oriented industry
with little contact with local firms. Inputs and
components are usually supplied by external (often
intra-company) sources or by MNC establishments in
Singapore (for example, Japanese electronics firms
have established local factories to supply
components to producers such as Matsushita) because
of factors such as established relationships,
technological knowhow or quality. Moreover local
firms are frequently small and therefore lack the
assets, managerial skills or organisation to
establish themselves as potential suppliers.
Indigenous firms do frequently act as wholesalers
and retailers for MNC products when these are sold
locally, but there is little capacity for
technology transfer in such circumstances. A
transfer of managerial and production skills does
occur, but a silicon valley effect (whereby ex-
employees of successful corporations set up their
own electronics firms) is unlikely. This is
because the learning-by-doing skill transfer does
not include research and development (R & D) or
product design: these activities are usually
conducted in industrialised countries, normally at
each multinational company's headquarters. (9)
A lack of R & D is in fact the chief cause of
Singapore's technological dependence and the
government needs to direct much effort into solving
this problem. In 1981 Singapore devoted a mere 0.3
percent of its GDP to R & D, (table 6.1) while
South Korea devoted 0.7 percent and the
industrialised countries expended a massive 2.4-2.5
percent of GDP. (In absolute terms Singapore's
expenditure is miniscule.) In 1980 only 52 private
companies (28 of them foreign) conducted any R & D
in Singapore. Philips was the biggest investor

with $4 million (20 percent of private R & D) and 200 research engineers. (10) Singapore's need to acquire and develop technology is urgent, particularly in the light of process-affecting new emerging technologies, such as microelectronics, biotechnology and materials technology. These technologies are best transferred directly (11) and, unfortunately for developing countries, are tending to shift the comparative advantage in many industries back to the industrialised nations. (12)

Table 6.1   Gross R & D Expenditure in Selected Countries, 1981

Country	Amount (US$ bn)	Proportion of GDP (%)
Singapore	neg.[a]	0.3
South Korea	n.a.	0.7
UK	6.0	2.4
Japan	14.4	2.4
USA	39.1	2.5
Germany	8.2	2.5

Sources: OECD and Science and Technology Quarterly, October 1983.

Note: a - $0.04 billion.

However shipbuilding, shiprepairing and other marine industries are examples of successful technology transfer. Chapter five showed that the chief bases for this success were: (i) an existing pool of labour with the appropriate skills; (ii) a joint venture technique of technology transfer which meant that the Japanese partners trained the indigenous partner and imported an appropriate organisational structure; and (iii) the role of the Singapore state in most joint ventures, ensuring adequate resources for the projects concerned and unwavering participation on the part of the foreign partner.

It would be worthwhile for the government to adopt a similar approach to other industries (13), particularly now that pools of partly trained workers in various industries (electronics, petroleum products) are available. Support should be given to private firms when the state is not directly involved and the marine industries experience should be drawn upon. Kwan and Lee (14) also argue the case for non-equity forms of technology transfer, including licensing agreements, management contracts and turnkey projects. Such options may not always be available, but the EDB should remain flexible in its approach. It is worth mentioning that firms from some countries (Japan, South Korea, perhaps India, West Germany and Scandinavia) may be more amenable to joint ventures or non-equity investments.

Vertical Linkages and Competitive Effects

From Singapore's point of view the potential benefits of MNC vertical linkages with suppliers of components, parts and other imports (15) are partial dis-intermediation and technology/skill transfer. (Employment creation is effectively attended to by the many EPZs.) Ideally backward linkages with indigenous firms reduce foreign imports of components and parts (16); these are produced locally and gradually production by indigenous firms extends forward into more complex parts, components and eventually complete products. What is necessary is some technological know-how (perhaps imparted by the foreign firm), organisation, entrepreneurship (17) and experience. Earlier remarks notwithstanding some strong vertical linkages have been created, especially in the electronics industry. Linda Lim and Pang Eng Fong (18) have shown that the local purchase of material imports by electronics MNCs varies from about 10 to 50 percent (19), with US firms buying the smallest proportion and European firms the largest. Some MNCs are particularly enlightened:

> Company B actively helps to set up and develop locally-owned supporting industries. Firms are encouraged to start supplying to the company by promises of guaranteed sales, and by technical training and advice by local and expatriate engineers and others specially

flown out from Europe. Years of training
are invested in some suppliers to help
them reach the required standards. When
new products and materials are introduced,
the suppliers have to be retrained.
Financial assistance is sometimes given,
e.g. for one supplier, by partially
deducting the cost of a machine from
deliveries over 5 years, or the company
itself buys the machines and hires them
out to the supplier. The company also
recommends satisfactory local suppliers to
other regional sister plants, and
introduces and recommends them to new
customers, including buyers in Europe,
which helps them to expand their export
markets. The suppliers' success benefits
the company itself because its suppliers
are more viable, less dependent on it, and
perhaps can produce cheaper inputs because
of economies of scale. Company B also
encourages its suppliers to upgrade,
integrate and automate their activities,
especially in Singapore's tight labour
market. (20)

However, though behaviour such as that of company
"B" should be encouraged, MNCs still import the
major proportion of their material inputs and this
situation is unlikely to change. Moreover, many
"locally" purchased inputs are either indirect
imports or produced by the local subsidiaries of
MNCs (see page 241); and, arguably, other
industries are less prone to vertical linkages than
electronics.
In fact most linkages between MNCs and local
firms appear to be "cross-industrial", with the
latter supplying the former with port facilities,
storage/warehousing, distributive services, marine
industry products (including shipbuilding and
equipment for the offshore oil industry), business
services, technical services etc. These linkages
apart, MNCs and indigenous firms essentially co-
exist in their respective commercial niches,
reducing the likelihood of either group producing
a competitive stimulus on the other. MNCs account
for 70 percent or more of tradeable goods and
services and their exports are destined for the
industrialised countries or the entire East Asian
region. Local firms are mainly domestically
orientated, while most exports, are destined for

nearby developing countries. (Where exports to industrialised countries do occur these are often via mass merchandisers such are Sears Roebuck). In effect multinational companies and domestic firms are separated both by market and by technology. This separation has already been discussed for the electronics industry (page 241) and a similar case can also be made for many other industries, including commercial banking. (21)

The financial, technological and market dominance of MNCs tends to raise fears about anti-competitive effects. Lim Joo-Jock has expressed these well:

> In these circumstances the question can be raised as to whether the sheer volume of foreign capital and its overall pervasiveness might restrict the opportunities, smothering local investment from currently desirable higher technology areas and immobilizing it in the present low technology and servicing sectors, thus relegating it to a subordinate role in the national economy, with accompanying political consequences. There is no doubt that high technology and highly capital-intensive industries, with assured overseas markets, are dominated, to the point of exclusivity, by the big transnationals. It is also quite clear that ownership of servicing industries such as the catering and tourist industry, as exemplified in equity holdings of the major hotels, is mainly in the hands of local ownership of smaller-scale back-up industries fabricating parts and components for the large MNCs. This adds further to the impression that local enterprise is cast in a subordinate role. (22)

Singapore's dependence on MNCs and the international community suggests that these fears of subordination are not mis-placed; and the value of an MNC-based stategy of development will increasingly be questioned by domestic firms and the populace. (23)

Towards Dis-intermediation

Despite the various costs and benefits of MNC

operations in Singapore (24) the issue of dependency remains salient. It is in the country's interest to reduce this by a policy of indigenisation and technological independence; and the potential effectiveness of such a policy is enhanced by the state's direct role in the economy. (Indeed cabinet ministers are also often chairmen/directors of state-owned enterprises.) Moreover, Singapore is relatively developed with a well trained, experienced work-force; and there are previous examples of successful technology transfer which can be used as guidelines for future action. (25)

Any move towards self-reliance is likely to be slow because of the dominance of multinational companies and the crucial role they play in the economy. (26) Further, even if such a policy were to succeed two crucial problems remain. First, it is likely that the main beneficiaries of an indigenisation policy will be state-owned enterprises and this is not necessarily in the interest of private domestic firms or the general population, particularly given the authoritarian nature of the regime. (See next section) Secondly, mere displacement of MNCs is not enough: Singapore would still remain an intermediate economy, heavily dependent on external forces. In particular the economy would still have to be wary of: (i) disruptions in supply (components, raw materials); (ii) disruptions in demand (protectionism in industrialised markets, for example); and (iii) competition from other developing countries (especially those in which MNC expansion is permitted!). It is such worries, of course, which always make the PAP rush, pell-mell, into the arms of the multinationals and make the "security" of a Pacific Community welcome; but alternatives are available, including dis-intermediation. Admittedly dis-intermediation is difficult for a tiny economy with no hinterland, but ASEAN can more than fill such a role. (27) In addition to its policy of indigenisation and technological independence, Singapore needs to alter its role in ASEAN from an exploitative one (in which it serves as an intermediate economy beteween ASEAN and the industrialised countries) to one which is much more co-operative in nature. ASEAN (including Singapore) can thereby become a comparatively self-reliant community of Nations.

THE PAP AND THE POPULACE

The denial of basic political and industrial rights was fundamental to the PAPs policy of attracting international capital and can be regarded as a major cost of foreign direct investment. (28) The Unions and the left (including a major part of the PAP) recognises' this and struggled vigourously against Lee Kuan Yew and his allies, but were ultimately defeated. (29) Chapter two has documented these events, including corollaries such as the militarisation of Singapore. During the late sixties and seventies, as workers discovered that they had "never had it so good" and a new generation came of age, civil liberation were not of prime concern; but a wealthier, sophisticated, go-getting populace is less inclined to accept restrictions and is beginning to question the regime's policies. Whether the PAP can come to terms with this contradictory consequence of its own authoritarian economic strategy is an issue already in the boiling pot. Popular discontent is emerging in various forms, of which three examples are given below:

Income, Income Distribution and Industrial Relations. Singapore offers multinational companies a low-risk environment with a very high rate of return (30) and, in the final analysis, it is this feature of the economy which encourages a continuing influx of foreign direct investment. However, in order to maintain high profit shares the regime has restricted the growth of wages and salaries by using a variety of instruments, including anti-union legislation, the PAP-sponsored National Trade Union Congress (NTUC) and the "tri-partite" National Wages Council (NWC). The results of this policy are confirmed by Table 6.2 which shows that though earnings increased in real terms over the period 1966-1982 this icrease was much slower than the growth in either GDP or indigenous GDP per worker. (31) Both private and state-owned enterprises have therefore increased their share of income (value added) generated by the economy; and, because GDP per worker has grown more rapidly than indigenous GDP per worker, foreign investors are obviously the chief beneficiaries.

Though an average gross wage of $99 per week in 1982 (production workers, $67; professionals, $225) means that Singapore is no longer a low-wage

Table 6.2   The Relative Growth of GDP, Wages and
             Prices, 1966-82

	Index of Growth				
	1966	1972	1975	1978	1982
GDP per Worker	100	185	277	320	530
Indigenous GDP per workers	100	159	233	257	428
Weekly Earnings	100	115	168	199	322
Consumer Price Level	100	108	162	172	219

Sources: Singapore Department of Statistics,
            Economic and Social Statistics 1960-1982
            and Yearbook of Statistics, 1982/83.

economy, workers are increasingly questioning the
fact that employers are appropriating the lion's-
share of productivity gains. (32) The island's
internationally travelled population especially
resents a developing country level of income
and income distribution (33) when the government is
constantly bragging about an "economic miracle"
which has thrust the country into the rank of
rich nations. This resentment is further amplified
by the heavy burden of contribution to the
Central Provident Fund (CPF) which reduces gross
wages by nearly a third.

The government's policies are aimed at
scotching incipient worker discontent by
strengthening state/employer control of the unions.
Thus the great majority of unions are now led by
non-union professionals (including PAP and employer
representatives) as per NTUC policy. (The NTUC is
itself led by PAP cadres and its General-Secretary
is a cabinet minister.) A current measure is to
encourage the development of company or house
unions (similar to those in Japan) which will
identify their interests with management and

thereby become divided from the larger union
movement. (34) However, resistance continues,
albeit sporadically. Three examples will
suffice: (i) in 1980 airline pilots in the
Singapore Airline Pilots Association (SIAPA) went
on a work-to-rule for a better contract, the first
major industrial action since the Metal Box house
union strike of 1977. Lee Kuan Yew personally
intervened on the grounds that the action was 'an
attempt to tear down the basis of Singapore's
industrial relations system built on a foundation
of mutual co-operation among government, management
and unions'. (35) SIAPA was deregistered, a new
pilots union formed and even more restrictive
legislation enacted (go-slows and work-to-rules
were made illegal), but notice had been served by
the labour movement. (ii) In 1981 Goh Keng Swee,
the First Deputy Prime Minister, advised the
teachers unions to become professional associations
because 'the need to strike had not, does not and
will not arise, nor the occasion to do so be
allowed to happen'. (36) Teachers considered this
a threat and new membership into the Singapore
Teachers' Union (STU) doubled in the next month.
(iii) In 1982 the 3,000 strong United Workers of
the Petroleum Industry voted against allowing its
members to form company unions, although pressure
from the NTUC (and the PAP) forced a climbdown
later in the year. (37)
     Tensions between workers and the government/
employers will remain potent because, as Evelyn
Wong puts it: 'the labour movement is
simultaneously facing greater restrictions and
controls on the one hand, and exhortations to adopt
a spirit of trust and cooperation with its
employers on the other.' (38) The question of
income and income distribution is central to this
apparent contradiction - and a sophisticated
population and workforce, intent on receiving a
fair income, has begun to recognise why.

Old Age, Pensions and the Central Provident Fund.
The problems of a rapidly "graying" population
which have recently beset all industrialised
countries have also come to the fore in Singapore.
In April 1984 the government published a policy
paper on the "Problems of the Aged" (39) and
controversy has raged ever since. The paper
pointed out that life expectancy on this island has
risen from only 50 years at birth in 1947 to 70
years in 1980. As a consequence there will be only

three working people to each retired person in 2030, as opposed to a ratio of 15 to 1 in 1980 and 34 to 1 in 1947. The paper also put forward a number of recommendations to solve the perceived difficulties created by this demographic transition. The most controversial recommendations were: (i) legislation to compel children to maintain their parents; (ii) proposals to raise retirement age from 55 to 60 and ultimately to 65 - and to defer withdrawals from the compulsory Central Provident Fund (a major source of government revenue and popular resentment, see page 54) to the new corresponding retirement ages; and (iii) the suggestion that institutional care and health/recreational needs should be met by voluntary and community organisations. The government was surprised by the overwhelmingly negative response of citizens and there were calls for a referendum and public debate. As Kulkarni puts it:

> The lack of public trust was evident in the case of some people over 55 who had left their money in CPF, who hastened to withdraw their savings and put them elsewhere where they would retain personal control. While the government had expected some criticism, the uniformly negative feedback seems to have surprised the authorities. The newspapers closed their hotlines abruptly after four days without explanation, and despite disclaimers that they were acting under direction, it was generally assumed that the government had heard enough. (40)

The government back-pedalled and toned down policy proposals, but the PAPs discomfiture was noted in many quarters. At the end of a three day debate on the recommendations in July, 19 of the 72 PAP MPs contrived to be absent. (41)

The PAP is only belatedly recognising that its heavy handed methods are no longer viable. Deep resentments have built up over a variety of issues, including the Central Provident Fund (CPF). Though the CPF has proved to be a highly successful device for harnessing the country's resources it is generally regarded as a tax on the poor: (i) contributions are not paid above a specified income level; (ii) contributions are tax exempt (therefore those in higher tax brackets benefit more); and

(iii) contributions are assessed only on income from labour (thus excluding, for example, returns on stocks and shares). (42) Kaye puts the matter thus:

> The regressive incidence of CPF levies might make good supply-side sense for those in the upper income brackets, but sceptics wonder about its motivational effect on the factory workers who remain Singapore's main drawing card for foreign investment. Locking away an ever-increasing proportion of their pay, only to be redeemed at a remote and ever-receding future date, could sap their "productivity will". And employers, for their part, are troubled by a surcharge on their wage bill that does not translate visibly into increased output or employee loyalty. (43)

The PAPs endearing conversion to Confucian values (e.g. children maintaining their elderly parents, community based welfare and Mandarin language television broadcasting) is also regarded cynically by the population as an ideological tool - rather like the Japanisation programme. (44)

Ironically the PAP got itself into a quandry over the age/pensions issue needlessly because, like many governments world-wide, it panicked and failed to recognise that similar transitions have occurred in the past. Agriculture and manufacturing, for example, have steadily become a smaller proportion of most economies through the course of the twentieth century, but both are still well capable of supporting "non-productive" sectors such as the services. Productivity is the key word: just as 15 Singaporeans today are immensely more productive than 34 in 1947, so 3 Singaporeans in 2030 will be sufficiently productive to support one elderly person between them. The key question is how the redistribution will be channelled, but this should be a social choice and not a matter of government decree.

Socio-biological Engineering. The PAP is an authoritarian party and though it is more beneficent than some, this is no recommendation. The leadership often claims that its authoritarian nature and desire for keen discipline is determined by international pressures, but there is considerable evidence to suggest otherwise. Of particular relevance is the leadership's view of society which is essentially akin to the social Darwinism of the nineteenth century. To put it prosaically, Lee Kuan Yew and many in the PAP are eugenicists and their attitudes are the cornerstone of the state's elitist ideology. The PAPs eugenical views are well attested (45) and in its hubris the party has attempted to put them into practise. In 1983 Lee Kuan Yew used the dubious research of psychologist Arthur Jensen to support his meritocratic world view:

> In his speech on national day, August 14th, Mr Lee quoted the Jensenists' key ratio for human performance - 80% nature, 20% nurture. He also noted that the cleverest women in Singapore, graduates with good jobs, were producing fewer children than their less bright sisters. He said 'if we continue to reproduce ourselves in this lop-sided way, we will be unable to maintain our present standards. Levels of competence will decline. Our economy will falter, the administration will suffer, and the society will decline'. (46)

Soon after this speech the government brought in a number of measures specifically designed to encourage middle class procreation and discourage child bearing in the lower classes. Most controversially educated mothers are given priority access to the education system (which is already highly selective [47]). There is differential access to top schools for the following categories (in descending order): graduate mothers with three or more children, graduates with two children, sterilised uneducated mothers with two children and unsterilised uneducated mothers. (48) Not unexpectedly this policy came under fire from all quarters, including the Roman Catholic church and graduate women themselves. Tony Tan, Minister for Education, recently confirmed that the policy was under review because of considerable public resentment. (49)

The increasing resistance to the People's Action Party, as discussed above, was convincingly demonstrated by the results of the general election in December 1984. (Table 6.3) In July, expecting

Table 6.3 Singapore's General Election, December 22, 1984

Party	Number of candidates	seats	votes (thousands)	Share of vote(%)[a]
People's Action Party (PAP)	79	77	558	64.4
Worker's Party	15	1	111	12.8
Singapore Democratic Party	4	1	25	3.7
Others	22	0	161	18.2

Source: The Times, December 24, 1984

Note: Not counting invalid ballots.

an electoral clean-sweep, the government had passed a bill creating three "non-constituency" seats for the three highest losers. (50) In the event the PAPs share of votes dropped from 75 percent to 63 percent and opposition seats increased from 1 to 2 out of a 79 seat parliament. Hardly a cause of concern in most countries, but in Singapore where the ruling party has enjoyed nigh absolute control for two decades, this result was regarded as a disaster. The PAPs initial reaction was to stress the youth vote and agree that the population wanted the party to 'be more generous in our policies, less austere.' (51) The authoritarian attitude soon resurfaced, however, and Lee was quoted as saying:

> It is necessary to put some safeguards into the way in which people use their votes to bargain, to coerce, to push, to jostle and get what they want without running the risk of losing the services of the government. (52)

More recently a number of "reforms" to th electoral system have been discussed, including wealth qualification, an income tax qualificatic and an age qualification. (People in thes categories would be given a greater share of th vote because of their "stability".) In any event proposal likely to become law in 1985 is an executive president directly elected by the population. It is likely that Lee Kuan Yew will fill this post himself and use the post as a "constitutional safeguard" - against the people! (53) The opposition was understandably overjoyed at the election result and claimed that the population wanted a change in policies as well as style. (Even some members of the PAP agree [54]) This will be put to the test in the next few years.

The PAPs normal response to popular dissent is to clamp dowm hard, excise centres of resistance and step up its propaganda effort. The instruments available for such an exercise are stronger than ever: the Internal Security Department possesses virtually unlimited power; the merger of the three biggest newspaper publishing houses in 1984 allows stricter control over what is published (55); and the government's monitoring powers will increase to almost "big brother" status when the state monopoly Telecoms completes its Integrated Services Digital Network (ISDN). (56) ISDN will allow the government to conduct telepolls (instant referenda on specific issues) and potentially give it access to "digitalised" mail and private electronic files. However, with an educated, sophisticated population such measures are likely to lead to a radicalisa- tion of large segments of the Nation, with various forms of resistance sapping the powers of the state. Nor can the communal card be played on a populace aware of the general regional situation - and, moreover, communalism could deal a fatal blow to Singapore's relations with its ASEAN partners. A further problem for the PAP is that it is in a transition from the old guard to a new group of leaders. The latter would do well to recall that the regime's authoritarian nature mainly springs from the need to attract MNCs (hence anti-union legislation, militarisation), the old communal enmities (callously exploited by Lee Kuan Yew and his cronies) and a eugenical view of society. It is in Singapore's interest to combat these factors and the policies and attitudes that arise. A switch to a self-reliant, ASEAN- oriented policy would create an excellent environment for the restructuring of Singapore into a co-operative, non-exploitative and tolerant society.

SINGAPORE AND ASEAN

Singapore is the nexus of intra-ASEAN economic

relations and this is most apparent in the pattern of trade. Eighty five percent of intra-ASEAN trade is with Singapore (table 5.9) and the commodity composition of this trade is along the lines suggested by the concept of peripheral intermediation, i.e. Singapore exports manufactured goods to its ASEAN partners in return for raw materials. This situation reflects Singapore's position as a bridgehead for multinational expansion into South East Asia, but is not in the country's long term interest. The problems associated with dependence on MNCs have already been discussed (pages 256ff); and its role as the Janus of ASEAN, facilitating the exploitation (57) of the region, is both uncomfortable and divisive (58).

As a regional community ASEANs economic prospects are excellent. The group has a large labour force (the population is nearly 300 million people, roughly equivalent to the EC), an abundance of raw materials, energy sufficiency and considerable technological competence. Of course, it is this very potential which attracts the major powers (59). Each country has much to gain through greater political and economic co-operation and Singapore should welcome the opportunities inherent in such a potentially powerful bloc of Nations. The development of the region would be enhanced considerably if Singapore's technology, industry and services were married whole-heartedly with the region's resources. Unfortunately, however, economic nationalism (and, perhaps, communal prejudices) prevents greater co-operation between ASEANs members; and Singapore (the most advanced) and Indonesia (the most resource abundant) are the countries most inclined to tarry. Nevertheless it is advisable that ASEAN proceeds rapidly in its efforts towards economic co-operation: the alternative is a dependent status within the Pacific Community. The organisation's first priority should be to establish a consensus on its longer-term objectives; and the report of the Independent Task Force on Economic Co-operation (presented in June 1983 [60]) could prove to be a viable basis for further discussion. The report recommended a variety of measures on: trade co-operation; industrial co-operation (e.g. treatment facilitating intra-ASEAN investment); finance and banking (e.g. a limited payments union and an ASEAN export - import bank); transport and communications (e.g. a reduction in tariffs and an improvement in intra - ASEAN shipping services); third country relations ('ASEAN should not be diverted by offers of assistance in areas of peripheral interest to ASEAN'); organisational structure (especially a stronger secretariat); and market sharing/resource pooling. (61) ASEANs evolution into a credible economic and political organisation could be furthered by heed to the progressive tenor of the report. (62)

CONCLUDING REMARKS

It is not possible to argue conclusively that Singapore has paid too high a price for its industrialisation and development. It is always the alternatives that justify a particular course of action - and these are difficult to assess in this case. (63) Nevertheless alternatives are not static and new options are constantly becoming available. This chapter has suggested that the regime's current strategy is fraught with danger and can be improved upon. In particular Singapore should embark upon policies stressing self-reliance, intra-ASEAN co-operation and the needs and aspirations of its people. Failure to do so could lead to disaster.

NOTES

1. As already related in chapters two to four.
2. See especially the discussion on the emerging international economic order and the Pacific Community in chapter five.
3. These international obstacles have been partly discussed elsewhere in this book. See also: "The Last Road to Survival", South, February 1985; Antonio Maria Costa (1984), "The Pressure Towards Protectionism : Is it Systemic? A Legacy of the Recession? The Result of Policy to Promote Recovery?", World Development, Vol. 12, No. 10; Hellmut Schutte (1984), "Question marks behind Asia's Export Successes", Euro-Asia Business Review, Vol. 3, No. 3; Vincent Cable (1983), "Low-cost Asian competition in Europe : How is Britain meeting the challenge?", Euro-Asia Business Review, Vol. 2, No. 3; UNCTAD (1984), Protectionism and Structural Adjustment, parts I and II, Geneva, TD/B/981; UNIDO (1983), Industrial Development

NOTES continued

Strategies and Policies for Developing Countries, Vienna, UNIDO/IS.431; and UNCTAD (1984), Anti-dumping and countervailing duty practises, Geneva, TD/B/979.

4. Some international restrictions are specifically aimed at Singapore. The USA has always maintained that incentives offered by the EDB are export-subsidies. In addition an "intellectual property rights" delegation was recently rebuffed by Singaporean officials over the "piracy" of copyrighted materials and patents by Singaporean concerns. The delegation departed promising retribution in the form of GSP curtailment, reduced high-technology investment etc. See Lincoln Kaye (1984), "Copycats unrepentant", Far Eastern Economic Review, May 31.

5. International Reports, December 28, 1984 forecast a 7-8 percent growth rate for Singapore in 1985, chiefly the result of rapid growth in electronics and financial services.

6. Of course it is true that many of these expenditures would have been required for a non-MNC based development strategy, but a more self-reliant state would not succumb to the pressure exerted by competitive foreign investment schemes in other developing countries. Singapore has to maintain an attractive investment promotion regime because of its reliance on potentially "foot-loose" multinationals. The type of expenditures on inputs, infrastructure etc. are indicated variously in chapters two to four. See also Paisal Sricharatchanya (1983), "Hospitality can hurt", Far Eastern Economic Review, May 12.

7. Martin Fransman (1984), "The Rise of Asia's Machinery Industry", Euro-Asia Business Review, Vol. 3, No. 3.

8. Konosuke Odaka (1984), "The 'Becak' and 'Jeepney' are best!", Euro-Asia Business Review, Vol. 3, No. 3, page 16.

9. A similar case could be made for service industries such as banking and technical services.

10. Science and Technology Quarterly, Vol No. 2, October 1981, page 10.

11. "Mimicry" and "piracy" are not enough!

12. Though, as mentioned in chapter five, if the appropriate skills can be generated in developing countries this will help maintain MNC activity there. See UNCTAD (1984), New and Emerging Technologies : Some economic, commercial

NOTES continued

and developmental aspects, Geneva, TD/B/C.6/120.

13.   Indeed the importance of the state sector in various industries implies that such an approach is being taken, if only on an ad hoc basis. See especially chapter three and the petroleum industry in chapter five.

14.   Kwan Kuen-Chor and Lee Soo Ann (1983), "Japanese Direct Investment in the Singapore Manufacturing Industry" in Sueo Sekiguchi (ed), ASEAN-Japan Relations : Investment, Institute of Southeast Asian Studies, Singapore, page 164.

15.   Backward vertical integration is much more likely because most MNCs are orientated towards exports.

16.   Though the import of raw materials and semi-processed products may increase.

17.   Entrepreneurship is a property that the government finds lacking in Singaporeans (who prefer a risk-free job in a large corporation!) and is attempting to instil. This lack also explains the major entrepreneural role played by the state.

18.   Linda Lim and Pang Eng Fong (1982), "Vertical Linkages and Multinational Enterprises in Developing Countries", World Development, Vol. 10, No. 7.; and Lim and Pang (1977), The Electronics Industry in Singapore : Structure, Technology and Linkages, Chopments Enterprises, Singapore.

19.   With the occasional firm buying a much lower or greater proportion.

20.   Lim and Pang (1982), op. cit., page 588.

21.   See Lincoln Kaye (1984), "Strong on History in Changing Singapore", Far Eastern Economic Review, September 20. Banking in Singapore is seen as a three-tiered market between the "big four" domestic firms, the two colonial-era "grandes dames" (Hong Kong bank and Chartered bank) and the recently arrived financial institutions.

22.   Lim Joo-Jock et al. (1977), Foreign Investment in Singapore : Economic and Socio-Political Ramifications, Institute of Southeast Asian Studies, page 122.

23.   Attacks by the media, though muted, are not rare. See also page 241 (on the attitude of local electronics producers) and Lim Joo-Jock (1977), "The Multinational Petroleum Companies and their Retailers in Singapore : a potential conflict situation" in Lim Joo-Jock (1977), op. cit.

24   For other potential benefits and costs see some of the literature cited above, especially

NOTES continued

Lim Joo-Jock (1977), Lim and Pang (1977) and Sekiguchi (1982). See also : Chong Li Choy (1983), Multinational Business and National Development, Maruzen Asia, Singapore; Yoshihara Kunio (1976), Foreign Investment and Domestic Response : A study of Singapore's Industrialisation, Eastern Universities Press; Basant K. Kapur (1983), "A short-term Analytical Model of the Singapore Economy", Journal of Development Economics, vol. 12; Peter S. Low (1984), "Singapore-Based Subsidiaries of US Multinationals and Singaporean Firms : A comparative management study", Asia Pacific Journal of Management, September; and Donald J. Lecraw (1984), "Pricing Strategies of Transnational Corporations", Asia Pacific Journal of Management, January. Low's study indicates the possible benefits resulting from the transfer of management and organisation structures; Lecraw looks at predatory pricing, intercountry price discrimination and price leadership in the ASEAN countries.

25. The marine industry is the obvious example, but both private and state-owned enterprises in Singapore have used joint-ventures (and other mechanisms) to expand into higher value added industries, including computers, aircraft, telecommunications and petrochemicals. See pages 54ff, 66 (EDB training courses), 70, and 108ff.

26. Of course lower costs of inducing foreign investment would release resources which could be used in R & D.

27. Dis-intermediation occurs in the sense that Singapore becomes an equal partner in ASEAN and economic specialisation occurs on the basis of the common good.

28. It could be argued that the PAPs authoritarian policies were incidental to its plans to attract MNCs, but this is not borne out by the facts. Unions and the left-wing had to be broken in order to attract multinationals; and therefore their emasculation was a consequence of foreign direct investment. For a further explanation of this "non-purposive intention" see Jack Meiland (1970), The Nature of Intention, Methuen and Co.

29. See also Hans Luther (1978), "Strikes and the Institutionalisation of Labour Protest : the Case of Singapore", Journal of Contemporary Asia, Vol. 8, No. 2.

NOTES continued

30. Indeed some MNCs' profit-share is 80 percent or more of value added. For profitability see the appropriate sections in chapters three and four.

31. During 1979-81 earnings increased at about the same rate as GDP per worker because the state was following a "high-wage" policy; but the previous trends have since re-emerged. See, for example, Lincoln Kaye (1984), "The Wages of Spending", Far Eastern Economic Review, June 7. In fact the NWCs 1984 award does not even keep pace with inflation.

32. Even the "tame" National Trade Union Congress (NTUC) has 'cautioned employers that if increased productivity and higher returns for companies were to make sense to workers, they must see fair play and receive a fair share of productivity gains through wage increases and improved conditions' : Evelyn S. Wong (1983), "Industrial Relations in Singapore", in Southeast Asian Affairs, 1983, Institute of South East Asian Studies, Singapore, page 272.

33. Income distribution here means both the relative income shares of capital and labour and household income distribution. For further information see : Peter Limqueco (1983), "Contradictions of Development in ASEAN", Journal of Contemporary Asia, Vol. 13, No. 3; V.V. Bhanoji and M. Ramakrishman (1980), Income Inequality in Singapore, Singapore University Press; and Jacques Lecaillon (1984), Income Distribution and Economic Development, International Labour Office, Geneva.

34. The formation of industry unions (as opposed to trade unions) along German lines in the early eighties was also a part of the PAPs policy of "rationalising" employer-worker relations.

35. Straits Times, December 27, 1980.

36. Straits Times, March 2, 1981. Cited in Wong (1983), op. cit., page 268.

37. See The Economist, "South East Asian Unions", December 10, 1983.

38. Wong (1983), op. cit., page 274.

39. Ministry of Health, (1984), Problems of the Aged, Singapore.

40. V.G. Kulkarni (1984), "In a Rage over Age", Far Eastern Economic Review, April 19.

41. See Lincoln Kaye (1984), "The People's Managers", Far Eastern Economic Review, July 19.

42. The CPF is also regarded as a cheap

NOTES continued

source of government funds because interest paid is at least 3 percent less than the market rate. Further, 14 percent of contributions are only recouped by the heirs of a fund member! See Kaye (1984), op. cit.

43. Kaye (1984), op. cit., page 80.

44. The ideological basis of Singapore's Confucianisation needs to be pointed out because many claim to have detected a "Confucian ethic" in East Asia and use this to explain the success of Japan and the Asian NICs. Such a notion is questionable. The ruling class of Singapore was moulded by British values and most are English educated. Lee and the liberal PAP actually fought the Chinese educated left wing for control of the island-state. Indeed, Lee and his cronies could be termed "Machiavellian" in their behaviour - but no Italian ancestry is immediately discernible! For further discussion on the Confucian ethic thesis see: G.L. Hicks and S.G. Redding (1983), "The story of the East Asian 'Economic Miracle'. Part 1 : Economic theory be dammed! Part 2: the Culture Connection", Euro-Asia Business Review, Vol 2, nos 3 and 4; and R. Hofheinz and K. Calder (1982), The East Asia Edge, Basic Books, New York.

45. See especially Chan Chee Khoon and Chee Heng Leng (1984), Designer Genes : IQ, Ideology and Biology, Institute for Social Analysis, Insan, Petaling Jaya, Malaysia.

46. The Economist (1983), "A Question of Breeding", September 24, page 50.

47. There is streaming from the age of nine on the basis that intelligence is largely inherited and is primarily associated with class.

48. The Guardian (1984) "Lee's Brighter Babies Plan Angers Wives", February 22.

49. The Guardian (1985), "Loving and Learning", February 4.

50. Deprived of voting rights this was to be a very tame opposition indeed! See Lincoln Kaye (1984), "Falling into Line", Far Eastern Economic Review, August 9; Lincoln Kaye (1984), "Custom-made criticism", Far Eastern Economic Review, July 12; and V.G. Kulkarni (1984), "Prudence and Presidency" Far Eastern Economic Review, September 6.

51. The Times, December 24, 1984.

52. V.G. Kulkarni (1985), "Unhappy and Glorious", Far Eastern Economic Review, January 10, page 13.

NOTES continued

53. The Economist, "The Thoughts of Lee Kuan Yew", January 26, 1985.

54. Founder Chairman of the PAP Toh Chin Chye has criticised various aspects of the government's policies. See V.G. Kulkarni (1984), "Cause seeks Rebels", Far Eastern Economic Review, October 4.

55. The Guardian, "Singapore Merger Dismays Journalists", July 18, 1984.

56. Lincoln Kaye (1984), "From Lion City to Wired City", Focus: Telecommunications/Office Technology, Far Eastern Economic Review, September 6.

57. See for example Amnuay Viravan (1984), "ASEANs role in the 1980s : A Bridge over Troubled Waters?", Euro-Asia Business Review, Vol 3 No. 1. The exploitation of South East Asia (especially by Japan and the USA) is widely acknowledged and continues even if some labour-intensive industries are being transferred to other ASEAN countries. Singapore maintains a technological lead, of course, in both industry and services.

58. Of course a wedge between Singapore and ASEAN is in the interest of industrialised countries.

59. It is this very potential which attracts the major powers. In terms of energy, for example, ASEAN has an abundance of petroleum; the grouping sits astride the major sea lanes between the Middle East and East Asia/North America; and the rivalry over the reserves in the South China sea includes some ASEAN states as well as China and Vietnam. No wonder, then, that the Superpowers are so deeply embroiled in South East Asia.

60. P. Sricharatchanya and S. Awanohara (1984), "An economic block.... and how to free it.", Far Eastern Economic Review, March 8.

61. Ibid.

62. With regard to MNCs for example a credible organisation would have considerable bargaining power. See also, Chia Siow Yue (1983) "Codes of Conduct for MNCs and Governments in ASEAN", Contemporary South East Asia, Vol 5 No. 2.

63. Nevertheless many would argue that preferable and feasible alternatives were available, expecially if Barisan sosialis had won the left-right conflict of the early sixties.

SELECT BIBLIOGRAPHY

End of chapter notes also refer to key material,
especially magazine articles.

Akrasanee, N. (1983), "ASEAN : Economic Trends and
        Potential", Contemporary South East Asia,
        Vol 5, No 2.
Asher, M. and Osborne M. (1980), Issues in Public
        Finance in Singapore, Singapore University
        Press.
Bhanoji Rao, V.V. and Ramakrishnan, M. (1980),
        Income Inequality in Singapore : Impact of
        Economic Growth and Structural Change, 1966-
        1975, Singapore University Press.
Broinowski, A. (ed) (1982), Understanding ASEAN,
        Macmillan, London.
Buchanan, I. (1972), Singapore in Southeast Asia,
        G. Bell and Sons, London.
Caldwell, M. (1978), "Oil in South East Asia :
        National Liberation versus Transnational
        Incorporation" in E. Utrecht, Transnational
        Corporations in South East Asia and the
        Pacific, Vol II, Transnational Corporations
        Research Project, University of Sydney.
Centre for Strategic and International Studies
        (1980), Asia-Pacific in the 1980s : Towards
        Greater Symmetry in Economic
        Interdependence, Jakarta.
Chan Chee Khoon and Chee Heng Leng (eds) (1984),
        Designer Genes : IQ, Ideology and Biology,
        Institute for Social Analysis, Insan,
        Petaling Jaya, Malaysia.
Chia Siow Yue (1983), "Codes of Conduct for MNCs and
        Governments in ASEAN" in Contemporary South
        East Asia, Vol 5, No 2.
Chong Li Choy (1983), Multinational Business and
        National Development : Transfer of

Bibliography

    Managerial Knowhow to Singapore, Maruzen
    Asia, Singapore.
Crouch, H. (1984), Domestic Political Structures and
    Regional Economic Cooperation, Institute of
    Southeast Asian Studies, Singapore.
Edgington, D.W. (1983), Japanese Transnational
    Corporations and the Economic Integration of
    Australia and the Asian-Pacific Region,
    Working Paper No. 15, Transnational
    Corporations Research Project, University of
    Sydney.
Far Eastern Economic Review (1985), Banking '85,
    Supplement, April 25.
Federation of United Kingdom and Eire Malaysian and
    Singaporean Student Organisations (FUEMSSO)
    (1976), Singapore : Behind the "Economic
    Miracle", London.
Floyd, R.H., Gray C.S. and Short, R.P. (1984),
    Public Enterprise in Mixed Economies : Some
    Microeconomic Aspects, International
    Monetary Fund, Washington.
Fransman, M. (1984), "The Rise of Asia's Machinery
    Industry", Euro-Asia Business Review, Vol 3,
    No 3.
George, T.J.S. (1973), Lee Kuan Yew's Singapore,
    Andre Deutsch, London.
Hagiwara, Y. (1982), Asia in the 1980s :
    Interdependence, Peace and Development,
    Institute of Developing Economies, Tokyo.
Hamilton, C. (1983), "Capitalist Industrialisation
    in the Four Little Tigers of East Asia" in
    P. Limqueco and B. McFarlane, Neo-Marxist
    Theories of Development, Croom Helm,
    London.
Haseyama, T., Hirata, A. and Yanagihara, T. (eds)
    (1983), Two Decades of Asian Development and
    Outlook for the 1980s, Institute of
    Developing Economies, Tokyo.
Heenan, D.A. (1983), The Re-United States of
    America, Addison-Wesley, Reading.
Hernadi, A. (1982), Japan and the Pacific Region,
    Hungarian Scientific Council for World
    Economy, Budapest.
Hicks, G.L. and Redding, S.G. (1983), "The Story of
    the East Asian Economic Miracle", parts one
    and two, in Euro-Asia Business Review, Vol
    2, Nos 2 and 4.
Hofheinz, R. and Calder, K.E. (1982), The Eastasia
    Edge, Basic Books, New York.
ILO (1982), Labour Relations and Development :
    Country Studies on Japan, the Philippines,

Singapore and Sri Lanka, Geneva.

Johns, R.A. (1983), Tax Havens and Offshore Finance : A Study of Transnational Economic Development, Frances Pinter, London.

Josey, L. (1974), Lee Kuan Yew : the Struggle for Singapore, Angus and Robertson, London.

Kemp, T. (1983), Industrialisation in the Non-Western World, Longman, London.

Kiel, G.C. and Howard C.A. (1984), "The Pacific Rim - Vision or Reality?" in European Journal of Marketing, Vol 18, No 4.

Krause, L.B. and Sekiguchi, S. (eds) (1980), Economic Interaction in the Pacific Basin, Brookings Institution, Washington.

Leaillon, J. et al. (1984), Income Distribution and Economic Development : An Analytical Survey, International Labour Office, Geneva.

Lee, S.Y. and Jao, Y.C. (1982), Financial Structures and Monetary Policies in Southeast Asia, Macmillan, London.

Legget C., Wong, E. and Ariff, M. (1983), "Changing Industrial Relations in Singapore" in A1SEC Business Executive, Vol 2.

Luther, H. (1978), "Strikes and the Institutionalisation of Labour Protest : the Case of Singapore", Journal of Contemporary Asia, Vol 8, No 2.

Lim Joo-Jock et al. (1977), Foreign Investment in Singapore : Economic and Socio-Political Ramifications, Institute of Southeast Asian Studies, Singapore.

Lim, Linda and Pang Eng Fong (1984), "Labour Strategies and the High-Tech Challenge : the Case of Singapore", Euro-Asia Business Review, Vol 3, No 2.

Lip Ping Thean and Sek Keong Chan (1982), "Singapore" in B. Brown (ed), International Banking Centres, Euromoney Publications, London.

McFarlane B. (1982), "Western Strategies in the Asia-Pacific Region" in E. Utrecht (ed), Transnational Corporations in South East Asia and the Pacific, Vol IV, Transnational Corporations Research Project, University of Sydney.

McMullen, N. (1982), The Newly Industrialising Countries : Adjusting to Success, British-North American Committee, Washington.

Maex, R. (1983), Employment and Multinationals in Asian Export Processing Zones, International Labour Office, Geneva.

Bibliography

Mehmet, O. (1984), "Industrial Adjustment in ASEAN", Euro-Asia Business Review, Vol 3, No 2.

Ministry of Health (1984), Problems of the Aged, Singapore.

National Computer Board (1983), Singapore Computer Industry Survey, Industry Development Department, Singapore.

Oborne, M.W. and Fourt, N. (1983), Pacific Basin Economic Cooperation, OECD, Paris.

Pang Eng Fong (1982), Education, Manpower and Development in Singapore, Singapore University Press.

Pang Eng Fong and Linda Lim (1977), The Electronics Industry in Singapore : Structure, Technology and Linkages, Chopmen Enterprises, Singapore.

Pillai N. Philip (1983), State Enterprises in Singapore : Legal Importation and Development, Singapore University Press.

Process Plant EDC (1983), Market Profile : Singapore, in the "Selling to the Energy Industries in South East Asia" Series, National Economic Development Office, London.

Riddle, D.I. and Sours, M.H. (1984), "Service Industries as Growth Leaders on the Pacific Rim", Asia Pacific Journal of Management, May.

Riedel, J. (1983), Trade as the Engine of Growth in Developing Countries, The World Bank, Staff Working Paper No 555, Washington.

Sabre Foundation (1983), Free Zones in Developing Countries : Expanding Opportunities for the Private Sector, A.I.D. Program Evaluation Discussion Paper No 18, U.S. Agency for International Development, Washington.

Saw Swee-Hock (1981), Demographic Trends in Singapore, Department of Statistics, Singapore.

Saw Swee-Hock and Bhathal, R.S. (1981), Singapore : Towards the Year 2000, Singapore University Press.

Sekiguchi, S. (ed) (1983), ASEAN-Japan Relations : Investment, Institute of Southeast Asian Relations, Singapore.

Seow, T.W. (1984), Shipbuilding and Shiprepairing Industry in Singapore, United Nations Industrial Development Organisation, ID/WG.413/14, Vienna.

Sklar, H. (ed) (1980), Trilateralism : The Trilateral Commission and Elite Planning for

World Management, South End Press.

Skully, M.T. (1982), Financial Institutions and Markets in the Far East, Macmillan, London.

Skully, M.T. (1983), Merchant Banking in ASEAN, Oxford University Press, Kuala Lumpur.

Smith, P. (1982), "The Union Engineers", Far Eastern Economic Review, June 25.

Snitwongse, K. and Paribatra, S. (1984). The Invisible Nexus: Energy and ASEAN Security, Executive Publications, Singapore.

Soesastro, H. and Han, S. (eds) (1983), Pacific Ecomomic Cooperation: The Next Phase, Centre of Strategic and International Studies, Jakarta.

Spinager D. (1984), "Objectives and Impact of Economic Activity Zones - Some Evidence from Asia" in Weltwirtschaftliches Archiv, Bd. CXX.

Tan Chwee Huat (1984), Financial Institutions in Singapore, Singapore University Press.

Tanzer A. (1983), "Asia plugs into the computer" in Far Eastern Economic Review, July 21.

Time Magazine (1982), Into the Ranks of the Rich, Feature Article, January 25.

UNCTAD (1984), Trade and Development Report, 1984, Geneva .

UNIDO (1984), World Industrial Restructuring and Redeployment, ID/Conf.5/3, Vienna.

Utrecht, E. (1978), "Australian Based Companies in Singapore" in E. Utrecht and K. Short, Transnational Corporations in South East Asia and the Pacific Vol I, Transnational Corporations Research Project, University of Sydney.

Wain, B. (ed) (1979), The ASEAN Report, The Asian Wall Street Journal. Dow Jones Publishing Co., Hong Kong.

Wong, E.S. (1983), "Industrial Relations in Singapore" in Southeast Asian Affairs 1983, Institute of Southeast Studies, Singapore.

Yoshihara, K. (1976). Foreign Investment and Domestic Response: A Study of Singapore's Industrialisation, Eastern Universities Press, Singapore.